TRAVEL AND HOSPITALITY

C A R E E R
D I R E C T O R Y

Visible Ink Press proudly presents the second edition of the acclaimed *Travel and Hospitality Career Directory*, first published by the Career Press. The hallmark of this volume, part of VIP's Career Advisor Series, remains the essays by active professionals. Here, industry insiders describe opportunities and challenges in all segments of travel and hospitality, including:

- Airlines
- Cruise lines
- Hotels and motels
- Travel agencies
- Corporate travel agencies
- Car rental firms
- Meeting planning firms
- Local convention and visitor bureaus
- State travel and tourism offices

In fully up-to-date articles, they describe:

- What to expect on the job
- Typical career paths
- What they look for in an applicant
- How their specialty is unique

New Edition Provides Greatly Enhanced Job-Hunting Resources

Once this "Advice from the Pro's" has given you a feel for travel and hospitality careers, the *Directory* offers more help than ever before with your job-search strategy:

- **The Job Search Process** includes essays on determining career objectives, resume preparation, networking, writing effective cover letters, and interviewing. With worksheets and sample resumes and letters. **NEW:** Resumes are now targeted to the realities of the travel and hospitality industries.

- **Job Opportunities Databank** provides details on hundreds of agencies that hire at entry level. **NEW:** More agencies are listed, and information on internships that they offer is now included.

- **Career Resources** identifies sources of help-wanted ads, professional associations, employment agencies and search firms, career guides, professional and trade periodicals, and basic reference guides. **NEW:** Resource listings are greatly expanded and now include detailed descriptions to help you select the publications and organizations that will best meet your needs.

New Master Index Puts Information at Your Fingertips

This edition is more thoroughly indexed, with access to essays and directory sections both by subject and by organization name, publication title, or service name.

CAREER ADVISOR SERIES

TRAVEL AND HOSPITALITY

CAREER DIRECTORY

A Practical, One-Stop Guide to
Getting a Job in Travel and Hospitality

2ND EDITION

Bradley J. Morgan

with Joseph M. Palmisano

VISIBLE
INK
PRESS

DETROIT • WASHINGTON, D.C. • LONDON

CAREER ADVISOR SERIES

TRAVEL AND HOSPITALITY

CAREER
DIRECTORY

Second Edition

A Practical, One-Stop Guide to Getting a Job in Travel and Hospitality

Published by **Visible Ink Press** ™
a division of Gale Research Inc.
835 Penobscot Building
Detroit, MI 48226-4094

ISBN 0-8103-9427-8

Art Director: Cynthia Baldwin
Cover and Interior Design: Mary Krzewinski
Career Advisor Logo Designs: Kyle Raetz

Printed in the United States of America

Contents

PART ONE

Advice from the Pro's

PART TWO

The Job Search Process

Job Opportunities Databank

Career Resources

Master Index

Acknowledgments

The editor would like to thank all the "pro's" who took the time out of their busy schedules to share their first-hand knowledge and enthusiasm with the next generation of job-seekers. A special thanks to Kathy Daniels, Assistant Director of the Career Planning and Placement office at the University of Detroit–Mercy, who provided much-needed help with the job search section on short notice.

Thanks are also owed to the human resources personnel at the companies listed in this volume, and to the public relations staffs of the associations who provided excellent suggestions for new essays. Pam Parker of the Airline Pilots Association and David Melancon of the Association of Flight Attendants deserve special mention.

Introduction

recent *New York Times* article reported that 1992 college graduates were facing the toughest job market the United States has seen in twenty years. An ongoing series by the *Detroit Free Press* tracked the progress of six recent University of Michigan graduates; despite beginning their job search months before graduation day, only one of the six had landed that elusive first job one month after graduation.

Clearly, job-hunting in the 1990s is a challenging and demanding proposition, one that benefits from assistance at each step. The *Travel and Hospitality Career Directory*, formerly published by the Career Press, was developed to provide job-seekers with all the help they need to break into the competitive travel and hospitality industry. It provides a comprehensive, one-stop resource for carrying out a successful job search, including:

- Essays by industry professionals that provide practical advice not found in any other career resource
- Job-search guidance designed to help you get in the door in the travel and hospitality industry
- Job and internship listings from leading companies in the United States
- Information on additional career resources to further the job hunt
- A **Master Index** to facilitate easy access to the *Directory*

idebars located throughout the *Directory* are intended to amplify the text or provide a counterpoint to information presented on the page. They'll help you build a context for your career and job-search efforts by bringing you discussions of trends in the travel and hospitality industries and the business world, labor statistics, job-hunting techniques, and predictions about our future worklife. These and other tips and tidbits were gleaned from a wide range of sources—sources you can continue to draw upon for a broader understanding of your chosen field and of the job-search process.

The *Directory* is organized into four parts that correspond to the steps of a typical job search—identifying your area of interest, refining your presentation, targeting companies, and researching your prospects.

Advice from the Pro's: An Invaluable Tool

Instead of offering "one-size-fits-all" advice or government statistics on what the working world is like, the *Travel and Hospitality Career Directory* goes into the field for first-hand reports from experienced professionals working in all segments of travel and hospitality.

This "Advice from the Pro's" is offered by people who know what it's like to land that first job and turn it into a rich and rewarding career. Learn about:

- how exciting working for a cruise line can be from Mary Fallon Miller, author of *How to Get a Job with a Cruise Line*
- what it takes to become an airline pilot from the Air Line Pilots Association, International
- the pros and cons of being a flight attendant from Dee Maki, a 28-year veteran as a flight attendant and current president of the Association of Flight Attendants, AFL-CIO
- and nine other areas of specialization, including:

Car rental	Corporate travel
Hotel management	Meeting planning
Hotel sales and marketing	Local travel and tourism
Travel agent	State travel and tourism

The essays cover the most important things a job applicant needs to know, including:

- Which college courses and other background experiences offer the best preparation
- Specific skills that are needed
- What companies look for in an applicant
- Typical career paths
- Salary information

The Job Search Process: Making Sense of It All

What is the first thing a new job hunter should do?

What are the different types of resumes and what should they look like?

Which questions are off limits in an interview?

These important questions are among the dozens that go through every person's mind when he or she begins to look for a job. Part Two of the *Travel and Hospitality Career Directory*, **The Job Search Process**, answers these questions and more. It is divided into five chapters that cover all the basics of how to aggressively pursue a job:

- **Getting Started: Self-Evaluation and Career Objectives**. How to evaluate personal strengths and weaknesses and set goals.
- **Targeting Prospective Employers and Networking for Success.** How to identify the companies you would like to work for and how to build a network of contacts.
- **Preparing Your Resume.** What to include, what not to include, and which style to use. Includes samples of the three basic resume types and worksheets to help you organize your information.
- **Writing Better Letters.** Which letters should be written throughout the search process and how to make them more effective. Includes samples.
- **Questions for You, Questions for Them.** How to handle an interview and get the job.

Job Opportunities Databank: Finding the Job You Want

Once you're ready to start sending out those first resumes, how do you know where to start? The **Job Opportunities Databank**, Part Three of the *Directory*, includes listings for more than 400 hotels, airlines, cruise lines, hotel chains, travel agencies and related companies in the United States that offer entry-level jobs. These listings provide detailed contact information and data on the companies' business activities, hiring practices, benefits, and application procedures—everything you need to know to approach potential employers. And since internships play an increasingly important role in the career research and employment process, information on the internship opportunities offered by the companies listed is also included.

For further information on the arrangement and content of the **Job Opportunities Databank**, consult "How to Use the Job Opportunities Databank" immediately following this introduction.

Career Resources: A Guide to Organizations and Publications in the Field

Need to do more research on the specialty you've chosen or the companies you'll be interviewing with? Part Four of the *Directory*, **Career Resources**, includes information on the following:

- Sources of help-wanted ads
- Professional associations
- Employment agencies and search firms
- Career guides
- Professional and trade periodicals
- Basic reference guides

Listings now contain contact information and descriptions of each publication's content and each organization's membership, purposes, and activities, helping you to pinpoint the resources you need for your own specific job search.

For additional information on the arrangement and content of **Career Resources**, consult "How to Locate Career Resources" following this introduction.

New Master Index Speeds Access to Resources

A **Master Index** leads you to the information contained in all four sections of the *Directory* by citing all subjects, organizations, publications, and services listed throughout in a single alphabetic sequence. The index also includes inversions on significant words appearing in cited organization, publication, and service names. For example, the "Association of Flight Attendants" would also be listed in the index under "Flight Attendants, Association of." Citations in the index refer to page numbers.

New Information Keeps Pace with the Changing Job Market

This new edition of the *Travel and Hospitality Career Directory* has been completely revised and updated. New essays in the **Advice from the Pro's** section were contributed by leading professionals in travel and hospitality on subjects of particular interest to today's job seekers. The best essays from the previous edition were reviewed and completely updated as needed by the original authors. All employers listed in the **Job Opportunities Databank** were contacted by telephone or facsimile to obtain current information, and **Career Resources** listings were greatly expanded through the addition of selected material from databases compiled by Gale Research Inc.

Special Thanks

Thanks to the many people at Visible Ink Press and Gale Research Inc. who helped to shape this book: Katherine Gruber and Linda Hubbard, whose guidance and skill made my job easy; Karen Hill, who kept the big picture in sight; Jennifer Arnold Mast and her staff; and the staff of the Sourcebooks team for their superior skill and assistance.

Comments and Suggestions Welcome

The staff of the *Travel and Hospitality Career Directory* appreciates learning of any corrections or additions that will make this book as complete and useful as possible. Comments or suggestions for future essay topics or other improvements are also welcome, as are suggestions for careers that could be covered in new editions of the Career Advisor Series. Please contact:

Career Advisor Series
Visible Ink Press
835 Penobscot Bldg.
Detroit, MI 48226-4094
Phone: 800-347-4253
Fax: (313)961-6815

Bradley J. Morgan

How to Use the Job Opportunities Databank

The **Job Opportunities Databank** comprises two sections:

Entry-Level Job and Internship Listings

Additional Companies

Entry-Level Job and Internship Listings

The first section provides listings for more than 400 hotels and hotel chains, airlines, cruise lines, travel agencies, convention and visitor bureaus, tourist boards, amusement parks and resorts, and car rental firms. Entries in the **Job Opportunities Databank** are arranged alphabetically by company name. When available, entries include:

- **Company name.**
- **Address and telephone number.** A mailing address and telephone number are provided in every entry.
- **Fax and toll-free telephone number.** These are provided when known.
- **Business description.** Outlines the company's business activities. The geographical scope of the company's operations may also be provided.
- **Corporate officers.** Lists the names of executive officers, with titles.
- **Number of employees.** Includes the most recently provided figure for total number of employees. Other employee-specific information may be provided as well.
- **Average entry-level hiring.** Includes the number of entry-level employees the company typically hires in an average year. Many companies have listed "Unknown" or "0" for their average number of entry-level jobs. Because of current economic conditions, many firms could not estimate their projected entry-level hires for the coming years. However, because these firms have offered entry-level positions in the past and because their needs may change, we have continued to list them in this edition.
- **Opportunities.** Describes the entry-level positions that the company typically offers, as well as the education and other requirements needed for those positions.
- **Benefits.** Lists the insurance, time off, retirement and financial plans, activities, and programs provided by the company, if known.

- **Human resources contacts.** Lists the names of personnel-related staff, with titles.
- **Application procedure.** Describes specific application instructions, when provided by the company.

Many entries also include information on available internship programs. Internship information provided includes:

- **Contact name.** Lists the names of officers or personnel-related contacts who are responsible for the internship program.
- **Type.** Indicates the type of internship, including time period and whether it is paid or unpaid. Also indicates if a company does not offer internships.
- **Number available.** Number of internships that the company typically offers.
- **Number of applications received.** Total number of applications received in a typical year.
- **Application procedures and deadline.** Describes specific application instructions and the deadline for submitting applications.
- **Decision date.** Final date when internship placement decisions are made.
- **Duties.** Lists the typical duties that an intern can expect to perform at the company.
- **Qualifications.** Lists the criteria a prospective applicant must meet to be considered for an internship with the company.

Additional Companies

Covers those companies that elected to provide only their name, address, and telephone number for inclusion in the *Travel and Hospitality Career Directory*. Entries are arranged alphabetically by company name.

How to Locate
Career Resources

The **Career Resources** chapter contains six categories of information sources, each of which is arranged alphabetically by resource or organization name. The categories include:

▼ **Sources of Help-Wanted Ads**

- **Covers:** Professional journals, industry periodicals, association newsletters, placement bulletins, and online services that include employment ads or business opportunities. Includes sources that focus specifically on travel and hospitality, as well as general periodical sources such as the *National Business Employment Weekly*.

- **Entries include:** The resource's title; name, address, and telephone number of its publisher; frequency; subscription rate; description of contents; toll-free and additional telephone numbers; and facsimile numbers.

▼ **Professional Associations**

- **Covers:** Trade and professional associations that offer career-related information and services.

- **Entries include:** Association name, address, and telephone number; membership; purpose and objectives; publications; toll-free or additional telephone numbers; and facsimile numbers. In some cases, the publications mentioned in these entries are described in greater detail as separate entries cited in the Sources of Help-Wanted Ads, Career Guides, Professional and Trade Periodicals, and Basic Reference Guides categories.

▼ **Employment Agencies and Search Firms**

- **Covers:** Firms used by companies to recruit candidates for positions and, at times, by individuals to pursue openings. Employment agencies are generally geared towards filling openings at entry- to mid-level in the local job market, while executive search firms are paid by the hiring organization to recruit professional and managerial candidates, usually for higher-level openings. Also covers temporary employment agencies because they can be a method of identifying and obtaining regular employment.

Includes sources that focus specifically on travel and hospitality, as well as some larger general firms.

- **Entries include:** The firm's name, address, and telephone number; whether it's an employment agency, executive search firm, or temporary agency; descriptive information, as appropriate; toll-free and additional telephone numbers; and facsimile number.

▼ **Career Guides**

- **Covers:** Books, kits, pamphlets, brochures, videocassettes, films, and other materials that describe the job-hunting process in general or that provide guidance and insight into the job-hunting process in travel and hospitality.

- **Entries include:** The resource's title; name, address, and telephone number of its publisher or distributor; name of the editor or author; publication date or frequency; description of contents; arrangement; indexes; toll-free or additional telephone numbers; and facsimile numbers.

▼ **Professional and Trade Periodicals**

- **Covers:** Newsletters, magazines, newspapers, trade journals, and other serials that offer information to travel and hospitality professionals.

- **Entries include:** The resource's title; the name, address, and telephone number of the publisher; the editor's name; frequency; description of contents; toll-free and additional telephone numbers; and facsimile numbers.

▼ **Basic Reference Guides**

- **Covers:** Manuals, directories, dictionaries, encyclopedias, films and videocassettes, and other published reference material used by professionals working in travel and hospitality.

- **Entries include:** The resource's title; name, address, and telephone number of the publisher or distributor; the editor's or author's name; publication date or frequency; description of contents; toll-free and additional telephone numbers; and facsimile numbers.

ADVICE
FROM THE
PRO'S

Flying the "Friendly" Skies

Dee Maki, National President
Association of Flight Attendants, AFL-CIO

Since the days when airlines advertised with posters touting, "Fly Me, I'm Cheryl," flight attendants have made dramatic strides in achieving the public's respect and recognition for their commitment. No longer are the women and men who work in the back of the plane considered "air waitresses"; the erroneous image of the pretty little stewardess who glamorously flew from city to city looking for a good time is a thing of the past.

Today's flight attendant is a dedicated safety professional responsible for the safety and well-being of every passenger on his or her airplane. Today's flight attendant is much more than just a smiling poster advertisement—she or he must be chef, bartender, trauma specialist, fire fighter, customer service representative, shrink, baggage handler, tour guide, and nursemaid all rolled into one.

So, what skills does one need to be one of these "superpeople"? Even more importantly, why would anyone want to? The flight attendant profession is one of hard work, grueling schedules and unrelenting stress. It is also one of the most rewarding and satisfying careers a person can choose to undertake. And all one needs to be successful is a positive attitude, a willingness to work as part of a team, and a healthy dose of gumption.

The Rewards: Travel and Flexibility

The most obvious benefit to a flight attendant career is the tremendous opportunity for travel. For someone who wishes to see the world, the life of a flight attendant may definitely be right. The job itself is constant travel, but not always to the places one wishes to go. The average flight attendant goes out for three- or four-day trips, landing in as many as ten cities with an overnight stay in a different place each night. A trip could include exotic cities in foreign countries or small cities dotted across the

Midwest. Each trip is as different and exciting as one chooses to make it, no matter what the stops.

Besides the travel involved with the job itself, there's also the benefit of travel afforded to each flight attendant as an airline employee. Flight attendants are allowed to "pass ride," or fly for free, on their airline in their off time. This travel is on a space-available basis, so it may involve waiting for a less-than-full flight, but it's fairly easy to get wherever one wishes to go. Additionally, many airlines have agreements with other carriers that allow flight attendants to fly very cheaply on an airline other than their own. This means that one's travel options aren't limited to one's own airline's destinations.

Another significant benefit to the flight attendant profession is a very flexible work schedule. After a four-day trip, one usually has five to six days off. Many flight attendants use this flexibility to spend time with their families, to travel for pleasure, or to pursue other educational or career goals. Flight attendants who work their way through college or graduate school while flying often don't want to give it up—the airlines have several doctors, lawyers, and dentists who balance dual careers, flying trips while still maintaining an active practice.

All trip scheduling for flight attendants is done on the basis of seniority, so beginning attendants may find themselves working a less-than-flexible schedule at first. This fledgling period is over quickly, however, as one accumulates the necessary seniority.

While flight attendant salaries still aren't commensurate with the rigors of the job, they have gotten much more equitable in the last decade. The first few years of a flight attendant's career are usually at low wages, but the average salary becomes much better as one gains experience. As a rule, the major airlines offer higher salaries, but are usually much more competitive when it comes to hiring.

The Drawbacks: Stress!

A flight attendant must be ready to deal with any emergency—from a crash to a passenger heart attack to a terrorist threat—at any moment. Being prepared for any eventuality, while dealing with the situations that do arise, are the cause of the number one drawback to the flight attendant profession: stress.

Commercial air travel is safer today than it's ever been, but accidents still happen. And a flight attendant must be prepared for the worst every time the plane takes-off or lands. Just being ready for an accident at any time causes a high level of stress that becomes routine to the veteran flight attendant. Actually being in an accident and carrying out the safety professional's responsibility to the passengers aboard is something that can't even be measured in terms of stress. It's something every flight attendant hopes never to experience, while constantly being ready for it.

But that stress is only part of the equation. The everyday stress of weather delays, hundreds of hurried and often cranky passengers, and gruelingly long hours on one's feet, are a flight attendant's normal world. It is stress that never really lets up, and it makes for a career that requires a very special candidate.

While stress has always been a by-product of life as a flight attendant, the other major drawback is much more recent. The advent of airline deregulation in 1978 made for the volatile airline industry of today, and unfortunately, job security has become a thing of the past. The demise of countless airlines, including Eastern, Pan Am, and Midway, has meant thousands of flight attendants and other airline employees have been put out of jobs. While employment opportunities at surviving air carriers are still good, the situation changes on a day-to-day basis. While some potential flight attendants still look at the job as two or three year proposition, the average flight attendant of today is looking for a long-term career. Deregulation has made this quest one often difficult to fulfill.

Tough Training Is a Requirement

Every flight attendant goes through an initial four-to-six weeks of rigorous training that includes safety and emergency procedures, as well as service methods. Fighting in-flight fires, performing evacuations, handling medical emergencies, and dealing with terrorist threats are all part of the curriculum. Additionally, flight attendants must go through an annual refresher training of these safety skills.

Currently, flight attendants in the U.S. are not licensed or certified. Many European countries do have certification, however, and we have long been fighting for it here. Certification would give flight attendants the same credibility held by other safety-sensitive occupations, such as pilots and mechanics, and anyone considering a career as an attendant should be prepared for this to happen in the near future.

Leading Foreign Destinations for U.S. Air Travellers

1. Mexico
2. United Kingdom
3. Germany
4. Bahamas
5. Japan
6. France
7. Dominican Republic
8. Jamaica
9. Italy
10. Netherlands Antilles

Source: *Travel Industry World Yearbook*

What Background Do You Need?

While a college degree isn't a requirement, almost half of the flight attendants currently on the line hold a four-year degree, and almost 70 percent of all flight attendants have some college experience. Because of the growing globalization of today's airline industry, fluency in a second language gives applicants a definite advantage, but is not usually mandatory.

While most airlines don't have strict educational requirements, the highly competitive nature of today's industry means that every thing counts. Because of the varied, often cosmopolitan nature of the flight attendant's customer, higher education is very definitely a plus.

Some physical qualifications are necessary to become a flight attendant. One must be fit enough to carry out one's safety and emergency responsibilities aboard an airplane. Additionally, most airlines have height and weight standards that must be met.

How to Look for Your First Job

Once one decides that the advantages of being a flight attendant outweigh the

drawbacks, where does he or she start to look for a job? If an airline is headquartered near one's home, that would be the obvious starting point. If not, the Future Aviation Professionals of America (1-800-JET-JOBS) keep an accurate listing of employment opportunities at all the airlines across the country. Once again, deregulation has made landing a spot as a flight attendant very competitive. But as air travel becomes more and more common, the opportunities will be there for the committed applicant.

A Unique Lifestyle Awaits You

Being a flight attendant is much more than flying from city to city, serving drinks and meals, and smiling at passengers. While the plane's captain has the authority of the law in the air, the flight attendant is in control of the cabin—and the safety and well-being of every passenger on that plane is her or his responsibility. The flight attendant's presence on that plane is mandated by Congress and required by law.

Flight attendants often speak of belonging to a subculture. The lifestyle and world of a flight attendant is one very few people are truly cut out for—the rigors certainly aren't for everyone. For this reason, flight attendants are most comfortable talking about their careers, their problems, and their joys with other flight attendants. Being a flight attendant is a lifestyle that "gets in your blood," and it is a responsibility that only the committed should undertake. For the few who do, it is the career—and the experience of a lifetime.

▼

DEE MAKI is a 28-year flight attendant and the National President of the Association of Flight Attendants, AFL-CIO, the world's largest flight attendant union, representing 33,000 attendants at 20 different airlines. During her tenure as a safety professional and labor leader, she has flown for three different airlines, and survived the mergers, acquisitions, and calamities of airline deregulation.

Introduction to Aviation

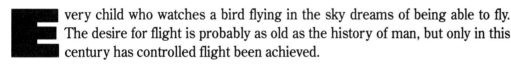

Air Line Pilots Association, International

Every child who watches a bird flying in the sky dreams of being able to fly. The desire for flight is probably as old as the history of man, but only in this century has controlled flight been achieved.

Commercial air passenger service began in 1926. In that year 6,000 passengers traveled to just a handful of cities. Now air transportation moves 400 million passengers a year to hundreds of cities all over the world.

The early commercial pilots flew their routes by looking for familiar landmarks—a certain barn, a river bend, a farmer's windmill. Sometimes they followed train tracks, and cases have been recorded of near-misses with onrushing locomotives during low visibility conditions.

Those pioneer airline pilots would be amazed at present-day cockpits. Technological advances have changed the speed and safety of travel, changed the aircraft, and changed the demands on the flight crew. Today's complex air traffic system and sophisticated aircraft demand skill, judgment, education, and—most importantly—experience.

Pilots control vehicles valued at millions of dollars, transporting as many as 400 persons plus tons of mail and freight. Such a huge aircraft takes off from a strip of pavement a mile or so long, touching down again hundreds or thousands of miles away on another strip of pavement about 150 feet wide. Often the entire journey is made with no sight of the ground from takeoff to landing.

A takeoff or a landing is made on the average of every three seconds by members of the Air Line Pilots Association, International. The scheduled airlines of the United States operate a fleet of over 3,000 aircraft, most of them jets.

The big business of air travel requires hundreds of thousands of workers. Many thousands are employed by airlines as mechanics, reservation agents, dispatchers, sales representatives, baggage handlers,office workers, and other important staff members. Additional thousands are employed at airports, in government, and in businesses that support aviation and air travelers.

But once the power is applied to the engines, the safety of the flight depends on the professional crew up front.

Three Pilot Positions

The three positions in the airline pilot profession are captain, first officer (copilot), and second officer (flight engineer). Not all aircraft operated by the airlines require a second officer; these are flown with the captain and first officer sharing all the duties.

On all reputable airlines, a pilot progresses into the captain's position of authority through experience. Experience is important because no two flights are ever alike. The manner in which a flight is conducted and how the aircraft is controlled depends on many factors, including visibility, wind direction and velocity, temperature, and aircraft loading. Only experience equips a pilot to meet these changing conditions safely and efficiently. Furthermore, only experience prepares the crew for those infrequent times when an emergency, if not dealt with promptly and with precision, can become a tragedy.

Each of the pilot positions requires a certificate from the Federal Aviation Administration (FAA) and a currently valid medical certificate.

Captain—Commands the aircraft and is responsible for the safety of its passengers, crew, and cargo. Requires an air transport pilot (ATP) certificate from FAA. The average ALPA captain is 48 years old with 20 years of service and earns about $110,000 annually.

First Officer (Copilot)—Assists or relieves the captain in the operation of the aircraft. Requires a commercial pilot certificate with instrument rating from FAA. The average ALPA first officer is 40 years old with 10 years of service and a yearly salary of about $58,000. At airlines that do not fly three-man-crew aircraft, the first officer is the starting position for new pilots. Beginning salaries at such airlines range from $10,000 to $24,000, depending on the size of the aircraft flown.

Second Officer (Flight Engineer)—Assists in flight operations and sees that the mechanical and electronic devices of the aircraft are in perfect working order. Requires a flight engineer's certificate from FAA. A second officer does not fly the aircraft, but airlines today require a second officer to have a valid pilot's certificate and to maintain proficiency as a pilot while working as a second officer. The second officer position is the entry-level job at many airlines. Second officers normally serve a one-year probationary period with their airlines and their entry-level salaries range from $12,000 to $25,000. Overall, the average ALPA second officer is 37 years old with 6 years of service and earns a yearly salary of about $38,000.

Preparing for an Airline Pilot Career

General Qualifications

All pilots are licensed by the FAA. A certificate can be refused or revoked if the individual is determined not to be of good character. Physical requirements vary with the level of the license, but all pilots must be able to pass a physical examination at regular, frequent intervals.

A good educational foundation is needed in mathematics, science, English, and geography. Most airlines prefers a four-year college degree.

Experience Requirements

In aviation, experience is judged in two ways: hours of flying and kind of flying. Most airlines require at least 1,500 hours of flying time, preferably in multi-engine aircraft. The average new-hire at regional airlines has over 3,000 hours; the average new-hire at the major airlines has almost 4,000. The averages are higher than the requirements because of high flying time of former military pilots.

Although flight instruction and similar work are good ways to build up the first hours of commercial flying experience, once a pilot has recorded 2,000 to 3,000 hours of flying, additional time confers no competitive advantage unless it is flown in large transport-type aircraft. A pilot with 6,000 hours as a crop duster is probably a very good crop duster—but the airlines want multi-engine experience.

Training

About 75% of the airlines pilots currently flying have had military training. However, at the present time the military services are training fewer pilots and requiring longer commitments. As a result, recently the number of newly hired pilots with civilian training surpassed that of the military-trained pilots. Both the Navy and the Air Force require a college degree for those trained as pilots; the Army does not.

If your goal is to be an airline pilot, you can reach it sooner with civilian training. Pilot training can be obtained in colleges with aviation courses or in privately operated flight schools. The FAA provides certification for both instructors and flight schools; be sure that the school and instructors you choose have current FAA certification.

Personal Requirements

The federal government establishes minimum and maximum ages for airline pilots. A commercial pilot must be at least 18 years of age and an applicant for an air transport pilot certificate must be at least 23 years of age. Federal law requires commercial airline pilots to retire at age 60.

Until very recently, airlines rarely hired pilots after age 32. Today, older pilots are being hired because of growing pilot shortage, but the airlines expect experience to be commensurate with age. In other words, older pilots with many hours of flight time who would not have been considered just a few years ago are now attractive to the airlines.

Airline pilots must meet stringent physical health requirements. Medical examinations required by the FAA are classified as first, second, or third class. The differences are based on the specific levels of physical requirements and the length of time the certificate is valid. A first class certificate requires the highest physical requirements and is valid for six months. It is required for an airline pilot in command of an aircraft (captain).

Before you begin training for any airline position, we strongly recommended that you take a first class physical from a physician who is a designated FAA examiner. You can obtain the names of FAA medical examiners from the FAA regional headquarters nearest you, or you can ask the operator of any FAA-approved training school in your area for the name of an examiner.

Heart, lungs, physical dexterity, and eyesight are the main concerns. Dependence on drugs—even most prescription drugs—is disqualifying. Almost every airline will now allow applicants to wear glasses or contact lenses to correct vision to 20/20 in each eye.

▼

Most Heavily Traveled Airline Routes

Ranked by number of passengers
1. New York—Los Angeles
2. New York—Boston
3. New York—Washington
4. New York—Miami
5. Los Angeles—San Francisco
6. New York—Chicago
7. Dallas—Houston
8. Honolulu—Kahului (Maui)
9. New York—San Francisco
10. New York—Orlando
Source: *New York Times*

Educational Requirements

The commercial airline pilot profession increasingly becomes more complex and technical. To meet the constant demands of constantly changing technology requires a high degree of mental dexterity. Airline pilots never stop learning—new systems, new aircraft configurations, new procedures. Because of the ever-changing aviation technology and the requirements for mastery of new systems, pilots must attend ground schools regularly and pass courses there as well as passing flight checks in simulators and aircraft.

Because the airline pilot works with technically complex systems of navigation and communications equipment, the pilot should have a thorough grasp of mathematics, aerodynamics, aeronautics, navigation, and meteorology. The pilot must be able to think clearly even in times of stress and to communicate accurately, understandably, and concisely while performing other duties.

The acquisition of these skills begins at the secondary level of education with an emphasis on the basic sciences, particularly math and physics. At the college level, preferred courses in preparations for an airline pilot career would include advanced math, English, sciences, aeronautical engineering, and other aviation-related studies.

Learning to fly an aircraft requires training and experience, but because pilots are in command of equipment valued at millions of dollars and responsible for hundreds of lives, they must also have good judgment and a good attitude.

License Requirements

The four kinds of basic pilot certificates issued by the Federal Aviation Administration are: (1) student, (2) private, (3) commercial, and (4) air transport pilot. Except for the pilot holding only a student certificate, a certificate holder may have different ratings or type certification. For instance, pilot may have ratings for single-engine, multi-engine, land, sea, helicopter, or instrument. A specific type rating in the model flown is required before a pilot can fly an aircraft weighing more than 12,500 pounds.

1. Student Pilot

Minimum age: 16

Privileges: May receive instruction and fly solo under the supervision of a certificated flight instructor. May not carry passengers.

Physical standards: Must possess a valid third class medical certificate prior to solo.

Education: Should have a good basic education in mathematics, sciences, and English.

After a minimum of 35 hours of training at an FAA-approved school or 40 hours at a non-FAA-approved school, including specified hours of training in cross-country, introduction to instruments, and emergency procedures, the student may be recommended for a private certification.

2. Private Pilot

Minimum age: 17

Privileges: May pilot any aircraft for which a rating is held and may carry passengers but not be paid or receive other compensation for activity as a pilot.

Physical standards: Must posses a valid third class medical certificate.

Education: Besides a basic education, must have specialized instruction in Federal Aviation Regulations, navigation, radio communications, weather observation and evaluation, aircraft loading, and flight planning.

Skill level: Must pass a written examination administered by the FAA and successfully demonstrate to an FAA-designated examiner pilot skills covering flight planning, preflight procedures, straight and level flight, climbing and gliding turns, soft field and short field takeoffs and landings, stall recovery from various attitudes, 720-degree turns with precision, and crosswind takeoffs and landings.

3. Commercial Pilot

Minimum age: 18

Privileges: May act as pilot in command of any aircraft for which a rating is held and receive compensation.

Physical standards: Must hold a valid and current second class medical certificate.

Aeronautical experience: Must have at least 250 hours of flight time, including at least 100 hours as pilot in command, 50 hours of cross-country, 10 hours of training in control of complex (adjustable landing gear and props) aircraft, 10 hours of instrument instruction, and an instrument rating.

Skill level: Must pass a detailed written examination and demonstrate to an examiner most of the skills required for a private certificate but performed with a higher degree of precision.

The Air Line Pilots Association, International has an associate membership program designed for commercially rated pilots working within the aviation profession, the Association of Independent Airmen (AIA). AIA is designed to offer pilots the professional benefits and services needed to be successful in today's aviation industry.

For more information about AIA membership, write a brochure to:

The Association of Independent Airmen
535 Herndon Pkwy.
PO Box 1671
Herndon, VA 22070800-842-2129

4. Air Transport Pilot

Minimum age: 23

Privileges: May serve as pilot in command of aircraft.

Physical standards: Requires a current and valid first class medical certificate.

Education: High school or its equivalent. (Most employers prefer a college degree.)

Aeronautical experience: 1,500 flight hours, 500 of which are cross-country, 100 at night, 75 in instrument category, of which 50 will be in actual instrument weather conditions. An instrument rating is required.

Aeronautical skill: Must successfully pass a written examination and demonstrate to an examiner his/her ability to pilot an aircraft under the complex situations applicable to airline-type flying.

All categories of licenses require recency of experience. All pilots must take a flight review with an instructor at least every two years. In addition to taking regular six-month FAA and company flight checks, and simulator and medical exams, an airline pilot is subject to unannounced spot checks by FAA inspectors.

Where to Go for Additional Information

Films, booklets, and brochures can be obtained from a variety of sources, including the airlines, government, aircraft manufacturers, libraries, schools, and associations.

Many home study courses are available, including visual and taped presentations. Aviation supply shops and some airports offer training books for sale.

Where you are in preparation for your aviation career will, of course, determine your next step. If you have not yet started to become a pilot, you may want to visit your nearest airport and talk with a flight instructor.

Airline Pilot Career Information

The Air Line Pilots Association, International has a program designed for aspiring airline pilots, the **Pilot Information Program (PIP).** The annual membership fee of $20.00 includes a subscription to the *Air Line Pilot* magazine, among other benefits.

For information about **PIP** membership, write for a brochure to:

Pilot Information Program
Education Department
Air Line Pilots Association, International
1625 Massachusetts Ave., NW
Washington, DC 20036
(703) 689-2270

Educational Materials

Aerospace Education Foundation
1501 Lee Hwy.
Arlington, VA 22209-1198
(703) 247-5839

Airline Information

Air Transport Association of America
1709 New York Ave., NW
Washington, DC 20006
(202) 626-4000

Aviation Training Capsules

Department of Transportation
Federal Aviation Administration
Office of Training and Higher Education
800 Independence Ave., SW
Washington, DC 20591
(202) 366-7503

Pilot Career Consultation

Future Aviation Professionals of America
4959 Massachusetts Blvd.
Atlanta, GA 30337
1-800-JET-JOBS

An excellent source for addresses and names of key personnel from all segments of aviation is the *World Aviation Directory.* It provides information on national/international airlines, manufacturers, airports, etc. It is published twice a year by Aviation Week Group, McGraw-Hill, Inc., 1156 15th St., NW, Washington, DC 20005, (202) 822-4600, and is available at most libraries.

Looking Ahead

Whatever path you may take for a career, aviation and air transportation will be an important part of life. Even though you may not become an airline pilot, air travel may be essential in another career.

We hope that the information in this essay has been helpful to you as you plan your future. As professionals dedicated to a continuance of professionalism, we at the Air Line Pilots Association, International welcome the opportunity to discuss the future of air transportation and the potential for your place in it.

By comparison to most other professions, the number of airline pilot positions is small, but there is always room for the dedicated individual who seeks to excel.

We wish you success in reaching your goals. Perhaps in the future we will see you at the controls and be able to welcome you as a member of ALPA.

The Lodging Industry Is Looking for a Few Good People—500,000 or So

Michele Kelley, Manager of Media Relations
American Hotel & Motel Association

The lodging industry is growing at a rapid pace throughout the United States and the world. So rapid that it's expected that, by the year 2000, there will be well over 500,000 additional positions for entry-level people, jobs offering excellent opportunities for advancement.

In less than a decade, travel and tourism, as a whole, will become the nation's number one employer, with one out of every five employed American workers working in some segment of the industry.

The Jobs to Shoot For

Entry-level jobs in all areas of the lodging industry offer competitive pay, rapid promotion, and access to a field offering more jobs than any other industry, except health care. To give you a better understanding of the structure and operation of a hotel or motel, the following are brief job descriptions of hotel management positions—the jobs you are probably aiming for:

General Manager
- Responsible to ownership for the efficient and effective operation of the hotel, motel, restaurant, and ancillary facilities;
- Guides and directs management team to achieve established goals and objectives;
- Responsible for the selection, coordination, and delegation of authority to all managers and department heads employed by the hotel;
- Hires new employees; discharges employees when necessary;
- Evaluates management personnel in order to upgrade when openings arise;
- Forecasts, budgets, and solves problems;

- Handles executive affairs of the hotel operation;

- Represents the hotel in public affairs and builds good will for the property.

Resident Manager

- Lives in the hotel and is on call 24 hours a day to take charge in resolving any problems or emergencies. Reports to the general manager and is responsible for supervising all hotel activities, including the efficient and effective operation of the Housekeeping Department, Room Reservations Department, Front Office, Bell Service Department, PBX Department, Food and Beverage Department, and Sales Office;

- Prepares occupancy forecasts to facilitate top management interpretation of future guest head counts and gross revenue expectancies;

- Performs the duties of "guest relations manager"—handling complaints or requests for guests and acting as the official host to VIP guests.

Food and Beverage Manager

- Reports to the general manager and is responsible for all food and beverage service within the hotel, supervising the Food, Banquet, and Beverage Departments through subordinate managers;

- Creates and develops menu food and beverage offerings, establishes prices and is responsible for selecting the condiments, linens, uniforms, and decor used within the facility;

- Standardizes portions and is responsible for controlling food, beverage and labor costs;

- Recommends equipment to be used and is responsible for the proper selection of all food and beverage products;

- Approves booked activities, such as banquets and conventions, where food and beverage service are required. Maintains liaison with the Sales Department in order to facilitate the proper handling of convention and banquet obligations;

- Responsible for public relations and customer satisfaction;

- Develops budgets for individual units and has primary responsibility for meeting profit objectives.

Restaurant Manager

- Reports to food and beverage manager and hires, trains, and supervises waiters, busboys, and captains;

- Maintains patron satisfaction;

- Occasionally may book or handle small functions serviced in the restaurant from the regular menu;

- Maintains records of personnel performance and dining room food and labor costs;

- Maintains a departmental time log and may check employee time cards against audits entered into the log;

- Assists the food and beverage manager and assistant food and beverage manager as a cost accountant, reviewing expenditures versus revenues in the food and beverage operation;

- Calculates the daily volume of business, prepares statements, and advises appropriate department heads of their daily and weekly labor costs versus gross volume of business;

- Checks food prices to confirm and keep up-to-date on the market fluctuations.

Front Office Manager

- Directly supervises all front office personnel and is responsible for all hotel front office activities: maintaining data of future room occupancy; setting up filing systems for correspondence; monitoring reservation systems; and maintaining liaison with sales, housekeeping, and accounting departments;

- Compiles daily, weekly, monthly, and yearly room forecasts;

- Controls opening and closing dates;

- Responsible for keeping data regarding future room occupancy, guest head counts, and convention guest count and keeping management informed of occupancy level so sound decisions can be made to keep the property's occupancy high (without overselling);

- Responsible for setting up and maintaining a filing system for all correspondence pertaining to future arrivals, reservation requests and refusals, past arrivals, no-show guests, and cancellations;

- Insures that guests are handled courteously and efficiently, complaints and problems resolved and requests for special services carried out;

- Responsible for inspecting guest accommodations, attending staff and operational meetings, and scheduling employee work assignments.

Controller

- Directly supervises all hotel accounting personnel and all phases of the Accounting Department;

- Controls the activities of the restaurant Cashiers Department, front office cashier, night auditor, Payroll Department and Credit and Accounting Departments;

- Responsible for hotel financial statements.

Accountant

- Makes appropriate recommendations for new accounts, revisions in reporting systems, and changes in instructions regarding the use of accounts;

- Makes decisions concerning the accounting treatment of various transactions;

- Recommends solutions to complex problems;

- Supervises office clerks in an assigned area.

Sales Manager

- Meets with individuals representing national, international, regional, and state organizations, local and wholesale markets, and travel agents to produce contacts and schedule desired bookings for conventions. Maintains records of such individuals;

- May also visit officials and representatives and attend conventions in other cities to generate conventions or group business. Maintains rapport with contacts who may produce or have produced conventions or group business for the hotel;

- Corresponds with numerous travel agencies throughout the United States and foreign countries concerning planned tours to the area. Distributes advertising material concerning the hotel's facilities, service, and package plans to such agencies;

- Conducts tours of the property and facilities to elicit commitments from clients for future conventions or group business.

Convention Coordinator

- Responsible for complete follow-up and coordination of all conventions, meetings, and banquets booked through the Sales Office. After a group has been booked by the sales force, it is the responsibility of the convention coordinator to contact the client, set up meeting dates, times, and needed number of sleeping and meeting rooms;

- Obtains guaranteed commitments for number of people attending banquets, meetings, and functions prior to the commencement of each particular function;

- Assists clients with the selection of suitable banquet menus;

- Works closely with the banquet manager and room reservations manager to coordinate group movements, avoid double booking a function room, and avoid overselling the property;

- Notifies all departments that may be involved with the execution of a convention of any changes in the original contract commitments. Prepares and distributes convention worksheet to all respective departments;

- Maintains a pleasant relationship with the clients and personally assists with any discrepancies they may have with the services offered by the hotel—changes in schedules, arrival times, rental equipment needed, time of registration, etc.

Chief Engineer

- Supervises operation for the entire building: refrigeration, heating, plumbing, water treatment, preventive maintenance, hotel rooms, heating and cooling systems, ice machines, swimming pools, lighting, kitchen equipment, emergency generators, water softeners, switch rooms, roof exhausts, electrical substations, etc.;

- Insures that all projects are completed on time and according to the necessary specifications;

- Works closely with each of the craft foremen to discuss any future projects, present operational, or personnel problems;

- Works closely with executive housekeeper and front office manager;

- Checks the daily log reports from each of the craftsmen to be familiar with the daily work and progress;

- Aids and instructs the craftsmen in scheduling work, ordering material, and completing assignments on schedule;

- Meets with the architects to discuss blueprints, contracts, and contractors to submit bids for new construction; meets with construction supervisors to discuss different phases of work.

Other managerial positions may be specialists responsible for activities such as personnel, office administration, marketing, security, recreational facilities, advertising, and public relations. These positions usually require specific knowledge and expertise in the particular field.

Do You Have What it Takes?

A bachelor's degree in hotel and restaurant administration provides particularly strong preparation for a career in hotel management. In 1988, over 150 colleges and universities offered bachelor's and graduate programs in this field. Over 600 community and junior colleges, technical institutes, vocational and trade schools, and other academic institutions also have hotel or restaurant management programs leading to an associate degree or other formal recognition. Graduates of such management programs usually start as **trainee assistant managers,** or, at the very least, advance to this position more quickly. Even if a college degree isn't mandatory for breaking into the hotel/motel business, it *is* essential if your goal is to make it to senior-level management. With the rapid advance in management techniques and technology in the industry, a solid education is a must. Needless to say, computer literacy is also extremely valuable.

Top Lodging Brands in Consumer Awareness

Based on percentage of frequent-travel survey respondents aware of brand name
1. Best Western, with 92.4%
2. Holiday Inns, 89.7%
3. Ramada Inns, 89.0%
4. Marriott Hotels, 86.9%
5. Days Inns of America Inc., 86.6%
6. Hilton Hotels, 85.5%
7. Hyatt Hotels, 85.2%
8. Howard Johnson, 84.1%
9. Sheraton Hotels, 83.4%
10. Motel 6, 80.7%

Source: *Lodging Hospitality*

And What You Still Have to Learn

Management positions almost always require knowledge of the business from "the bottom up." Hardworkers with what it takes might expect to be at a management level within five years, with an increase in starting pay from 20% to 100%.

Most managers are promoted from the ranks of front desk clerks, housekeepers, waiters, chefs, and salespeople. While some persons still advance to hotel management positions without the benefit of education or training beyond high school, post-secondary education is increasingly required and specialized hotel or restaurant training is preferred. Experience working in a hotel, even part-time while in school, is a great asset to anyone hoping to begin a hotel management career. Restaurant management training or experience is also a good background for entering hotel management, because the success of a hotel's restaurant and cocktail lounge are often key to the profitability of the entire establishment.

In *this* industry, it is not "news" when someone starts at the bottom of the career ladder and makes it to the top. There are success stories in every functional area: the housekeeper who works her way up to executive housekeeper in a 1,200 room hotel, the waiter who eventually becomes food and beverage manager, the reservations clerk promoted to front office manager and the bellman who becomes general manager.

Personality and stamina are key factors to hotel industry success. No matter what your job might be, you are there to service the guests. During the busy times, this could mean double shifts, loss of days off, even staying overnight in the hotel just to catch a few hours sleep. Hotels are not just looking for young and beautiful people to work in a beautiful environment; they are looking for people with good common sense and a willingness to work hard.

Managers are promoted frequently and often relocated to other properties in the United States and abroad. These managers must be able to get along with all kinds of people, even in stressful situations. They need initiative, self-discipline, and the ability to organize and direct the work of others, solve problems, and concentrate on details.

There Are Good Training Programs

Many large hotels and hotel corporations offer specialized, on-the-job management training programs that enable trainees to rotate among various departments and gain a thorough knowledge of the hotel's operation. Some offer free courses to employees to help them advance in their careers. Other hotels may even finance the necessary formal training in hotel management for outstanding employees. Newly-built hotels, particularly those without well-established, on-the-job training programs, often prefer experienced personnel for managerial positions.

While large hotel and motel chains may offer better opportunities for advancement than small, independently-owned establishments, they may also require frequent relocation. The large chains have more extensive career ladder programs and offer managers the opportunity to transfer to another hotel or motel in the chain or to the central office if an opening occurs. There is no business in the world that offers so much opportunity to move upwards rapidly.

Working in the hotel industry is exciting, even humorous at times, no matter what your job might be. It is a fast career track offering on-the-job training, the chance to meet new people everyday and an atmosphere that encourages individuality and scheduling flexibility.

You don't often hear about a hotel professional "burning out" on the job. Rather, once they start a career in the lodging industry, most people never want to leave!

▼

A veteran of the lodging industry for the past 12 years, MICHELE KELLEY has served as spokesperson for the lodging industry for the last four years in her role as Director of Communications for the American Hotel and Motel Association. During her tenure with the Association, she has implemented several award programs, such as an industry response to the economic effects of the Persian Gulf War entitled,

"Travel the Perfect Freedom;" an awareness program to the importance of tourism to the economic well-being of the United States; and a booklet explaining the various segments of the lodging industry, *Shopping for a Hotel*.

Prior to her work with the American Hotel and Motel Association, Ms. Kelley opened the public relations department for the Sheraton New Orleans Hotel, a 1200-room property in the heart of downtown New Orleans.

CHAPTER FOUR

The Real Hotel Business: A Lot More Exciting Than the TV Version

James P. Manley, Area Director—Personnel
Inter•Continental Hotels, Americas & Pacific/Asia

The hotel industry is more interesting, more complicated and much more exciting than the denizens of TV's fictional St. Gregory Hotel would ever believe. Not only may you specialize in a functional discipline like finance, marketing, human resources, food and beverage, etc., but the vast range of types, sizes and quality of hotel operations offers virtually unlimited career choices and opportunities.

This industry has traditionally been one in which you could rise progressively through the ranks to the most senior position—hotel general manager. In fact, I doubt you would find many general managers who did not begin their careers at or near the bottom of the career ladder. In the staunch European tradition of hotel management, not much followed today in the U. S. industry, it would not be uncommon for newcomers to spend years in apprenticeship before being promoted to even the most junior management positions.

Industry statistics indicated that the top 25 lodging chains in North America collectively control approximately 10,000 properties that offer roughly one million jobs. Add the many smaller lodging chains and the hundreds of independent hotels and the number of workers in this industry becomes truly staggering. So does the range of opportunities for you.

The Typical Hotel

From roadside motels to oceanside resort hotels, the industry has grown and segmented, providing an array of facilities and services for the most frugal vacation traveller and the most discriminating business traveller. Career opportunities may vary considerably depending on the segment of the industry you enter. But to at least give you a basic look at the industry, let's discuss a typical hotel, its organizational structure, positions, and career paths.

At the Top

The top position in the hotel is the general manager. Reporting to him or her may be an executive assistant or resident manager, although this layer of management may, in some hotels, not be necessary. The next management layer includes the controller, director of marketing and sales, food and beverage manager, rooms division (or front office) manager, executive housekeeper, human resources director, and chief engineer. These positions make up the executive committee of the hotel and, under the leadership of the general manager, are responsible for the hotel's efficient and profitable operation.

Other departments within the hotel include public relations, security, laundry, computer systems, and purchasing. The successful operation of the hotel takes a great deal of communication and teamwork between all departments.

The major operating departments of a hotel—food and beverage, sales and marketing, human resources, accounting, rooms and housekeeping—generally offer the greatest percentage of entry-level positions and provide the most clear-cut career paths.

▼

Best Mid-Priced Sector Hotels

1. Sheraton Inns
2. Courtyard by Marriott
3. Holiday Inns
4. Signature Inns
5. Clubhouse Inns of America
6. Ramada Inns
6. Dillon Inns
8. Harley Hotels
9. Drury Inns
10. Quality Inns

Source: *Business Travel News*

Food and Beverage

The type and size of the hotel will greatly influence the size and functions of the food and beverage department. Within the kitchen operation, you will find a culinary team, directed by the executive chef, responsible for all food preparation, and a stewarding department, commanded by an executive steward, responsible for the proper maintenance and storage of the hotel's china, glass, and silverware. Executive chefs manage the entire food production side of the kitchen and report directly to the food and beverage director. (Detailed discussion of a career in the culinary area is beyond the scope of this article—it is a profession unto itself that requires special training and dedication. While executive chefs have continued their careers into other areas, such movement is not the industry norm.)

The executive steward is faced with a most challenging dilemma—the workforce he or she oversees is generally unskilled and uneducated, yet the value of the inventory for which they are responsible may easily exceed $100,000. Not surprisingly, success in this area demands exceptional people and organizational skills—it is not a job for a prima donna or someone afraid to (literally) get their shirt sleeves wet. An entry-level position as an assistant executive steward provides immediate exposure to the challenge of managing people. It will also give you an understanding of the major supply line to the food and beverage operation—insight which will prove valuable as you continue your career path up the departmental ladder.

Other career opportunities in the food and beverage department exist in restaurant management. A hotel typically has at least one restaurant—often more—as well as room service. These restaurants may vary from informal breakfast and lunch cafes to jacket-and-tie gourmet dining rooms. The degree of food and beverage product and service knowledge required may vary considerably, therefore, depending on the type of restaurant in which you wind up working.

The restaurant manager is responsible for the profitable management of the restaurant including hiring, scheduling, coaching, counseling of staff, monitoring the operation in terms of service and product quality, forecasting and budgeting, and staff training. An assistant restaurant manager is a good entry-level management position; it may lead to assistant positions in other types of hotel restaurants, as well as to the position of restaurant manager. Typically, a food and beverage management career will lead to the position of assistant food and beverage manager and on to manager. The areas of room service and banqueting are also part of a career path to be pursued in preparing for upper-level food and beverage positions.

Rooms Division

The rooms division is composed of the front office, reservations, telephone, guest services, housekeeping, laundry, and uniformed services (i.e., bellstaff). The entire department may be managed by a rooms division manager or its management may be divided between front office, housekeeping, and laundry. The latter is more typically the case. In this situation, the front office would manage the front desk, reservations, telephone, guest services, and uniformed services.

Entry-level management positions are generally in the front office area. The assistant manager position may lead to assistant front office manager and front office manager. The assistant manager oversees the reception and reservations area in the absence of department management and, in particular, responds to guests' needs and related problems. This position provides exposure not only to the front office area, but to the entire hotel as well, since guests' problems are not confined to the front office. Its high frequency of guest interaction provides an excellent training ground not only for "customer handling" skills, but for a heightened awareness of who the customer is and what he or she wants and needs.

Housekeeping

The housekeeping department is second in size (staff-wise) only to the food and beverage department. As you would expect, this department is responsible for the cleanliness of the hotel, including guest rooms, restaurants, public areas, and the "back of the house"—the offices, laundry, locker rooms, etc.

Due to its lack of "glamour" status, housekeeping is not pursued as a career path as frequently as other operating departments. This, in my opinion, is unfortunate. The entry-level candidate looking to gain managerial experience will find it quickly in the housekeeping department. The experience gained from supervising this work group will accelerate the learning curve when it comes to understanding basic managerial skills—coaching, counseling, motivating, and scheduling. Furthermore, the expense budget of the housekeeping department is extremely large, and any exposure to managing a large budget will prove invaluable to your career climb.

This particular area offers very good opportunities to someone trying to break in to the hotel industry. A typical career path may begin as a housekeeping supervisor and may lead to assistant housekeeper, executive assistant housekeeper, and, finally, to executive housekeeper. Once you reach this latter position, you may decide to remain in housekeeping as a "professional" or choose (at this stage or prior) to pursue opportunities in the front office which were discussed earlier. Gaining housekeeping experience on the way to becoming rooms division manager is an excellent choice.

Sales and Marketing

The sales and marketing department is generally composed of a director of marketing and a director of sales (or one person with both titles) who, in turn, manage a team of sales managers. In many hotels, entry-level sales positions are titled account executives or sales associates. Another entry point may be as a sales and marketing assistant or researcher.

The task of this department is quite simple—they must sell the hotel facilities, hopefully well into the future. There is generally not a great deal of career cross-over from sales to marketing, though the converse may be true. After gaining a couple of years experience in one of the above entry-level positions, the next step would be to sales manager (this may or may not have a specific geographic or market segment attached to it). From sales manager, one would aspire to director of sales, or if with a chain, to a regional sales position, which would involve selling a number of hotels as opposed to one.

Career paths from a hotel's top sales and marketing position may be either through operations as an executive assistant manager or resident manager or as a sales and marketing professional within a large chain's corporate structure. Sales and marketing tends to hold a "glitz and glamour" image and, therefore, competition for entry-level positions is keen.

Accounting

The accounting department is commanded by a controller who is generally responsible for all hotel accounting and financial reports. Ample opportunities exist for someone seeking a career in the accounting and finance field, and your career would be greatly enhanced by education in this area. Some titles or positions to look for include:

- Cost Accountant—responsible for overall cost accounting reporting and relevant record keeping.

- Financial Accountant—responsible for a variety of accounting and financial analysis (perhaps obtained after entry-level position).

- Credit Manager—responsible for monitoring day-to-day credit practices, enforcing established credit policies and properly setting up account billing for groups and other credit related items.

Other positions which may provide entry into the department are income auditor, accounts receivable, or accounts payable supervisor. Career advancement would tend to follow a path from one or more of these positions to assistant controller and then to controller.

Human Resources

A typical human resources department is composed of a director (sometimes known as personnel director or manager), training manager, employee benefits administrator, employee relations manager (or assistant human resources manager, depending on the size of the hotel), and, possibly, a recruiter. Your career here depends greatly on your previous experience, due to the small size of the department. The position of benefits administrator often serves as an entry point for someone with little or no experience. In organizations where a management training program exists, it may be possible to enter a program designed to prepare the trainee for an assistant personnel or training coordinator position, titles generally found in the smaller hotels.

Given the labor intensity of the hotel business, the human resources department is as busy as any other operating department. The director is charged with managing a function with hundreds of internal customers—the employees. A well-managed department can contribute significantly to the profitability of the hotel—especially when you consider that a large hotel's annual payroll may be in the millions.

Education and Training

While it is not an absolute requirement, I would strongly urge anyone serious about a career in the hotel industry to attend one of the many available hotel schools. Most hotel chains offer structured management training programs, varying from year-long rotational assignments in all departments to specialized programs lasting up to six months in a specific department. Many of the candidates for these programs are uncovered by the chains' recruitment efforts at the major hotel schools.

Which training program you choose will greatly depend on your having made (or not made) a decision to concentrate in a particular department. There is no right or wrong choice in this regard; it's really simply what you want to do.

If you're fresh out of school with little or no industry experience, such training programs offer the fastest career path into management. A number of these schools also have graduate programs which provide the same advantages and enhance your marketability.

Which hotel school should you attend? Simply keep in mind that those with the best reputation will draw the most recruiters and, therefore, enhance your career opportunities. An additional benefit is the strong alumni network of the well-known hotel schools.

If you have gone through the required course of study at a school offering a major in hotel/restaurant management, you would be ready to enter a hotel's manager training program and spend approximately six to eight months "getting down and learning the business." After this training period is over, you may obtain an entry-level position in a major hotel chain with a salary in the low $20,000 range.

As in any other job, experience always pays off. If you have worked in any area of the hotel industry but not participated in a hotel school's program, you can still qualify for an entry-level job and, in fact, will probably begin at a higher salary level than a trainee with no experience. As the proverb says, "Only the wearer knows where the shoe pinches." There is no substitute for experience, and the reward for this would be a starting salary in the mid- to upper-twenties (depending on the amount of experience you have acquired).

▼

Test Out Your Career

Fortunately, the hotel industry offers many opportunities for you to "try out" a hotel career before you actually graduate. This is generally accomplished through a summer position in one of the many nonmanagerial positions often available. If you're still in school and considering a career in the hotel industry, take the opportunity to work in a hotel during the summer. Not only will you get a feel for what it's like, but you will begin to build relevant industry experience. I know one person who worked for the housekeeping department during her summers at college and is now the reservations manager at a very respectable hotel.

Be Ready to Be Flexible

Have I convinced you to consider a career in the hotel industry? Are you ready to work unusual hours? Spend some extremely long days? Work during your favorite holidays?

You'd better be. The hotel industry is not meant for people who cannot be flexible—flexibility is as important as the job itself. Especially when you get to a department head level, mobility is essential. You could easily move to another hotel when assuming a higher position, and candidates must be ready to take this into account when starting their careers.

If everything still sounds wonderful, come join this exciting and growing industry!

▼

JAMES P. MANLEY received his BA in Business Administration from Glassboro State College and a Masters in Professional Studies from the Cornell School of Hotel Administration.

Mr. Manley has been working for InterContinental since July, 1981, beginning as a manager in the corporate training department and moving to director of manpower planning and selection. In 1988, he was appointed to his current position. In addition to the daily job responsibilities, Mr. Manley has conducted training programs all over the world and has also provided human resources support to 35 hotels in his area.

A Career in Hospitality Sales:
Is it the One for You?

**Kevin P. Kelley, Director of Sales and Marketing,
Grand Hyatt Washington**

Sales & Marketing Careers in the Hotel Business

A sales career in the hotel industry is one that can be very rewarding and exciting, however, it may not be as easy as sometimes perceived. Sales positions in the hotel industry are perceived as the "glamour" or "fun" positions, and while the career can be enjoyable, there is another side.

Entering into Sales

A career in hotel sales is in very high demand. The competition to enter into sales is growing increasingly stronger and making sales positions more difficult to obtain. Before you convince yourself that sales is the career you want, you should ask yourself, "Am I really cut out for sales?" In order to do this you may want to honestly ask yourself some of the following questions:

1. Am I a highly competitive person? Would it bother me to lose a sale to another sales manager at a competing hotel property?

2. Am I the type of person that can sit on the phone for 5-7 hours a day and make calls to people that I may not know, in order to see if they are interested in my product?

3. Can I work under the pressure of a quota and the fact that, if I don't meet my quotas, my job could be in jeopardy?

4. Is traveling and being away from my family, along with coming to work early and staying late to entertain customers, something that I would enjoy? (Keep in mind that when you are traveling, you are not on vacation, rather on sales calls for 10 hours per day, and you rarely have time to see much of

anything. In addition, when you are entertaining, you are moving toward closing a sale; you are not out for a casual dinner or breakfast.)

These are just a few of the questions you have to ask. While sales is not a physically demanding job, it is mentally demanding.

How Do I Find Out if Sales Is for Me?

As mentioned earlier, the competition for sales positions is very keen. In order to find out if sales is for you, and in order to pick up some experience in sales, there are several ways you can approach getting some much needed experience.

Largest Hotel Chains in Food and Beverage Sales

1. Sheraton Corp.
2. Marriott Lodging
3. Hilton Hotels
4. Holiday Inns
5. Hyatt Hotels Corp.
6. Days Inns of America Inc.
7. Westin Hotels & Resorts
8. Inter-Continental Hotels Corp.
9. Quality Inns
10. Radisson Hotel Corp.

Source: *Restaurants & Institutions*

1. Starting in January, look for a summer internship position. Many hotel sales departments look to summer interns to do a variety of projects which would include, but are not limited to: market research, database projects of accounts, organize sales projects, and a host of other projects. These are projects that may have been put off or may not have been finished. Many sales departments do not have the budgets to hire a full-time staff person to assist with these projects, therefore, many departments will take on someone at or around minimum wage to assist them. While it may not be a well-paying job, it is a step up that you will have on those competing for a sales position later.

2. Offer to coordinate a telemarketing or blitz campaign for a hotel sales department. Through the college or university, contact a variety of hotels or resorts and let them know your class or a group of those interested in hotel sales management are interested in doing a telemarketing campaign. Most hotels will welcome you with open arms and will work with you to develop the campaign in order for it to be effective.

For either program mentioned, you should contact the director of sales and/or marketing at the hotels that you decide to work at and, in either case, be persistent with your goals. Any director of sales appreciates an aggressive, relentless, and tenacious person, some of the qualities necessary for a successful sales manager.

Will these Programs Help Me Determine if Sales Is for Me?

Perhaps not 100%, however, working in these environments will give you a feel for making calls and experiencing the types of situations sales managers face on a daily basis.

A good sales person demonstrates many different attributes, some of which include:

- self-confidence
- self-starter
- will to win
- aggressive

- works well under pressure
- empathetic
- high self-esteem
- ego driven

In order to succeed in sales, you must really know in your mind that it is what you want. If you have the attitude that you just want to try it to see if you like it, or are unsure if it's for you, the chances for failure are high. You have to determine before you enter into a sales management position that this is for you, or you are wasting your career time and the hotel's time.

Are There Any Other Ways of Entering into Sales?

You may have succeeded in doing one or both of the programs mentioned above, however, when you go to look for a sales job, there may not be any available. Where do we go from here? Many people with successful and prominent careers in the hospitality industry have started as secretaries, pool attendants, night auditors, or hotel operators, and now direct entire corporations. They just wanted to get their foot in the door. From there, they made their careers happen with hard work, determination, and the desire to succeed.

If you are faced with not being able to acquire the job you want, settle for another position that will at least get you into the organization. You should also let the appropriate persons know that you took this job to get into the business, however, your goal is to be in sales. Make sure they know it, and make sure you keep reminding them!

To make the picture a little more attractive, it is an added benefit to your sales career that you experience how other positions and departments work. The better sales people in the hospitality industry know what the other departments need, how they work, how they like to see information communicated, and how the hotel runs best. These areas are critical when making commitments on the hotel's behalf to our customers. Working in other departments can only benefit you in your job.

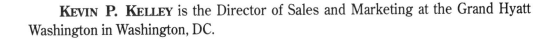

KEVIN P. KELLEY is the Director of Sales and Marketing at the Grand Hyatt Washington in Washington, DC.

Meet the Meeting Planners

Tina Berres Filipski, Manager of Communications
Meeting Planners International

Companies and associations throughout the world are meeting more often in more places to achieve a greater variety of objectives than ever before. Recent surveys reveal that over $56 billion is spent annually in the U.S. alone on meetings and conventions, making it one of the top industries in the country. As the number of meetings increases, so, obviously, does the demand for qualified professionals to plan and manage them.

As the title implies, meeting planners may plan and manage a variety of meetings—from intimate seminars and conferences requiring a room, a lunch, and a slide show to massive conventions, trade shows, and symposiums involving thousands of participants.

The profession is a relatively new one, and today's meeting planners come from a varied background. Most of the "pioneers" in meeting planning entered the meetings industry "through the back door"—they had jobs with limited planning responsibilities that expanded over the years until meeting planning became a major part of their job function. Even now, most meeting planners do not simply plan meetings full-time; many are also responsible for some combination of communications, public relations, marketing, general administrative, and other such duties.

But as meetings have become more important and expensive to the business world, a new breed of meeting planners have emerged—well-educated individuals who have entered the industry through the front door and have every intention of making their careers as *meetings* professionals.

The meetings field is highly competitive, and well-educated, aggressive individuals who plot strategies for obtaining planner positions are usually the ones who are successful. A key part of that strategy is determining what sort of qualifications potential employers are seeking in their meeting planners, then plotting a course of action to obtain them.

Typically, meeting planners entering the profession today possess a four-year college degree with an emphasis on business. Their written and verbal communication skills are impeccable, as is their ability to make quick decisions and interact with all types of people.

In addition to these "basic" requirements, knowledge of the travel industry would be most helpful. And you must be ready and able to take frequent business trips. If you have an eye for detail and organization and can work well under pressure, meeting planning can be a very interesting career choice.

The Job of a Planner

Meeting planners have a wide variety of duties. Depending on their specific job responsibilities and the complexity of their organizations' meetings, meeting planners typically:

- Prepare budgets
- Select meeting sites and facilities
- Negotiate group rates for accommodations and all transportation (both air and ground)
- Develop meeting programs and agenda
- Book reservations for participants
- Develop meeting specifications and secure actual meeting space
- Obtain and coordinate any entertainment
- Plan food and beverage functions
- Coordinate production of any printed and audio-visual support materials
- Administer the meetings on site once they are underway

Additionally, meeting planners must work closely with top management to determine what each meeting is supposed to achieve and to ensure that the agreed-upon objectives are actually met.

Educational Preparation and Opportunities

Effective meeting planners are versatile, well-educated individuals who know how to function as businesspeople first and meeting planners second. So a four-year college degree—preferably one in business administration with an emphasis on marketing, management or communication—is recommended, if not virtually mandatory. Some colleges and universities offer degree programs in hotel/motel management that may include elementary meeting planning courses. Such a program may well be a helpful way to build a planning knowledge base.

There are also many professional associations that offer meeting planners, and aspiring meeting planners, a wide variety of educational and training opportunities. Many of these organizations conduct national educational conferences and have local chapters that meet frequently.

Getting Started and Getting Paid

Although the specific responsibilities in any sample of planner jobs will still vary quite significantly, entry-level planner salaries usually average in the low twenties. Add some experience and these salaries can progress relatively quickly. For example, the average salary for U.S. planners in 1991 was $34,580.

Current hiring practices for even entry-level planner positions show that applicants with experience—*any experience*—are getting the jobs. How do you get experience if you're still a full-time student? Here are a few ideas:

- Find a part-time or summer job working for a hotel that is active in hosting meetings.

- Start in a clerical or administrative position with limited planning responsibilities at an association or corporation that plans a number of meetings.

- Find an internship or get a first job with a planner who is willing to be a mentor.

- Volunteer to plan activities such as office parties, church outings and other civic organization events.

These ideas may not result in a job as a meeting planner, but they will give you valuable meeting planning experience to put on your resume or job application. They also will create an enhanced awareness of what's involved in meeting planning.

Virtually every U.S. association or corporation has one or a group of individuals planning its meetings. These individuals may not have the job title "meeting planner," but they are, in fact, just that. They may be unaware of it themselves, but they have embarked on a career in the meetings industry that holds much promise for the future.

Here are some other ideas for finding entry-level openings:
- Check with current or past employers to see if opportunities exist.
- Check with other local employers—both corporations and associations that place an emphasis on meetings and education.
- Carefully review classified ads in a variety of publications and categories—look for positions that require detail-oriented individuals capable of coordinating promotions, special events and other similar functions. These may provide some initial planning experience.

TINA BERRES FILIPSKI is director of publications for Meeting Planners International and editor of MPI's monthly newsmagazine, *The Meeting Manager*. MPI is the largest educational association of meeting professionals with more than 10,500 members in 32 countries. It is committed to excellence in meetings, international growth, education, research, chapter, and high ethical standards.

How to Specialize in Corporate Travel

Stuart J. Faber

You receive a frantic call from the secretary of a leading industrialist in your city. The boss has been summoned to an urgent meeting in Kansas City, a destination with which neither the secretary nor the boss has any familiarity.

"What's the most expeditious way to get to Kansas City?"

"Can a charter aircraft be arranged?"

"Can you arrange limousine service from the airport to hotel?"

"Can you recommend the most luxurious hotel in town and arrange for video conferencing, a computer rental, and the use of one of the hotel's boardrooms?"

"Does the hotel have a fitness center and a business center?"

"What is Kansas City's most popular restaurant for a power lunch?"

"What is the weather like in Kansas City, and how do business people dress?"

"What recreational activities can you recommend for the boss's leisure time?"

Can you provide accurate answers to these questions? If you can, and are also capable of giving accurate responses about other major domestic and international cities at a moment's notice, you may be on your way to becoming a specialist as a business travel agent. The difference between a general travel agent and a business travel specialist is: 1) the possession of a thorough knowledge of what a business traveler will require on his or her mission; and 2) the ability to service the needs of the executive traveler by offering efficient and appropriate planning of transportation, hotel accommodations, meals and conferences.

The focus of this article will be on the travel agent who is seeking new avenues of revenue. Keep in mind, however, that the achievement of the knowledge and skills discussed in this article offer other career opportunities. For example, an employee of a travel agent could, with this knowledge and skill, develop a new corporate travel department for the travel agency. Opportunities also exist in private industry. Your knowledge and skill could convince a manager of a large corporation that you can save them money and provide superior service by setting up a special travel department in their corporation.

As an agent, once these skills are acquired, you can increase your business in a variety of ways:

1. You can offer full service to your leisure clientele who, from time to time have need for the services of a business travel specialist. This is important. If the leisure traveler calls a specialist for the occasional business trip, that client may later defect entirely and also take his or her leisure business to the specialist;

2. Your knowledge and skill not only enables you to retain your existing executive clientele, but could result in their defection from another travel agent to you for their leisure travel requirements;

3. Your knowledge and skill provide you with the weaponry with which to solicit new business from other travel agents;

4. If you are seeking employment in a travel agency, or would like to elevate yourself to a higher position in your current agency, your specialized skills will make you very marketable.

Benefits from this Specialty

1. Stability and Consistency

a. Leisure travel is discretionary, and susceptible to economic fluctuations. True, the economy also affects the volume of business travel, but many business trips are mandatory regardless of economic downturns, or even political unrest.

b. Leisure travelers take trips depending upon their mood, finances, and health. Business travelers frequently have to travel whether they want to or not. And if one executive is ill, another can usually take his or her place. Such substitutions are not generally made in leisure travel.

2. More Sophisticated Clientele

Most travel agents agree that it is easier and often more pleasant to work with clients for whom travel is not so esoteric. The more experienced the traveler, generally the easier it is to communicate with that client. Business travelers usually know what they want and make decisions quickly. Furthermore, because of the diversity of services offered, the challenge to the travel agent is greater and the vicarious aspect of the mission is heightened. Most travel agents agree that it is exciting to be a participant in the planning of a business mission.

3. Revenue Enhancement

   a. Business travel offers new avenues of revenue for the travel agent. In addition to the usual commissionable services, commission negotiations can be made with travel providers for your participation in the planning of meetings, business dinners, and transportation services.

   b. Most leisure clients travel only once a year. Business travelers may travel as many as fifty times a year, and spend as much money on each mission as the leisure traveler spends in an entire year. For example, many business travelers use first class air service, the cost of which often exceeds coach fares by three times.

Training for this Specialty

I assume that the reader is a travel agent, or has already acquired the skills to become one. How do you enhance those skills so that you can become a specialist?

1. Learn About the Most Popular Business Traveler Destinations

Surveys we have conducted reveal that approximately 30 American cities receive 90% of all business travelers. Add to that another 10 cities in Asia, and 10 in Europe. Most of the host domestic cities have populations in excess of 500,000. The United States has approximately 60 additional cities with populations in excess of 250,000 that also may be likely hosts. Obviously it is difficult to learn about each of these cities. But it is important that you acquaint yourself with as many possible.

Discover where the major areas of business activity exist in each city—where the banking and financial centers are, the industrial complexes and business parks, the location of specialized industries such as automotive, garment, electronic, etc. For example, did you know that one of the most heavily populated business communities in the Kansas City, Missouri, area is actually in Overland, Kansas?

Your next step is to locate the hotels near the individual business centers and obtain detailed information about them, either by writing for brochures or by consulting a hotel encyclopedia. Learn as much a you can about the hotels, such as the year of construction, the date of the last major renovation, the size of the guest rooms, the configuration of the meeting rooms, and features about their restaurants and recreational facilities. For example, is shuttle service offered from the airport? Are computer modem hookups provided in the rooms? Determine the distance from the hotel to the airport and the easiest way to get there. Finally, obtain a general knowledge about dress, customs, and weather for each destination.

Then, when a client calls and tells you he or she is going to Milwaukee, Pittsburgh, Tulsa, Kansas City, or Birmingham, although you may never have been to any of those cities, you can, nevertheless, provide a service most travel agents are not equipped to offer. First, ask the client where his or her business activities will center. If for example your client says, "I will be near the Pittsburgh Gateway Center," your quick and impressive response might be, "The Pittsburgh Hilton is in the center of the complex and is just twenty minutes from the Pittsburgh International Airport. The hotel was renovated last year and has a new fitness center. I can get you a special corporate rate." You can further tell the traveler that a 50-passenger bus departs the airport every 20 minutes at a cost of $10.00, or a taxi ride is approximately $25.00. Finally, check the weather and offer tips on what clothes to bring. Will that client be impressed? You bet.

2. Learn How to Find New Clients

Your home town may be populated by travel-driven businesses you never knew about. How can learn the business demographics and ferret out these companies?

Most Expensive Cities for Business Travel
1. New York, NY
2. Boston, MA
3. Washington, DC
4. Chicago, IL
5. Los Angeles, CA
6. Santa Barbara, CA
7. Houston, TX
8. Newark, NJ
9. Philadelphia, PA
10. Dallas, TX
Source: *Corporate Travel*

Start with a business encyclopedia such as *Standard and Poor's Register of Corporations, Directors and Executives* or *Dun and Bradstreet's Million Dollar Directory*. Most public library reference departments have these publications, which list businesses in a number of categories—annual gross income, product or service, or geographic location. From the list of businesses in your city, select companies whose activities would most likely include business travel. Businesses with branch offices, sales forces, or those who sell products to out-of-town companies are likely candidates.

The natural tendency is to survey the larger companies, but don't be fooled. A one-person company could be engaging in millions of dollars of business generated from his or her sales trips to other cities. Discovering these potential clients can only come with further in-depth investigation.

Once you gather a list of companies, call each firm and ask who handles business travel. The rest depends upon your skill, personality, and sales ability.

3. Learn the Skills of a Meeting Planner

Your client may be hosting an out-of-town function which could include attendance by executives from several other cities. (Perhaps you can make their travel arrangements, too). These various attendees may require several rental cars, or a limousine. You can earn yourself extra commissions by providing limousine, bus, and car rental service—which historically pay commissions. Restaurant operators are not at all adverse to showing their gratitude with a commission.

In essence, not only can you serve as a business travel agent, you can function as a meeting planner. Meeting planners arrange air and ground transportation, meeting rooms, special audiovisual equipment, meal functions, and recreational and entertainment activities. Professional meeting planning, especially as it applies to large functions, is a specialty in itself and requires a greater expanse of skill. However, the planning of small functions (i.e., for up to 25 attendees) is something you can readily learn. You will become acquainted with new terms such as classroom seating for meetings, break-out sessions, flip-charts, teleconferencing, and spouse activities.

The best way to acquire this knowledge is to become friendly with a local hotel sales manager who can serve as your tutor. Take a tour of a local hotel and use it as your classroom. Try planning a meeting at a hotel in your city. There are no rules against a travel agent organizing a function for a meeting to be held in his or her own city to be attended by local attendees. A local hotel sales manager not only can help you plan the meeting, but can teach you how to plan future meetings, either in your town or another city.

There is no substitute for a personal visit to as many major cities as possible. Your own experiences can be far more valuable to your client than anything you might read in a brochure or directory.

Servicing the Requirements of the Business Traveler

1. Develop Out-of-Town Relationships with Travel Providers

Personal relationships with travel providers is of primary importance. For example, once a hotel manager in another city is convinced that you mean business and can send business, his or her providing an upgraded room or arranging a personal greeting for your client at the front desk will become standard procedure. Solving problems of your clients that may arise at his or her hotel comes easier with a such personal contact. Can you imagine how impressed your client will be when he or she learns that you and the hotel general manager are buddies?

2. Offer Social Transportation Service from Home and Back

Perhaps you can make arrangements for transportation from the executive's home to the airport. How many travel agents perform that service? This article assumes you have the skills to make flight arrangements. But you can do even more for your clients. A call to the airline will provide you special information about the flight such as seat size, meals, etc,. Make arrangements to get your client a special seat or a special meal. Pass that information on to your client before departure.

3. Help Make Your Client Comfortable at the Hotel

Make arrangements at the destination hotel for something special for your client—a greeting at the front desk, a fruit basket or a bottle of wine in the room with a greeting from you. Send a directive to the hotel to inform the staff of the special needs or preferences of your client, such as a room on a lower floor, a fax machine in the room, or a stock of bottled water.

Learn as much as you can about your client's needs and preferences. Then, prepare a questionnaire for each client and keep it on file. Will he or she want the same room on subsequent visits? Do they want rooms with views? Do they prefer rooms on lower floors or near the elevators? Will they require fax machines, ironing boards, bottled water, or other special equipment in the room?

How to Obtain New Business, Plus Keep the Business You Already Have

1. Impress potential clients with your specialized knowledge. Once you have targeted your market in the method described above, the first thing to do is to impress potential clients with your specialized knowledge. For example, send them one of your sample questionnaires to show that you are interested in their special requirements and preferences, and are sensitive to the needs of the business traveler.

2. Once you have determined the cities to which they travel, learn as much about those cities as you can and make it clear that you are familiar with those cities. Tell them also that, should they require a visit to a city which is unfamiliar to them, chances are the city is familiar to you.

3. Suggest that they contact other clients who can serve as references and give testimonials to your special skills. A word from a third party is your best advertisement.

4. Send monthly reminders of your services. Advertising experts will tell you that repetitive exposure eventually pays off. A monthly profile of a different city each month, updated airline news, or business trends in other cities not only displays your knowledge and interest, but keeps your name in front of them.

How do you obtain these materials? A potential client may have so much business, he or she may be worthy to a gift subscription to a trade magazine or a publication such as the *Wall Street Journal* or *Fortune Magazine*. A gift of a book of restaurants, a travel periodical, or information about airlines is something you should consider. The public relations department of airlines, hotels, restaurants, and other travel providers will happily furnish you with brochures, which you in turn you can send on to your clients with your compliments.

You may want to consider your own newsletter in which you might include information you have gathered about a number of cities.

The most important thing to remember is that once you have acquired the client, you must be able to provide the service. Acquiring the client is the easy task. Keeping the client is more difficult.

You might consider a special 800 number just for your business travel clients. This will enable them to call you anytime should a problem arise in their destination or should they need unexpected travel arrangements from that destination to another.

I am not telling you anything new when I stress that the secret of success in the travel business is service. Any travel agent, for example, can place their client on an American Airlines flight from Chicago to New York and put the client up in the New York Hilton Hotel. The ticket cost will probably be the same, and the airplane will be the same airplane and the Hilton will be the same Hilton. The extra you are providing is:

1. Is the Hilton where they should be staying?

2. Were their seats and meals properly selected for the flight?

3. Was there a special amenity in the room when your client arrived? Did you negotiate an upgraded room for the same price?

4. Can a fortuitous problem be handled by a phone call from you to the manager of the hotel?

5. Did you select a special restaurant for your client about which he or she had no previous knowledge, and which pleased them immensely?

6. Have you made your client feel at home in a town with which he or she was previously unfamiliar?

7. Was the room on the correct floor, was the bottled water waiting in the room, was the fax machine in place?

8. Were the teleconferencing arrangements adequately made, did the board room have enough chairs, note pads and pencils?

Affirmative answers to these questions are what will distinguish you from the run-of-the-mill travel agent.

You Are on Your Way to an Enhanced Career

Once you have developed the skills of a business travel specialist, new career avenues should open for you. Whether you operate your own agency, are employed by a travel agency, or desire to work in a private industry, these new skills will increase your income, pave the way to an enhanced career, plus provide many exciting hours of work that is never routine.

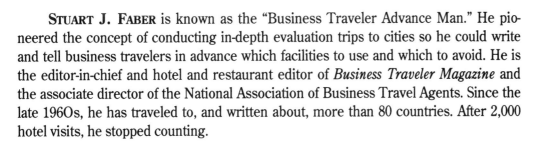

STUART J. FABER is known as the "Business Traveler Advance Man." He pioneered the concept of conducting in-depth evaluation trips to cities so he could write and tell business travelers in advance which facilities to use and which to avoid. He is the editor-in-chief and hotel and restaurant editor of *Business Traveler Magazine* and the associate director of the National Association of Business Travel Agents. Since the late 1960s, he has traveled to, and written about, more than 80 countries. After 2,000 hotel visits, he stopped counting.

With his team of travel evaluators, he now publishes the *FabeReport:,* a concise outline of every major U.S. and foreign city with evaluations of hotels restaurants and other travel facilities.

CHAPTER EIGHT

If You Love to Travel, Have I Got a Job for You

Leslie Ann Berryman, Thomas Cook Travel

f you love to travel, or think you would love to travel, becoming a travel agent would be one of the most rewarding, yet challenging, career choices you could make. The "glamour" and excitement of a travel agency career is enough to entice many people—young and old, male and female. Yes, you do get many chances to travel, and yes, it is often exciting and glamorous, but it does require a lot of hard work and dedication!

The travel industry is constantly changing, which means that anyone entering the industry must be very adaptable and open to change. In the present world of mega-agencies (i.e., American Express Travel, Thomas Cook Travel, and Rosenbluth Travel) and the rapid decline of the local "mom and pop" agencies, the industry requires a well-prepared, very adaptable candidate to fill staff positions. Therefore, it is now almost imperative to attend a travel school in order to be considered for a travel agency position.

Look for a Good Travel School

When investigating travel schools, look for a curriculum that concentrates on geography, phone skills, and most importantly, airline computer training (at least one month of computer usage is recommended). I cannot emphasize enough the importance of geographic knowledge. Too many human resource representatives and managers meet applicants with very poor geographic knowledge, and this area is very heavily weighed when making hiring decisions.

Another important aspect of travel school programs is the "on the job" experience. A good travel school with an established internship program deals with many agencies that accept travel school students on an internship basis. The agency benefits by being able to evaluate potential employees without having to endure the costly cycle of hiring, training, and, sometimes, firing inadequate employees. They also benefit by observing how the potential employee interacts with other staff members. The student benefits by experiencing the hectic, fast-paced, and ever-changing day-to-day office operations of a travel agency. Consequently, an internship is usually the "make or break" point when a student is pursuing a travel agency career!

As travel school counselors will advise (and agency managers will confirm) entry-level travel industry positions are low-paying. So, those interested in fast advancement, independence, and higher income potential will be better suited to the large mega-agency. Those looking for supplemental income and opportunities to travel frequently will be better suited to the smaller, local agency.

Entry-Level Positions Open the Door

Typically, an entry-level position in a large agency is a support staff member. Duties include ticket packaging and delivery, brochure stamping and filing, opening mail, answering and directing phone calls, and ordering and distributing office supplies.

U.S. States with the Most Travel Agencies

1. California
2. New York
3. Florida
4. Texas
5. Illinois
6. New Jersey
7. Pennsylvania
8. Massachusetts
9. Ohio
10. Michigan

Source: *Travel Industry World Yearbook*

In a smaller agency, you may be asked to quote airfares over the telephone and to call hotels, car rental firms, and tour company vendors for simple bookings. Once in a support position for six months to one year, you could advance to a quality control position, which requires much more work on the airline computer system. Duties include accessing flight reservations made by the staff reservationists and checking them for accuracy, data continuity, documentation of fare options, seat assignments, and frequent flyer data. A quality control agent is also responsible for ticket issuance. A quality control agent should expect to remain in this position for six months to one year. From this point, an exceptional employee can expect to advance to domestic reservationist, which involves answering phones and dealing directly with the traveler and travel arrangers. Given the responsibilities of this position, a good, productive, and accurate reservation agent is the cornerstone to a successful relationship between an agency and its clients. Duties include making flight, hotel, car, tour, and limousine reservations. Accurate quoting of airfares is an important aspect of this position. This position tends to be the most stressful position in the travel agency, but usually the most rewarding. Excelling in a reservationist position is the quickest way to get recognized for further advancement. A domestic reservation agent can advance to international reservationist, lead agent, supervisor, tariff coordinator, and even manager! However, in large mega-agencies, the operations department (support, quality control, reservations, and upper management) are only one part of the organization. Career opportunities can also lead to customer services, client liaison, sales, training, accounting, and technology development.

Entry-level positions in a smaller, local agency are usually as a file clerk and/or reservationist. Duties include answering phones, ordering brochures, stamping and filing, observing other staff members' sales techniques, and performing minor computer projects. Advancement comes with experience in booking flights, tours, packages, cruises, etc. A fast learner can advance to leisure agent very quickly. From leisure agent, an individual can progress to manager. Be mindful though, that advancement in smaller agencies tends to be very limited. Many agents spend several years in a smaller agency, gathering knowledge and experience in hopes of someday opening their own agency.

An added benefit of entering the travel industry with a smaller, local agency is that it provides a great opportunity for later transferring to a large mega-agency. Given the competitive state of the travel industry, there are many agencies looking for reservationists with a minimum of two years industry experience.

What is the greatest benefit of a career in the travel industry? The economical travel opportunities have been, and always will be, the major attraction of the industry. Airlines, tour vendors, cruise lines, and resorts encourage travel agents to experience their product first-hand so that they can more confidently sell it to the client. Discounts range from 50% off to 90% off, and, once in a great while, 100% off!

▼

Biggest Airline Computer Reservation Systems

Percent of market share, based on number of agency terminals
1. Sabre, with 34.7%
2. Apollo, 28.1%
3. Worldspan, 22.4%
4. System One, 14.8%
Source: *Wall Street Journal*

But an excellent candidate must also be attracted to a fast-paced, ever-changing environment. Ever-changing air fares, airline bankruptcies, new and lost business, and technological advancements all contribute to the operations of both large and small travel agencies.

In conclusion, travel agencies look for the following qualifications when hiring new employees: love of travel, adaptability to change, a thorough knowledge of geography, good phone and interpersonal skills, patience, and a willingness to advance. Possessing these qualifications will put you on the right track to a rewarding career in the travel industry!

▼

LESLIE BERRYMAN graduated from Grand Blanc (MI) High School in 1976. After one year at Michigan State University, she began her career in the travel industry with Red Carpet Travel, where she was promoted to office manager in 1981. In 1988, she joined Rosenbluth Travel as lead international agent and was promoted to office manager of the on-site corporate office in Toledo, OH. Leslie is currently the branch manager of a Thomas Cook Travel office in Detroit, MI.

How to Get a Job with a Cruise Line

Mary Fallon Miller, Author, *How to Get a Job with a Cruise Line*

1. What are my chances of landing a job with a cruise line?

If you've dreamed of becoming Julie the Cruise Director or Captain Steubing on the Love Boat, you can make your fantasy into a real, paying job. Instead of getting stuck at the same red light on your way to work, you'll travel around the world and get paid for it. Now is the best time to get started on your cruise line job search because, while other industries are laying off and downsizing, cruise lines are booming. There are thirty-four major cruise lines (members of Cruise Lines International Association) and many significant smaller lines. The cruise industry is betting that more people will choose to cruise—we'll see twenty-three new ships in the next four years. This means new positions, turnover, and more entry-level opportunities.

2. What are the different jobs that cruise lines need people for?

Many people find their skills may apply to cruise line jobs. A cruise ship is like a floating resort employing people with a variety of educational and work experience. Passengers are treated like kings and queens by the cruise director staff, hostess, gift shop, purser's staff (hotel and financial management team), cabin stewards, and bar and restaurant staff. Casino operators keep the high rollers happy, and junior cruisers receive the royal treatment from the youth counselor staff. Cruises are famous for entertainment, and that means jobs for singers, dancers, musicians, disc jockeys, comedians, and magicians.

The popularity of health and fitness programs aboard cruise ships has created excellent opportunities for aerobics instructors, fitness directors, massage therapists, and spa managers. Photographers, watersports instructors, and stage technicians complement the staff, and every ship must sail with a nurse and doctor aboard. Cruise line headquarters also need qualified, enthusiastic people for reservations, sales, marketing, public relations, and administration.

3. Who are cruise lines looking for?

Cruise lines want "people people!" There are opportunities for career changers, college students, and retired people. Cruise lines do their hiring for peak sailing periods—December through March, summer, and the holidays. Education majors Rick and Renee take summers off from college to work as youth counselors in the Caribbean. Paul Dickens went from being a local wedding photographer to a position as ship's photographer for the *Sovereign of the Seas.* Now he takes his passion for photography on location. Annie Fraraccio earned her aerobics certification, graduated from college, and travels as manager of a luxury liner health spa.

Career changers find new lives aboard ship: Suzann Christensen, a registered nurse, decided to leave hospital pressures and now travels Alaska and the Caribbean as a shipboard nurse. "My husband and brother are very supportive of me because it's something I've always wanted to do," says Suzann. Pam Jaye knew the nine-to-five office life wasn't for her. She combined her training as a dance instructor with her office management skills and now works as a member of the cruise director's staff.

If you're an expert at something, you might be able to trade your talents for travel. The popularity of theme cruises has opened up jobs for entertainers and other specialists. Cruises often feature workshops and lectures on ports-of-call, finance, cooking, health, fitness, gaming, and many other topics.

For retired gentlemen, sailing for free as a host may be your best bet. Several cruise lines offer the popular "host program", where select retired gentlemen act as dancing and dining companions for single women passengers.

Leading Cruise Lines

Based on share of total beds, in percent
1. Carnival, with 24.6%
2. Royal Caribbean, 12.6%
3. Kloster, 12.1%
4. Princess, 10.8%
5. Chandris, 6.1%
6. Costa, 6.0%
7. Cunard, 5.8%
8. Others, total 22.0%

Source: *Travel Agent*

4. Is it difficult to land a job aboard a cruise ship?

Yes, it is competitive—it's a dream come true for many people to get away from it all, travel around the world, and get paid for it. To land your dream job, prepare yourself by becoming knowledgeable about the jobs and cruise lines, and follow the advice of employees and personnel directors.

5. What tips do cruise employees and personnel directors give?

I personally interviewed cruise line employees in my book, *How to Get a Job with a Cruise Line,* and they tell how they got their job, their work and educational background, and specific tips that will help you get your dream job. I also interviewed cruise personnel directors who give their advice on how to stand out from the competition. Here's their advice:

A. Learn about the cruise industry: read the travel section of your newspaper; ask your travel agent to lend you copies of travel trade magazines; and attend travel shows.

B. Start preparing now. Take hospitality courses, work at a resort or restaurant, parks and recreation department or school, and polish your customer relations, language, communication, and entertainment skills. Get certification and training.

C. Target your job search. Determine what jobs interest you—and how your skills match those positions. Which jobs can you contribute to?

D. Start your own personal sales campaign. Prepare a professional resume, with references, a photo, and possibly a simple video of your work. Review your personal contacts and let them know you're interested in working with a cruise line.

6. What exciting places can I travel to?

As a cruise line employee, you'll have an opportunity to see the world. Destinations vary by the length of the cruise and by season. A three-night cruise may take you to the Mexican Riviera or the Bahamas; a seven-night cruise, to the Eastern or Western Caribbean. On the other hand, you may sail around South America or the South Pacific on a longer voyage. On her second cruise ship, gift shop manager Lee Ann Hansen traveled the Caribbean in the winter and Alaska in the summer. "People move around so they can see different parts of the world," says Hansen. Mike Messick swore he'd be an expedition leader by the age of twenty, and at age twenty-five, he had already traveled to 125 countries!

Some of the most popular Caribbean destinations include Cancun, Cozumel, Acapulco, Ocho Rios, Grand Cayman, San Juan, St. Thomas, Aruba, Bermuda, and the Bahamas. Other hot ports-of-call are found in Orient, the Mediterranean, the South Pacific, Russia, Hawaii, and Alaska. Southeast Asia has also opened its ports to cruise travel, and Cuba may be the next hot spot on the horizon.

7. How can you expect to be paid?

You travel for free, your accommodations and meals are free! As with any job, your salary will be based on your previous experience and the level of your position. The pay differs with each cruise line and for each job. You have the option of banking your money or spending it as you please. For example, cruise director Catherine Chastain sends her paycheck home to her mother. When I commented how generous she was, she laughed and told me she had already saved enough money for a down payment on her own house "shoreside" and her mother deposits her mortgage payments for her. Cosmetologist Ann Taylor enjoys spending her tips in the duty-free shops of St. Thomas.

"You can really put money away," says Larry Cavanaugh, Director of Casino Operations. "For your first couple years you like the travel the best and beyond a year and a half its the savings—the money you make."

8. What can I do with my time off? (Travel-Adventure-Romance!)

You'll visit the places the rich and famous travel to, meet new people, learn new cultures, and of course, go shopping. You'll visit exciting foreign countries, tropical islands, and historic cities. Youth counselors from Royal Caribbean ships hit the beach and go snorkeling or parasailing. Most importantly though, "You'll make a lot of good friends," says Tess Blake, ship's hostess. "I know people from all over the world!" As your world expands, you'll grow personally as well. Joyce Gleeson, an assistant cruise director, now speaks conversational Greek, Spanish, and Italian.

9. Is it really like the Love Boat? How do I make my dream job come true?

Cruise ship life is demanding, and you will put in some long days. But it's also very rewarding because you travel the world, get paid for it, and you are part of an important team. There's a camaraderie on a ship that you don't find in other nine to five jobs. As a member of the cruise staff, you are what makes the magic of cruising happen.

It's a job you can love. "I love working on a cruise ship," says Ronn McDonald, cruise director. "I'll be an entertainer until I'm so old they tell us we can't use canes." It's a lifestyle, not just a job, and it really is an adventure.

Two final tips:

Be polite and persistent!

For first hand knowledge—take a cruise!

▼

MARY FALLON MILLER has owned a cruise travel agency for six years. Her close contacts with the cruise lines make her uniquely qualified to give you the most accurate, inside information on cruise line jobs. Her second edition of *How to Get a Job with a Cruise Line*, from which this essay is excerpted, is recommended by *The New York Times* and the Cruise Lines International Association, the most recognized organization for cruise industry professionals.

Ms. Miller speaks nationally on cruise line employment, is a member of the Cruise Lines International Association, and races sail boats competitively as a member of the Boca Ciega Yacht Club of St. Petersburg, FL. Readers are invited to contact her with questions regarding the cruise industry.

Her book, *How to Get a Job with a Cruise Line*, may be ordered from Ticket to Adventure Publishing, Inc., PO Box 41005, St. Petersburg, FL 33743; or by phone at 800-929-7447. The book is also available at Waldenbooks, B. Dalton, and other major bookstores.

The Center of the Travel Industry—Getting Started in Car Rental

**Carol Riley, Director—Equal Opportunity & WHQ Employment
Avis Rent A Car System, Inc.**

n several respects, the rent a car companies are in the middle of the travel industry. Most travelers start their journey on an airplane and end the trip at a hotel or at home; they rent cars in between.

The airlines hold top honors as the "glamour" part of the travel industry. And hoteliers are in the business of providing life's necessities, food, and shelter. What, then, does the car rental field offer?

To its customers—service, convenience, and independence. To its employees—a fast-paced, ever-changing, exciting workplace. And to new graduates—you—the opportunity to immediately join front-line management.

Getting Started in the Field

A recent college graduate would begin his or her career in the rent a car operations group (in the "field") as a **shift manager** at one of the company's larger locations. The main function of the shift manager is to insure that the rental operation runs smoothly and that equipment, vehicles, and personnel are all in position to deliver world-class customer service.

The shift manager's other duties and responsibilities include customer service (answering customer complaints, comments, and concerns), employee discipline, increasing the overall operational quality of the vehicles and buses, ensuring efficient and professional counter sales techniques, solving problems unique to each location and, ultimately, renting as many cars as possible and producing a profit.

As a shift manager masters the rental operation, he or she may take on added responsibilities such as payroll preparation, car accountability reports, hiring of non-management personnel, conducting training exercises, and accountability for gas and supplies.

Shift managers generally earn their first promotions after two to three years on the job. Advancement within the field organization progresses through **station manager, agency manager, fleet manager, maintenance and damage manager, airport manager,** and **city or district manager.** Promotions generally involve a change of location—managers move frequently between large, medium, and small facilities.

A Shift Manager's Typical Day

Long hours and a varied schedule are the "order of the day" for shift managers. Many airport locations are open 24 hours per day, 365 days per year, so shift managers may be required to work midnight, weekend, and/or holiday hours. Larger locations tend to rotate managers' schedules to give everyone an equal proportion of desirable and less-than-desirable shifts.

A typical day at a busy airport location will find the shift manager performing these duties:

- **7 AM:** Ensure all employees have reported to work and the work force is large enough to handle the day's business. Gather the reports and information necessary to determine the actual amount of business anticipated;

- **8 AM:** Vehicles must be accounted for and ready to rent, plus necessary supplies (i.e., gas, fluids, towels, etc.) available to clean additional vehicles as the day progresses;

- **9 AM:** Prepare and reconcile receipts from the previous day: coupons received, vouchers used, cash received, checks written and charge cards used;

- **10 AM:** Reconcile car accountability reports (cars out for repairs, missing, sold, overdue or moved to other locations);

- **11 AM:** Continue monitoring the ongoing operation and respond to customer comments, complaints or concerns;

- **1 PM:** Allow time for customer service functions—phone calls to customers, mailed responses, billing problems and errors, lost and found items, and mini-lease agreement updates.

- **2 PM:** Prepare for afternoon work force; ensure employees arrive to work and information is gathered to determine afternoon business demands;

- **3 PM:** (when customers begin to return vehicles) The shift manager will organize the return parking lot to ensure maximum number of vehicles with the least amount of confusion for the customer, try to reduce customers wait-in-line time as much as possible, and prepare for the evening rental business (which begins late in the afternoon);

- **4 PM:** At this point of the day, a shift manager with an interest and ability in operations management will face all facets of the rental car operation simultaneously. There are never two days in a row exactly alike. This is a fast-paced, always-changing, exciting field of management;

- **5 PM:** The afternoon management shift arrives to continue the day's activities in much the same manner as the morning manager.

Compensation

The starting salary for a shift manager will vary based on experience, education, and the city in which the job opening occurs. Where the cost of living and taxes are high, salaries tend to be higher. Likewise, salaries tend to be lower in cities with a lower cost of living. Starting salaries can range from $20,000 to $25,000; the compensation package, however, may also include a performance bonus and the use of a company car (and, at Avis, an annual Employee Stock Ownership Plan stock allocation).

Every year, each manager's performance is appraised by his or her supervisor; pay raises are based on the individual's merit reviews.

A manager who leaves the car rental industry would likely find a welcome in any industry that serves the public. And because of the operational aspects of the job, a shift manager moving to a manufacturing or production environment will benefit from the management and scheduling expertise he or she will develop in a car rental firm.

The Ideal Entry-Level Candidate

The ideal candidate for an entry-level shift management position would be:

- Self-motivated, with a high energy level
- Oriented towards working with people, both customers and subordinates
- Willing to work long hours if necessary
- Quick-witted and able to make decisions independently

While a college degree is not necessary for the shift manager position, having one does serve a few useful purposes. The knowledge gained in college courses is always useful. And the time devoted to earning a degree and the difficulty of the coursework shows employers that the candidate has successfully managed pressure and time constraints before he or she even enters the work force.

Most Expensive Cities for Car Rental Costs

1. New York, NY
2. Birmingham, AL
3. Newark, NJ
4. Chicago, IL
5. Albany, NY
6. Mobile, AL
7. Toledo, OH
8. Houston, TX
9. El Paso, TX
10. Detroit, MI

Source: *Corporate Travel*

The most useful college majors are those in the business field (as opposed to liberal arts, education, the sciences, etc.). Human resources management, personnel, operations management, even marketing are useful majors. A knowledge of finance and accounting will help to increase one's later "promotability."

Internship positions are not available in the operations area, though part-time, non-management positions often are. These function in much the same way as an internship, exposing you to many facets of the industry and giving you a "foot in the door" for potential future management employment. Part-time jobs are available as **rental sales agents, service agents, bus drivers** and **car shuttlers.** The rental sales agent position offers the greatest learning opportunity.

Opportunities at the Reservation Center

Avis employs a large staff of reservation agents and managers at its Worldwide

Reservation Center in Tulsa, Oklahoma. These employees have the very complex task of matching the needs of customers to the products and services offered by Avis throughout the world. All managers have had specialized training and experience recent college graduates probably lack.

While no direct entry-level positions into management exist at the Reservation Center, a recent college graduate who is willing to work six months to a year as a reservation sales agent can gain the training and experience necessary to enter reservation management. Entry-level managers are selected by a process known as the Avis Reservation Management Assessment Program. Successful candidates become first-line supervisors with career paths available in Telecommunications, Finance, Human Resources, and Training, as well as management positions in more specialized reservation departments.

Opportunities at Headquarters

Headquarter staff positions run the gamut from attorneys, bankers, and controllers to worldwide implementation analysts. Entry-level positions for new college graduates include **junior accountants, computer programmer trainees,** and **customer service representatives.**

Finance and Accounting

A **junior accountant** will learn that several career paths exist within the finance and accounting areas. Car rental companies have departments devoted to internal auditing, vehicle accounting, customer accounting, finance, treasury, corporate accounting, and tax matters.

Information Services

The large car rental companies are heavily automated. Computers process reservations, rentals and invoices, and produce reports on everything from a day's rental transactions to how many seconds were spent on each telephone reservation. Avis hires the best and brightest computer science graduates into an IMS Computer Trainee Program. Individualized training generally lasts 18 to 24 months after which trainees are assigned to **associate programmer** positions.

Administration

The people who run the company are the top executives from each of the staff departments and the senior executives of the field operations group. These are definitely not entry-level positions; they are the jobs you will work towards. Getting there (or even near there) will take most of your career.

Communications

This area is responsible for both internal communications to employees and external public relations. The training, management development, and quality control functions are also represented. This is not an area of opportunity for new graduates as heavy car rental business experience is necessary for all jobs in this department. This area does, however, represent opportunities for field operations employees who may decide to pursue careers in staff functions.

Support Functions

Rent a car companies employ people from a variety of professional disciplines including attorneys, architects, engineers, insurance specialists, security managers, and buyers of automotive and other products. The Human Resources area is involved in employee relations, benefits, compensation, administration, labor relations, and employment issues. Management entry-level positions for college graduates in these areas are generally limited to **employment interviewers** and **junior compensation analysts.**

Opportunities in Sales and Marketing

Sales

This department straddles Headquarters staff and Field operations. Employees across the country sell Avis' services to other travel industry companies such as airlines, wholesale and retail tour operations, travel agents, and hotels, as well as large national commercial accounts, associations, and governments. Avis hires people with sales experience and provides extensive classroom and on-the-job training for its sales staff.

Marketing

The Marketing department has two missions: to develop and communicate an image for the company and to develop and implement marketing programs and communication plans to create demand for Avis in its major markets. The organization is structured by function such as Market Research, Product Development, Program Management, Advertising, and Direct Marketing.

Internships or entry-level positions are generally not available in the Marketing department. Avis primarily hires college graduates with three to five years specific experience in these functional areas.

Is the Car Rental Business for You?

If you:

...are self-motivated, have a high energy level and love interaction with other people

...are willing to work really hard, often at odd hours

...like an exciting, fast-paced, never-the-same-day-twice sort of career

...are not afraid to assume responsibility and make decisions

...have a talent for solving problems under pressure

...then you sound like the sort of person who would thrive and prosper in the car rental industry.

▼

CAROL RILEY is responsible for the equal opportunity and affirmative action programs for the entire company, as well as for recruiting and hiring staff employees at the headquarters office in Garden City, New York. She joined Avis in 1976 and held positions as a secretary, paralegal, EEO coordinator, and EEO manager before assuming her present duties two years ago. She is a business management/communications graduate of Adelphi University, New York. Carol wishes to acknowledge the contributions to this article of two of her colleagues at Avis—Michael Emery and David Olson. Michael Emery was hired by Avis directly out of school to be a shift manager at Chicago's O'Hare Airport. He has worked in the same capacity at Midway Airport and is currently a yield analyst for the Great Lakes Zone. David Olson started his 20-year Avis career as a service agent in Washington. He has been a station manager and fleet manager in Seattle, WA; a city manager in Boise, ID, and Maui, HI; a district manager in San Jose, CA; and is currently a yield analyst for the West Coast Zone.

Getting Everybody to Visit Your City

The Communications Department
International Association of Convention and Visitor Bureaus

Almost every city or community in the United States has a convention and visitor bureau to market itself—to "sell" the area to out-of-towners, telling them about its facilities, attractions and special events. In general terms, a convention and visitor bureau is a sales and marketing organization that serves a city's entire meeting and visitor industry.

How Bureaus Are Staffed

In smaller communities, a convention and visitor bureau may have a staff of only one or two and concentrate on promoting and assisting local tourism. In larger cities, there will often be a large staff of specialists involved in convention marketing, convention services and community relations, in addition to tourism promotion. In major metropolitan areas, separate suburbs may even have their own bureaus and compete with the center city for visitors.

Because bureaus serve communities of varying sizes, it's not surprising that their budgets cover a very broad range. In fact, convention and visitor bureau annual budgets range from $200,000 to more than $5 million. Consequently, bureau sizes range from a one- or two-person staff to organizations that employ 50 or more.

A typical convention and visitor bureau in a community of approximately 185,000 will employ, on average, seven people:

- 1 executive director
- 1 marketing director
- 2 convention sales managers
- 1 tourism manager
- 1 bookkeeper/secretary
- 1 secretary/receptionist

A bureau in a metropolitan area of approximately 350,000 has a much larger staff:

- president
- 3 national convention sales managers
- apprentice convention sales manager
- convention services coordinator
- 10 part-time registration personnel
- director of tourism
- tourism administrative assistant
- visitor information receptionist
- 4 visitor information personnel
- executive assistant/bookkeeper
- word-processing specialist
- part-time intern

In an even larger metropolitan area, the bureau staff will be almost double—50 people or more.

▼

U.S. Cities with the Most Expensive Hotel Room Rates

1. New York, NY
2. Boston, MA
3. San Francisco, CA
4. Washington, DC
5. Honolulu, HI
6. New Orleans, LA
7. Chicago, IL
8. San Diego, CA
9. Miami-Hialeah, FL
10. Los Angeles-Long Beach, CA

Source: *Meeting News*

Bureau Operations

A convention and visitor bureau typically operates in five primary areas—**convention sales & service, tourism sales & service, marketing & communications, finance & administration** and **membership services.** In smaller organizations, one person may wear many hats, whereas larger staffs usually feature a large number of specialists.

Convention Sales and Service

Convention sales & service is generally the primary focus of a bureau in a large- or medium-sized community. Individual conventions, meetings, and tradeshows can attract large numbers of people who generate vast sums of money. According to the 1991 Convention Income Survey update from the International Association of Convention & Visitor Bureaus, this can be as much as $253 or more per person per day. Because meetings and conventions are so valuable, bureaus invest substantially in soliciting and servicing them.

A bureau's convention sales force identifies those companies, associations and clubs that regularly hold meetings, determines each organization's requirements and then develops sales presentations to show them how the city can serve their meeting needs. After a successful "sale," the bureau continues working with the organization by providing convention services. For smaller meetings, this may require no more than putting the meeting planner in contact with appropriate local suppliers. For major conventions in large cities, the convention services functions may include arranging site visits, providing a housing bureau, assisting in identifying and hiring on-site registration personnel and much more.

Convention sales and service personnel must maintain contact with all the members of the local hospitality industry and be familiar with every aspect of their city. They must be intimately familiar with their city's hotels, restaurants, attractions and meeting facilities and maintain cordial relations with a host of potential suppliers. Their major purpose is to ensure a successful meeting, because successful meetings mean that the organizations will return again and the meeting planners will have favorable things to say about the destination when they talk with their peers in other organizations.

Entry-level positions in convention sales & service include sales trainees, sales assistants, convention registrars, and convention cashiers. Many bureaus employ convention service personnel on a part-time basis, which may provide you with the opportunity to learn about this aspect of bureau activity while you are still in school.

Tourism Sales and Service

Instead of soliciting meetings, tourism sales and service personnel work to influence visits by pleasure travelers, both individual vacationers and group tours. Although they may have similar reasons for visiting a particular city, successfully soliciting individuals and group tours requires two distinct marketing approaches.

Individual pleasure travelers are generally reached by advertising on radio and television, in newspapers, general- and special-interest magazines, and via direct mail and other methods of literature distribution.

Individual tour operators, on the other hand, can bring scores of people to a city during the course of a year. By convincing tour operators to include its city in their itineraries, a bureau can dramatically increase the number of visitors to its community. For this reason, group tour solicitation includes a greater use of target marketing, telephone and personal solicitations, and familiarization tours (**"FAM" trips**).

Entry-level positions in tourism sales & service include **sales trainees, sales assistants, visitor center receptionists, tour guides** and **inquiry fulfillment personnel.** In areas of the country where tourism activity is somewhat seasonal, you may find summer and holiday employment opportunities in this area of specialization as well.

Marketing & Communications

Marketing and communications functions in a convention and visitor bureau include:
- Developing and implementing advertising and sales promotions.
- Creating and producing ads and brochures.
- Writing and distributing newsletters and other bureau publications.
- Developing and analyzing market research.
- Planning and executing public relations and publicity.

Depending on the size of a bureau and how it operates, there could also be opportunities for **writers** and **artists,** as well as **managers, secretaries,** and **researchers.**

Finance and Administration

There is little difference in the finance and administration functions at a convention and visitor bureau vs. most other service-related organizations. Employees perform such tasks as accounting, planning, budgeting, personnel, payroll and general clerical operations. In large bureaus, each activity would likely be assigned to a specialist. In smaller bureaus, the functions are usually combined, leaving one or two people responsible for the entire operation.

Entry-level positions for high school graduates are mainly clerical; college graduates with expertise in finance, personnel, purchasing, and/or business administration may be able to enter higher up the professional ladder.

Membership Services

Some (though not all) bureaus are membership organizations, recruiting members from among community businesses and featuring them in sales materials and presentations. Membership personnel identify prospects, make presentations, and serve as liaison between the members and the bureau.

Many bureaus consider membership sales and support positions as entry-level opportunities that can lead to assignments in convention or tourism sales and service.

Getting Your Foot in the Door

Convention and visitor bureaus generally fall into one of three categories—a division of a chamber of commerce, an arm of local government or a private, nonprofit corporation. Whichever type is in your community, rest assured that it is always understaffed. Many bureaus solicit—and most bureaus welcome—volunteer workers, generally in convention services, tourism services and clerical positions. If you're interested in a career in the travel industry, a volunteer position with the bureau in your city offers a wonderful opportunity to learn more about the industry and gain invaluable experience that could help you eventually secure a paid position after graduation.

There are over 900 convention and visitor bureaus in the United States. One near your home might be a great place to start your career in the travel industry!

The "State" of Travel and Tourism

Peter B. Lee, Director of Marketing Services
Massachusetts Office of Travel & Tourism

By the year 2000, travel and tourism will become the single largest segment of the world economy. The related growth of the travel and tourism industry in Massachusetts will make it an increasingly significant sector of the state economy—creating jobs, supporting new businesses and services, and generating critically important tax revenues. I expect that similar growth will occur in many other states, offering myriad opportunities for those of you hoping to establish a career attracting visitors to your state.

Every state is different—boasting different attractions and facilities, needing to solve different problems, having larger or smaller promotional budgets, approaching travel and tourism in different ways. Even though all of my pertinent experience has been with just one state, I suspect, that there aren't that many *broad* differences from state to state. After all, we're all trying to do exactly the same thing—attract more visitors. So I think you'll find a look at the way we work in Massachusetts to be informative and useful if you're planning a career in state tourism promotion.

Additionally, if you're seeking an internship, you'll find that interns are hired to work in the same areas discussed below as entry-level opportunities, so this discussion is very pertinent to you, too.

Opportunities

The Massachusetts Office of Travel & Tourism (MOTT) manages a year-round advertising and marketing program to increase travel to Massachusetts from domestic and foreign markets and from within the state. In simple terms, our focus is to promote Massachusetts as a travel destination—to increase the vacationing public's awareness of what our state has to offer as a vacation destination.

Opportunities are available for energetic, enthusiastic, and motivated people looking to capitalize on a uniquely educational and exciting job or internship experience.

Exactly what you will be doing—on the job or during an internship—will, to a great extent, depend on the specific department to which you apply. MOTT (and most other similar state tourism offices) is divided into the following departments:

Marketing

Domestic Marketing—Oversees a comprehensive marketing campaign including direct response television and print ads, direct mail, special print advertising supplements, familiarization trips, cooperative promotions, and consumer travel publications.

International Marketing—International travelers represent the fastest growing market segment of the state's travel industry. This year, international visitors accounted for an estimated 5.2% of the total visitors and over 13% of the total visitor spending.

In cooperation with the Massachusetts Port Authority, the New England-USA Foundation and other public and private partners, the Office of Travel and Tourism actively markets Massachusetts in Great Britain, Japan, and France. Activities include trade shows, development of fly/drive packages, public relations, and print advertising supplements. In Britain (our current number one source of overseas visitors), Massachusetts advertises on television with TWA, the other New England states, and the United States Travel and Tourism Administration.

As a **marketing assistant** in domestic or international marketing, you will assist in the efforts to promote year-round travel, do support work in the record-keeping area, and participate in some of the planning involved. One function specific to international marketing is to develop and update a resource book for international vacationing consumers.

Group Tour

Group tour marketing programs include the promotion of Massachusetts at major travel trade shows and conventions, as well as the publication of a group tour manual, newsletter, and sales guide for travel agents. The Office of Travel and Tourism also provides business leads and information about the group tour market to the state's regional tourist councils and to Massachusetts' travel-related businesses.

The main focus of an internship or job in group tour marketing would be to provide information about the activities and attractions in Massachusetts to group tour operators and travel agents so they can, in turn, sell packages or make recommendations to their clients. An **assistant** in this department would primarily be involved with customer service, compiling, and maintaining mailing lists, updating the Group Tour Manual and assisting in the organization of familiarization trips.

Public Relations

A public relations program provides consumer and trade support for our advertising and marketing efforts. A library of color and black/white photographs and copies of TV ads are available for use by the press, travel agents, and tour operators. Interns would assist in managing this library and maintaining a press clipping file.

In addition to generating substantial regional, national, and international press, public relations activities include special events, press conferences, an industry newsletter, press kits and fact sheets, familiarization trips, coordination of promotional activities with regional tourist councils, co-op programs, public information services, and a minority marketing program.

Publications

The Office of Travel and Tourism publishes a series of consumer and trade publications:

- Massachusetts Accommodations Guide
- Massachusetts Attractions Guide
- Calendar of Events
- Massachusetts Highway Map
- Massachusetts Group Tour Manual

A **publications assistant** participates in the production process, which includes proofreading the copy, making phone calls to verify the accuracy of the information, and making sure all production deadlines are met.

Research

The Office of Travel and Tourism conducts and commissions research programs to track the economic impact of travel on the state's economy, to monitor travel trends, and to evaluate visitor perceptions of Massachusetts. A statewide economic report is published annually based on data from the United States Travel Data Center. Entry-level candidates or interns may be able to work in this area, assisting with tabulation, compilation, and data entry.

What You Can Earn and Learn

Funding for the Massachusetts Office of Travel and Tourism (and other states' similar organizations) comes from the state government. The budget allocated affects the number and extent of programs that can be undertaken and the number of personnel that can be hired.

Salaries for entry-level people are around $20,000 per year. How far and high you go will, to a great extent, depend not only on your own specific capabilities and skills, but also on the particular area in which you specialize. The potential for those of you in public relations or international marketing, for example, may be greater than for those in other areas.

How do these numbers compare with the private sector—working for a hotel, airline, etc.? In general, salaries in the private sector could be 25% (or more) higher than in the public sector (of which we and most other state tourism offices and city/area convention and visitor bureaus are a part).

The Availability of Internships

An internship gives you the chance to work with and define skills applicable to many careers. Attracting visitors to any destination is a fiercely competitive business. Getting people involved in your state is a challenge. In addressing this challenge, you will be developing skills in public relations, advertising, and other communication areas that will help you get your first job in this (or any other) industry.

Approximately sixteen paid internships are offered each year in my office, a number I suspect may not be out of line with other states' tourism departments. Students can work anywhere from fifteen to twenty hours (fall and spring semesters) to thirty-eight hours a week (summers) and are paid hourly. Of course, credit programs through your school would benefit you as much as us, and we're always willing to work out some such arrangement, if your school will. Volunteer positions are extremely unlimited—unpaid volunteers are *always* welcome!

Whether you're looking for a job or a summer internship, I would recommend that you join the pertinent professional organizations or associations and become as active as you can. This will give you a chance to both interact with professionals in your chosen field and network with them. They may well be the source for your internship or job!

Necessary Educational Background

It is not absolutely necessary that you have a college degree to get hired at an office such as ours, though some college level course work and/or the equivalent professional experience in a relevant industry would be required. Course work in marketing, promotions, advertising, public relations, and business are recommended. Participation in extracurricular activities relevant to your major would also be an asset to being hired for an internship or a permanent position. If you have done postgraduate work and have, for example, an MBA, you probably would be overqualified and, therefore, not strongly considered for an *entry-level* position.

Where Do You Go Next?

What happens after a year or two working for the state? Well, you will have had the opportunity to gain pertinent experience promoting it and its attractions. Furthermore, if you were specifically involved in any promotion work, the skills you will have developed are immensely transferrable—they could help you land a job in public relations, advertising, many areas of the hospitality industry, etc. At the very least, they could be very useful in promoting yourself in your job search.

PETER B. LEE has held his current position since July, 1988. His previous experience has been in several different industries, each with a common marketing emphasis, including responsibilities in advertising and financial services.

Mr. Lee has been profiled in several prestigious publications, including *Who's*

Who among Young American Professionals, Who's Who of Emerging Leaders in America, Who's Who in Advertising, and *Who's Who in the East.* He received a BBA in marketing with an economics minor from the University of Massachusetts in Amherst.

THE JOB
SEARCH
PROCESS

Getting Started: Self-Evaluation and Career Objectives

etting a job may be a relatively simple one-step or couple of weeks process or a complex, months-long operation.

Starting, nurturing and developing a career (or even a series of careers) is a life-long process.

What we'll be talking about in the five chapters that together form our Job Search Process are those basic steps to take, assumptions to make, things to think about if you want a job—especially a first job in some area of the travel and hospitality industries. But when these steps—this process—are applied and expanded over a lifetime, most if not all of them are the same procedures, carried out over and over again, that are necessary to develop a successful, lifelong, professional career.

What does all this have to do with putting together a resume, writing a cover letter, heading off for interviews and the other "traditional" steps necessary to get a job? Whether your college graduation is just around the corner or a far distant memory, you will continuously need to focus, evaluate and re-evaluate your response to the ever-changing challenge of your future: Just what do you want to do with the rest of your life? Whether you like it or not, you're all looking for that "entry-level opportunity."

You're already one or two steps ahead of the competition—you're sure you want to pursue a career in some area of the travel business. By heeding the advice of the many professionals who have written chapters for this *Career Directory*—and utilizing the extensive entry-level job, organization, and career resource listings we've included—you're well on your way to fulfilling that dream. But there are some key decisions and time-consuming preparations to make if you want to transform that hopeful dream into a real, live job.

The actual process of finding the right company, right career path and, most importantly, the right first job, begins long before you start mailing out resumes to potential employers. The choices and decisions you make now are not irrevocable, but this first job will have a definite impact on the career options you leave yourself. To help you make some of the right decisions and choices along the way (and avoid some of the most notable traps and pitfalls), the following chapters will lead you through a series of organized steps. If the entire job search process we are recommending here is properly executed, it will undoubtedly help you land exactly the job you want.

If you're currently in high school and hope, after college, to land a job with a hotel, convention and visitor bureau, tourist board, travel agency, cruise line, airline, etc., then attending the right college, choosing the right major, and getting the summer work experience many such companies look for are all important steps. Read the section of this *Career Directory* that covers the particular field and/or job specialty in which you're interested—many of the contributors have recommended colleges or graduate programs they favor.

If you're hoping to jump right into any of these fields without a college degree or other professional training, our best and only advice is—don't do it. As you'll soon see in the detailed information included in the **Job Opportunities Databank,** there are not that many job openings for students without a college degree. Those that do exist are generally clerical and will only rarely lead to promising careers.

The Concept of a Job Search Process

As we've explained, a job search is not a series of random events. Rather, it is a series of connected events that together form the job search process. It is important to know the eight steps that go into that process:

1. Evaluating yourself

Know thyself. What skills and abilities can you offer a prospective employer? What do you enjoy doing? What are your strengths and weaknesses? What do you want to do?

2. Establishing your career objectives

Where do you want to be next year, three years, five years from now? What do you ultimately want to accomplish in your career and your life?

3. Creating a company target list

How to prepare a "Hit List" of potential employers—researching them, matching their needs with your skills and starting your job search assault. Preparing company information sheets and evaluating your chances.

4. Networking for success

Learning how to utilize every contact, every friend, every relative, and anyone else you can think of to break down the barriers facing any would-be travel professional. How to organize your home office to keep track of your communications and stay on top of your job campaign.

5. Preparing your resume

How to encapsulate years of school and little actual work experience into a professional, selling resume. Learning when and how to use it.

6. Preparing cover letters

The many ordinary and the all-too-few extraordinary cover letters, the kind that land interviews and jobs.

7. Interviewing

How to make the interview process work for you—from the first "hello" to the first day on the job.

8. Following up

Often overlooked, it's perhaps the most important part of the job search process.

We won't try to kid you—it is a lot of work. To do it right, you have to get started early, probably quite a bit earlier than you'd planned. Frankly, we recommend beginning this process one full year prior to the day you plan to start work.

So if you're in college, the end of your junior year is the right time to begin your research and preparations. That should give you enough time during summer vacation to set up your files and begin your library research.

Whether you're in college or graduate school, one item may need to be planned even earlier—allowing enough free time in your schedule of classes for interview preparations and appointments. Waiting until your senior year to "make some time" is already too late. Searching for a full-time job is itself a full-time job! Though you're naturally restricted by your schedule, it's not difficult to plan ahead and prepare for your upcoming job search. Try to leave at least a couple of free mornings or afternoons a week. A day or even two without classes is even better.

The Self-Evaluation Process

Learning about who you are, what you want to be, what you can be, are critical first steps in the job search process and, unfortunately, the ones most often ignored by job seekers everywhere, especially students eager to leave the ivy behind and plunge into the "real world." But avoiding this crucial self-evaluation can hinder your progress and even damage some decent prospects.

Why? Because in order to land a job with a company at which you'll actually be happy, you need to be able to identify those firms and/or job descriptions that best match your own skills, likes and strengths. The more you know about yourself, the more you'll bring to this process and the more accurate the "match-ups." You'll be able to structure your presentation (resume, cover letter, interviews, follow up) to stress your most marketable skills and talents (and, dare we say it, conveniently avoid your weaknesses?). Later, you'll be able to evaluate potential employers and job offers on the basis of your own needs and desires. This spells the difference between waking up in the morning ready to enthusiastically tackle a new day of challenges and shutting off the alarm in the hopes the day (and your job) will just disappear.

Creating Your Self-Evaluation Form

If your self-evaluation is to have any meaning, you must first be honest with yourself. This self-evaluation form should help you achieve that goal by providing a structured environment to answer these tough questions.

Take a sheet of lined notebook paper. Set up eight columns across the top—Strengths, Weaknesses, Skills, Hobbies, Courses, Experience, Likes, Dislikes.

Now, fill in each of these columns according to these guidelines:

Strengths: Describe personality traits you consider your strengths (and try to look at them as an employer would)—e.g., persistence, organization, ambition, intelligence, logic, assertiveness, aggression, leadership, etc.

Weaknesses: The traits you consider glaring weaknesses—e.g., impatience, conceit, etc. Remember: Look at these as a potential employer would. Don't assume that the personal traits you consider weaknesses will necessarily be considered negatives in the business world. You may be "easily bored," a trait that led to lousy grades early on because teachers couldn't keep you interested in the subjects they were teaching. Well, many entrepreneurs need ever-changing challenges. Strength or weakness?

Skills: Any skill you have, whether you think it's marketable or not. Everything from basic business skills—like typing, word processing, and stenography—to computer, or teaching experience and foreign language literacy. Don't forget possibly obscure but marketable skills like "good telephone voice."

Hobbies: The things you enjoy doing that, more than likely, have no overt connection to career objectives. These should be distinct from the skills listed above, and may include activities such as reading, games, travel, sports and the like. While these may not be marketable in any general sense, they may well be useful in specific circumstances.

Courses: All the general subject areas (history, literature, etc.) and/or specific courses you've taken which may be marketable (computer, business, marketing, hotel management, etc.), you really enjoyed, or both.

Experience: Just the specific functions you performed at any part-time (school year) or full-time (summer) jobs.

Likes: List all your "likes," those important considerations that you haven't listed anywhere else yet. These might include the types of people you like to be with, the kind of environment you prefer (city, country, large places, small places, quiet, loud, fast-paced, slow-paced) and anything else which hasn't shown up somewhere on this form. Try to think of "likes" that you have that are related to the job you are applying for. For example, if you're applying for a job at a bank, mention that you enjoy reading the Wall St. Journal. However, try not to include entries which refer to specific jobs or companies. We'll list those on another form.

Dislikes: All the people, places and things you can easily live without.

Now assess the "marketability" of each item you've listed. (In other words, are some of your likes, skills or courses easier to match to a financial job description, or do they have little to do with a specific job or company?) Mark highly marketable skills with an "H." Use "M" to characterize those skills which may be marketable in a particular set of circumstances, "L" for those with minimal potential application to any job.

Referring back to the same list, decide if you'd enjoy using your marketable skills or talents as part of your everyday job—"Y" for yes, "N" for no. You may type 80 words a minute but truly despise typing or worry that stressing it too much will land you on the permanent clerical staff. If so, mark typing with an "N." (Keep one thing in mind— just because you dislike typing shouldn't mean you absolutely won't accept a job that requires it. Almost every professional job today—especially those involving stocks and bonds—requires computer-based work that make typing a plus.)

Now, go over the entire form carefully and look for inconsistencies.

To help you with your own form, consult the sample form on the next page that a job-hunter might complete.

The Value of a Second Opinion

There is a familiar misconception about the self-evaluation process that gets in the way of many new job applicants—the belief that it is a process which must be accomplished in isolation. Nothing could be further from the truth. Just because the family doctor tells you you need an operation doesn't mean you run right off to the hospital. Prudence dictates that you check out the opinion with another physician. Getting such a "second opinion"—someone else's, not just your own—is a valuable practice throughout the job search process, as well.

So after you've completed the various exercises in this chapter, review them with a friend, relative, or parent—just be sure it's someone who knows you well and cares about you. These second opinions may reveal some aspects of your self description on which you and the rest of the world differ. If so, discuss them, learn from them and, if necessary, change some conclusions. Should everyone concur with your self evaluation, you will be reassured that your choices are on target.

Establishing Your Career Objective(s)

For better or worse, you now know something more of who and what you are. But we've yet to establish and evaluate another important area—your overall needs, desires and goals. Where are you going? What do you want to accomplish?

Strength	Weakness	Skill	Hobby	Course	Experience	Like	Dislike
Marketable?							
Enjoy?							
Marketable?							
Enjoy?							
Marketable?							
Enjoy?							

If you're getting ready to graduate from college or graduate school, the next five years are the most critical period of your whole career. You need to make the initial transition from college to the workplace, establish yourself in a new and completely unfamiliar company environment, and begin to build the professional credentials necessary to achieve your career goals.

If that strikes you as a pretty tall order, well, it is. Unless you've narrowly prepared yourself for a specific profession, you're probably most ill-prepared for any real job. Instead, you've (hopefully) learned some basic principles—research and analytical skills that are necessary for success at almost any level—and, more or less, how to think.

It's tough to face, but face it you must: No matter what your college, major, or degree, all you represent right now is potential. How you package that potential and what you eventually make of it is completely up to you. It's an unfortunate fact that many companies will take a professional with barely a year or two experience over any newcomer, no matter how promising. Smaller firms, especially, can rarely afford to hire someone who can't begin contributing immediately.

So you have to be prepared to take your comparatively modest skills and experience and package them in a way that will get you interviewed and hired. Quite a challenge.

There are a number of different ways to approach such a task. If you find yourself confused or unable to list such goals, you might want to check a few books in your local library that have more time to spend on the topic of "goal-oriented planning."

But Is this Industry Right for You?

Presuming you now have a much better idea of yourself and where you'd like to be, let's make sure some of your basic assumptions are right. We presume you purchased this *Career Directory* because you're considering a career in some area of the travel and hospitality industries. Are you sure? Do you know enough about the industry as a whole and the particular part you're heading for to decide whether it's right for you? Probably not. So start your research now—learn as much about your potential career field as you now know about yourself.

Start with the essays in the Advice from the Pro's section—these will give you an excellent overview of a number of the specific types of companies—hotels, cruise lines, travel agencies, etc.—some very specialized (and growing) areas, and some things to keep in mind as you start on your career search. They will also give you a relatively simplified, though very necessary, understanding of just what people who work in all these areas of financial services actually do.

Other sources you should consider consulting to learn more about this business are listed in the **Career Resources** section of this book.

In that section, we've listed trade associations and publications associated with the travel and hospitality industries (together with many other resources that will help your job search. Consult the **Career Resources** section in the front of this directory for a complete description). Where possible in the association entries, we've included details on educational information they make available, but you should certainly consider writing each of the pertinent associations, letting them know you're interested in a career in their area of specialization and would appreciate whatever help and advice they're willing to impart. You'll find many sponsor seminars and conferences throughout the country, some of which you may be able to attend.

The trade publications are dedicated to the highly specific interests of the various areas of the travel and hospitality community. These magazines are generally not available at newsstands, but you may be able to obtain back issues at your local library (most major libraries have extensive collections of such journals) or by writing to the magazines' circulation/ subscription departments. We've also included regional and local magazines.

You may also try writing to the publishers and/or editors of these publications. State in your cover letter what area of the travel industry you're considering and ask them for whatever help and advice they can offer. But be specific. These are busy professionals and they do not have the time or the inclination to simply "tell me everything you can about the hotel business."

If you can afford it now, we strongly suggest subscribing to whichever trade magazines are applicable to the specialty you're considering. If you can't subscribe to all of them, make it a point to regularly read the copies that arrive at your local public or college library.

These publications may well provide the most imaginative and far-reaching information for your job search. Even a quick perusal of an issue or two will give you an excellent "feel" for the industry. After reading only a few articles, you'll already get a handle on what's happening in the field and some of the industry's peculiar and particular jargon. Later, more detailed study will aid you in your search for a specific job.

Authors of the articles themselves may well turn out to be important resources. If an article is directly related to your chosen specialty, why not call the author and ask some questions? You'd be amazed how willing many of these professionals will be to talk to you and answer your questions, and the worst they can do is say no. (But *do* use common sense—authors will not *always* respond graciously to your invitation to "chat about the business." And don't be *too* aggressive here.)

You'll find such research to be a double-edged sword. In addition to helping you get a handle on whether the area you've chosen is really right for you, you'll slowly learn enough about particular specialties, companies, the industry, etc., to actually sound like you know what you're talking about when you hit the pavement looking for your first job. And nothing is better than sounding like a pro—except being one.

Travel Is It. Now What?

After all this research, we're going to assume you've reached that final decision—you really do want a career in some aspect of the travel and hospitality industries. It is with this vague certainty that all too many of you will race off, hunting for any firm willing to give you a job. You'll manage to get interviews at a couple and, smiling brightly, tell everyone you meet, "I want a career in the hotel business." The interviewers, unfortunately, will all ask the same awkward question—"What *exactly* do you want to do at our company?"—and that will be the end of that.

It is simply not enough to narrow your job search to a specific industry. And so far, that's all you've done. You must now establish a specific career objective—the job you want to start, the career you want to pursue. Just knowing that you "want to get into the travel industry" doesn't mean anything to anybody. If that's all you can tell an interviewer, it demonstrates a lack of research into the industry itself and your failure to think ahead.

Interviewers will *not* welcome you with open arms if you're still vague about your career goals. If you've managed to get an "informational interview" with an executive whose company currently has no job openings, what is he or she supposed to do with your resume after you leave? Who should he or she send it to for future consideration? Since *you* don't seem to know exactly what you want to do, how's he or she going to figure it out? Worse, that person will probably resent your asking him or her to function as your personal career counselor.

Remember, the more specific your career objective, the better your chances of finding a job. It's that simple and that important. Naturally, before you declare your objective to the world, check once again to make sure your specific job target matches the skills and interests you defined in your self evaluation. Eventually, you may want to state such an objective on your resume, and "To obtain an entry-level position as a salesperson at a major hotel chain," is quite a bit better than "I want a career in travel." Do not consider this step final until you can summarize your job/career objective in a single, short, accurate sentence.

CHAPTER FOURTEEN

Targeting Prospective Employers and Networking for Success

As you move along the job search path, one fact will quickly become crystal clear—it is primarily a process of elimination: your task is to consider and research as many options as possible, then—for good reasons—eliminate as many as possible, attempting to continually narrow your focus.

Your Ideal Company Profile

Let's establish some criteria to evaluate potential employers. This will enable you to identify your target agencies, the places you'd really like to work. (This process, as we've pointed out, is not specific to any industry or field; the same steps, with perhaps some research resource variations, are applicable to any job, any company, any industry.)

Take a sheet of blank paper and divide it into three vertical columns. Title it "Target Company—Ideal Profile." Call the lefthand column "Musts," the middle column "Preferences," and the righthand column "Nevers."

We've listed a series of questions below. After considering each question, decide whether a particular criteria must be met, whether you would simply prefer it or never would consider it at all. If there are other criteria you consider important, feel free to add them to the list below and mark them accordingly on your Profile. (We have included a sample grid to help you set up your own.)

1. What are your geographical preferences? (Possible answers: U.S., Canada, International, Anywhere). If you only want to work in the U.S., then "Work in United States" would be the entry in the "Must" column. "Work in Canada or Foreign Country" might be the first entry in your "Never" column. There would be no applicable entry for this question in the "Preference" column. If, however, you will consider working in two of the three, then your "Must" column entry might

read "Work in U.S. or Canada," your "Preference" entry—if you preferred one over the other—could read "Work in U.S.," and the "Never" column, "Work Overseas."

2. If you prefer to work in the U.S. or Canada, what area, state(s) or province(s)? If Overseas, what area or countries?

3. Do you prefer a large city, small city, town, or somewhere as far away from civilization as possible?

4. In regard to question 3, any specific preferences?

5. Do you prefer a warm or cold climate?

6. Do you prefer a large or small company? Define your terms (by sales, income, employees, offices, etc.).

7. Do you mind relocating right now? Do you want to work for an company with a reputation for *frequently* relocating top people?

8. Do you mind travelling frequently? What percent do you consider reasonable? (Make sure this matches the normal requirements of the job specialization you're considering.)

9. What salary would you *like* to receive (put in the "Preference" column)? What's the *lowest* salary you'll accept (in the "Must" column)?

10. Are there any benefits (such as an expense account, medical and/or dental insurance, company car, etc.) you must or would like to have?

11. Are you planning to attend graduate school at some point in the future and, if so, is a tuition reimbursement plan important to you?

12. Do you feel that a formal training program is necessary?

13. If applicable, what kinds of specific accounts would you prefer to work with? What specific products?

It's important to keep revising this new form, just as you should continue to update your Self-Evaluation Form. After all, it contains the criteria by which you will judge every potential employer. Armed with a complete list of such criteria, you're now ready to find all the companies that match them.

Targeting Individual Companies

To begin creating your initial list of targeted companies, start with the **Job Opportunities Databank** in this directory. We've listed major U.S. hotels (including all major chains), airlines, cruise lines, convention and visitor bureaus, chambers of commerce, car rental firms, and more, all of which were contacted by telephone for this edition. These listings provide a plethora of data concerning the companies' overall operations, hiring practices, and other important information on entry-level job opportunities. This latter information includes key contacts (names), the average number of entry-level people they hire each year, along with complete job descriptions and requirements.

One word of advice. You'll notice that some/many of the agencies list "0" under average entry-level hiring. This is more a reflection of the current economic times than a long-range projection. In past editions of this book, these companies did list an average number of new hires, and they will again in the future. We have listed these companies for three reasons: 1) to present you with the overall view of prospective employers; 2) because even companies that don't plan to do any hiring will experience unexpected job openings; and 3) things change, so as soon as the economy begins to pick up, expect entry-level hiring to increase again.

We have attempted to include information on those major companies that represent most of the entry-level jobs out there. But there are, of course, many other companies of all sizes and shapes that you may also wish to research. In the **Career Resources** section, we have listed other reference tools you can use to obtain more information on the companies we've listed, as well as those we haven't.

The Other Side of the Iceberg

You are now better prepared to choose those companies that meet your own list of criteria. But a word of caution about these now-"obvious" requirements—they are not the only ones you need to take into consideration. And you probably won't be able to find all or many of the answers to this second set of questions in any reference book—they are known, however, by those persons already at work in the industry. Here is the list you will want to follow:

Promotion

If you are aggressive about your career plans, you'll want to know if you have a shot at the top. Look for companies that traditionally promote from within.

Training

Look for companies in which your early tenure will actually be a period of on-the-job training, hopefully ones in which training remains part of the long-term process. As new techniques and technologies enter the workplace, you must make sure you are updated on these skills. Most importantly, look for training that is craft or function-oriented—these are the so-called **transferable skills**, ones you can easily bring along with you from job-to-job, company-to-company, sometimes industry-to-industry.

Salary

Some industries are generally high paying, some not. But even an industry with a tradition of paying abnormally low salaries may have particular companies or job functions (like sales) within companies that command high remuneration. But it's important you know what the industry standard is.

Ask the Person Who Owns One

Some years ago, this advice was used as the theme for a highly successful automobile advertising campaign. The prospective car buyer was encouraged to find out about the product by asking the (supposedly) most trustworthy judge of all—someone who was already an owner.

You can use the same approach in your job search. You all have relatives or friends already out in the workplace—these are your best sources of information about those industries. Cast your net in as wide a circle as possible. Contact these valuable resources. You'll be amazed at how readily they will answer your questions. I suggest you check the criteria list at the beginning of this chapter to formulate your own list of pertinent questions. Ideally and minimally you will want to learn: how the industry is doing, what its long-term prospects are, the kinds of personalities they favor (aggressive, low key), rate of employee turnover, and the availability of training.

Benefits

Look for companies in which health insurance, vacation pay, retirement plans, 401K accounts, stock purchase opportunities, and other important employee benefits are extensive—and company paid. If you have to pay for basic benefits like medical coverage yourself, you'll be surprised at how expensive they are. An exceptional benefit package may even lead you to accept a lower-than-usual salary.

Unions

Make sure you know about the union situation in each industry you research. Periodic, union-mandated salary increases are one benefit nonunion workers may find hard to match.

Making Friends and Influencing People

Networking is a term you have probably heard; it is definitely a key aspect of any successful job search and a process you must master.

Informational interviews and **job interviews** are the two primary outgrowths of successful networking.

Referrals, an aspect of the networking process, entail using someone else's name, credentials and recommendation to set up a receptive environment when seeking a job interview.

All of these terms have one thing in common: Each depends on the actions of other people to put them in motion. Don't let this idea of "dependency" slow you down, however. A job search *must* be a very pro-active process—*you* have to initiate the action. When networking, this means contacting as many people as you can. The more you contact, the better the chances of getting one of those people you are "depending" on to take action and help you out.

So what is networking? How do you build your own network? And why do you need one in the first place? The balance of this chapter answers all of those questions and more.

Get your telephone ready. It's time to make some friends.

Not the World's Oldest Profession, But...

As Gordon Gekko, the high-rolling corporate raider played by Michael Douglas, sneers in the movie *Wall Street:* "Any schmuck can analyze stock charts. What separates the players from the sheep is information." Networking is the process of creating your own group of relatives, friends, and acquaintances who can feed you the information you need to find a job—identifying where the jobs are and giving you the personal introductions and background data necessary to pursue them.

If the job market were so well-organized that details on all employment opportunities were immediately available to all applicants, there would be no need for such a process. Rest assured the job market is *not* such a smooth-running machine—most applicants are left very much to their own devices. Build and use your own network wisely and you'll be amazed at the amount of useful job intelligence you will turn up.

While the term networking didn't gain prominence until the 1970s, it is by no means a new phenomenon. A selection process that connects people of similar skills, backgrounds, and/or attitudes—in other words, networking—has been in existence in a variety of forms for centuries. Attend any Ivy League school and you're automatically part of its very special centuries-old network.

Major law firms are known to favor candidates from a preferred list of law schools—the same ones the senior partners attended. Washington, D.C. and Corporate America have their own network—the same corporate bigwigs move back and forth from boardroom to Cabinet Room. The Academia-Washington connection is just as strong—notice the number of Harvard professors who call Washington their second home? No matter which party is in power, certain names just keep surfacing as Secretary of This or Undersecretary of That. No, networking is not new. It's just left its ivory tower and become a wellpublicized process *anyone* can and should utilize in their lifelong career development.

And it works. Remember your own reaction when you were asked to recommend someone for a job, club, or school office? You certainly didn't want to look foolish, so you gave it some thought and tried to recommend the best-qualified person that you thought would "fit in" with the rest of the group. It's a built-in screening process.

Creating the Ideal Network

As in most endeavors, there's a wrong way and a right way to network. The following tips will help you construct your own wide-ranging, information-gathering, interview-generating group—*your* network.

Diversify

Unlike the Harvard or Princeton network—confined to former graduates of each school—your network should be as diversified and wide-ranging as possible. You never know who might be in a position to help, so don't limit your group of friends. The more diverse they are, the greater the variety of information they may supply you with.

Don't Forget...

...to include everyone you know in your initial networking list: friends, relatives, social acquaintances, classmates, college alumni, professors, teachers, your dentist, doctor, family lawyer, insurance agent, banker, travel agent, elected officials in your community, ministers, fellow church members, local tradesmen, and local business or social club officers. And everybody they know!

Be Specific

Make a list of the kinds of assistance you will require from those in your network, then make specific requests of each. Do they know of jobs at their company? Can they introduce you to the proper executives? Have they heard something about or know someone at the company you're planning to interview with next week?

The more organized you are, the easier it will be to target the information you need and figure out who might have it. Begin to keep a business card file or case so you can keep track of all your contacts. A small plastic case for file cards that is available at any discount store will do nicely. One system you can use is to staple the card to a 3 x 5 index card. On the card, write down any information about that contact that you might need later—when you talked to them, job leads they provided, specific job search advice, etc. You will then have all the information you need about each company or contact in one easily accessible location.

Learn the Difference...

...between an **informational** interview and a **job** interview. The former requires you to cast yourself in the role of information gatherer; *you* are the interviewer and knowledge is your goal—about an industry, company, job function, key executive, etc. Such a meeting with someone already doing what you soon hope to be doing is by far the best way to find out everything you need to know—before you walk through the door and sit down for a formal job interview, at which time your purpose is more sharply defined: to get the job you're interviewing for.

If you learn of a specific job opening during an informational interview, you are in a position to find out details about the job, identify the interviewer and, possibly, even learn some things about him or her. In addition, presuming you get your contact's permission, you may be able to use his or her name as a referral. Calling up the interviewer and saying, "Joan Smith in your Convention Sales department suggested I contact you regarding openings for reservation clerks," is far superior to "Hello. Do you have any job openings at your hotel?"

(In such a case, be careful about referring to a specific job opening, even if your contact told you about it. It may not be something you're supposed to know about. By presenting your query as an open-ended question, you give your prospective employer the option of exploring your background without further commitment. If there is a job there and you're qualified for it, you'll find out soon enough.)

Don't Waste a Contact

Not everyone you call on your highly-diversified networking list will know about a job opening. It would be surprising if each one did. But what about *their* friends and colleagues? It's amazing how everyone knows someone who knows someone. Ask— you'll find that someone.

Value Your Contacts

If someone has provided you with helpful information or an introduction to a friend or colleague, keep him or her informed about how it all turns out. A referral that's panned out should be reported to the person who opened the door for you in the first place. Such courtesy will be appreciated—and may lead to more contacts. If someone has nothing to offer today, a call back in the future is still appropriate and may pay off.

The lesson is clear: Keep your options open, your contact list alive. Detailed records of your network—whom you spoke with, when, what transpired, etc.—will help you keep track of your overall progress and organize what can be a complicated and involved process.

Informational Interviews

So now you've done your homework, built your network, and begun using your contacts. It's time to go on your first informational interview.

A Typical Interview

You were, of course, smart enough to include John Fredericks, the bank officer who handled your dad's mortgage, on your original contact list. He knew you as a bright and conscientious college senior; in fact, your perfect three-year repayment record on the loan you took out to buy that '77 Plymouth impressed him. When you called him, he was happy to refer you to his golfing buddy, Bob Jones, sales manager director at Huge Hotels, Inc. Armed with permission to use Fredericks' name and recommendation, you wrote a letter to Bob Jones, the gist of which went something like this:

> *I am writing at the suggestion of Mr. Fredericks at Fidelity National Bank. He knows of my interest in hotel sales and, given your position at Huge Hotels, Inc. thought you may be able to help me gain a better understanding of your field and the career opportunities it presents.*
>
> *While I am majoring in marketing and minoring in business, I know I need to speak with professionals such as yourself to learn how to apply my studies to a work environment. If you could spare a half hour to meet with me, I'm certain I would be able to get enough information about your field to give me the direction I need.*
>
> *I'll call your office next week in the hope that we can schedule a meeting.*

Send a copy of this letter to Mr. Fredericks at the bank—it will refresh his memory should Mr. Jones call to inquire about you. Next step: the follow-up phone call. After you get Mr. Jones' secretary on the line, it will, with luck, go something like this:

> *"Hello, I'm Mr. Paul Smith. I'm calling in reference to a letter I wrote to Mr. Jones requesting an appointment."*
>
> *"Oh, yes. You're the young man interested in our sales rep training program. Mr. Jones can see you on June 23rd. Will 10 A.M. be satisfactory?"*
>
> *"That's fine. I'll be there."*

Well, the appointed day arrives. Well-scrubbed and dressed in your best (and most conservative) suit, you are ushered into Mr. Jones' office. He offers you coffee (you decline) and says that it is okay to light up if you smoke (you decline). The conversation might go something like this:

You: "Thank you for seeing me, Mr. Jones. I know you are busy and appreciate your taking the time to talk with me."

You: "As I stated in my letter, my interest in hotel sales is very real, but I'm having trouble seeing how all of my studies fit into the big picture. I think I'll be much better prepared to evaluate future job offers if I can learn how everything works at a hotel such as yours. May I ask you a few questions about the sales function at Huge Hotels, Inc?"

Jones: "Well it's my pleasure since you come so highly recommended. I'm always pleased to meet someone interested in my field."

Jones: "Fire away, Paul".

Mr. Jones relaxes. He realizes this is a knowledge hunt you are on, not a thinly-veiled job interview. Your approach has kept him off the spot—he doesn't have to be concerned with making a hiring decision. You've already gotten high marks for not putting him on the defensive. From this point on, you will be able to ask anything and everything you need to find out—not just about the sales function at hotels in general, but specifically about the training program at Huge Hotels, Inc. (which is what you're really interested in).

You: "I have a few specific questions I'd like to ask. First, at a hotel such as yours, where does an entry-level person start?"

Jones: "In this company, we rotate new people interested in sales through all the areas we work in—convention, resort, and room sales. You'd spend about two months in each area, then specialize in the one you're most interested and/or where we need you most."

You: "Where and how fast does someone progress after that?"

Jones: "Obviously, that depends on the person, but given the proper aptitude and ability, that person would simply get more and bigger projects to work with. How well you do all along the way will determine how far and how fast you progress."

You: "What is the work environment like—is it pretty hectic?"

Jones: "We try to keep the work load at an even keel. The comfort of our workers is of prime importance to us. Excessive turnover is costly, you know. But the hotel business is an exciting one and things change sometimes minute-to-minute. It's not a profession for the faint-hearted!"

You: "If I may shift to another area, I'd be interested in your opinion about the hospitality field in general and what you see as the most likely areas of opportunity in the foreseeable future. Do you think this is a growth career area, despite the many changes that have occurred in the last 18 months?"

Jones: "Well, judging by the hiring record of our company, I think you'll find it's an area worth making a commitment to. At the entry level, we've hired a number of new people in the past three or four years. There always seems to be opportunities, though it's gotten far more competitive."

You: "Do you think someone with my qualifications and background could get started in sales at a major hotel? Perhaps a look at my resume would be helpful to you." *(Give it to Mr. Jones.)*

Jones: "Your course work looks appropriate. I especially like the internships you've held every summer. I think you have a real chance to break into this field. I don't think we're hiring right now, but I know a couple of hotels that are looking for bright young people with qualifications like yours. Let me give you a couple of phone numbers." *(Write down names and phone numbers.)*

You: "You have been very generous with your time, but I can see from those flashing buttons on your phone that you have other things to do. Thank you again for taking the time to talk with me."

Jones: "You're welcome."

After the Interview

The next step should be obvious: **Two** thank-you letters are required, one to Mr. Jones, the second to Mr. Fredericks. Get them both out immediately. (And see the next chapter if you need help writing them.)

Keeping Track of the Interview Trail

Let's talk about record keeping again. If your networking works the way it's supposed to, this was only the first of many such interviews. Experts have estimated that the average person could develop a contact list of 250 people. Even if we limit your initial list to only 100, if each of them gave you one referral, your list would suddenly have 200 names. Presuming that it will not be necessary or helpful to see all of them, it's certainly possible that such a list could lead to 100 informational and/or job interviews! Unless you keep accurate records, by the time you're on No. 50, you won't even remember the first dozen!

So get the results of each interview down on paper. Use whatever format with which you're comfortable. You should create some kind of file, folder, or note card that is an "Interview Recap Record." If you have access to a personal computer, take advantage of it. It will be much easier to keep you information stored in one place and well-organized. Your record should be set up and contain something like the following:

Name: Huge Hotels, Inc.
Address: 333 Michigan Ave., Chicago, IL 60606
Phone: (312) 666-6666
Contact: Robert L. Jones
Type of Business: Full-service hotel chain
Referral Contact: Mr. Fredericks, Fidelity National Bank
Date: June 23, 1992

At this point, you should add a one- or two-paragraph summary of what you found out at the meeting. Since these comments are for your eyes only, you should be both objective and subjective. State the facts—what you found out in response to your specific questions—but include your impressions—your estimate of the opportunities for further discussions, your chances for future consideration for employment.

"I Was Just Calling To..."

Find any logical opportunity to stay in touch with Mr. Jones. You may, for example, let him know when you graduate and tell him your grade point average, carbon him in on any letters you write to Mr. Fredericks, even send a congratulatory note if his company's year-end financial results are positive or if you read something in the local paper about his department. This type of follow up has the all-important effect of keeping you and your name in the forefront of others' minds. Out of sight *is* out of mind. No matter how talented you may be or how good an impression you made, you'll have to work hard to "stay visible."

Why Should You Network?

- To unearth current information about the industry, company and pertinent job functions. Remember: Your knowledge and understanding of broad industry trends, financial health, hiring opportunities, and the competitive picture are key.
- To investigate each company's hiring policies—who makes the decisions, who the key players are (personnel, staff managers), whether there's a hiring season, whether they prefer applicants going direct or through recruiters, etc.
- To sell yourself—discuss your interests and research activities—and leave your calling card, your resume.
- To seek out advice on refining your job search process.
- To obtain the names of other persons (referrals) who can give you additional information on where the jobs are and what the market conditions are like.

There Are Rules, Just Like Any Game

It should already be obvious that the networking process is not only effective, but also quite deliberate in its objectives. There are two specific groups of people you must attempt to target: those who can give you information about an industry or career area and those who are potential employers. The line between these groups may often blur. Don't be concerned—you'll soon learn when (and how) to shift the focus from interviewer to interviewee.

To simplify this process, follow a single rule: Show interest in the field or job area under discussion, but wait to be asked about actually working for that company. During your informational interviews, you will be surprised at the number of times the person you're interviewing turns to you and asks, "Would you be interested in...?" Consider carefully what's being asked and, if you *would* be interested in the position under discussion, make your feelings known.

If the Process Scares You

Some of you will undoubtedly be hesitant about, even fear, the networking process. It is not an unusual response—it is very human to want to accomplish things "on your own," without anyone's help. Understandable and commendable as such independence might seem, it is, in reality, an impediment if it limits your involvement in this important process. Networking has such universal application because **there is no other effective way to bridge the gap between job applicant and job.** Employers are grateful for its existence. You should be, too.

Whether you are a first-time applicant or reentering the work force now that the children are grown, the networking process will more than likely be your point of entry. Sending out mass mailings of your resume and answering the help-wanted ads may well be less personal (and, therefore, "easier") approaches, but they will also be far less effective. The natural selection process of the networking phenomenon is your assurance that water does indeed seek its own level—you will be matched up with companies and job opportunities in which there is a mutual fit.

Six Good Reasons to Network

Many people fear the networking process because they think they are "bothering" others with their own selfish demands. Nonsense! There are good reasons—six of them, at least—why the people on your networking list will be happy to help you:

1. **Some day you will get to return the favor.** An ace insurance salesman built a successful business by offering low-cost coverage to first-year medical students. Ten years later, these now-successful practitioners remembered the company (and person) that helped them when they were just getting started. He gets new referrals every day.

2. **They, too, are seeking information.** An employer who has been out of school for several years might be interested in what the latest developments in the classroom are. He or she may be hoping to learn as much from you as you are from them, so be forthcoming in offering information. This desire for new information may be the reason he or she agreed to see you in the first place.

3. **Internal politics.** Some people will see you simply to make themselves appear powerful, implying to others in their organization that they have the authority to hire (they may or may not), an envied prerogative.

4. **They're "saving for a rainy day".** Executives know that it never hurts to look and that maintaining a backlog of qualified candidates is a big asset when the floodgates open and supervisors are forced to hire quickly.

5. **They're just plain nice.** Some people will see you simply because they feel it's the decent thing to do or because they just can't say "no."

6. **They are looking themselves.** Some people will see you because they are anxious to do a friend (whoever referred you) a favor. Or because they have another friend seeking new talent, in which case you represent a referral they can make (part of their own continuing network process). You see, networking never does stop—it helps them and it helps you.

Before you proceed to the next chapter, begin making your contact list. You may wish to keep a separate sheet of paper or note card on each person (especially the dozen or so you think are most important), even a separate telephone list to make your communications easier and more efficient. However you set up your list, be sure to keep it up to date—it won't be long before you'll be calling each and every name on the list.

CHAPTER FIFTEEN

Preparing Your Resume

Your resume is a one-page summary of you—your education, skills, employment experience and career objective(s). It is not a biography, but a "quick and dirty" way to identify and describe you to potential employers. Most importantly, its real purpose is to sell you to the company you want to work for. It must set you apart from all the other applicants (those competitors) out there.

So, as you sit down to formulate your resume, remember you're trying to present the pertinent information in a format and manner that will convince an executive to grant you an interview, the prelude to any job offer. All resumes must follow two basic rules—excellent visual presentation and honesty—but it's important to realize that different career markets require different resumes. The resume you are compiling for your career in travel and hospitality is much different than one you would prepare for a book publishing career. As more and more resume " training" services become available, employers are becoming increasingly choosy about the resumes they receive. They expect to view a professional presentation, one that sets a candidate apart from the crowd. Your resume has to be perfect and it has to be specialized—clearly demonstrating the relationship between your qualifications and the job you are applying for.

What does this mean? It means the resume you use to get that first travel or hospitality job should highlight the skills that demonstrate your ability to work with people (especially the public!), your flexibility, and your ability to handle a number of varied jobs. While "travel and hospitality" covers a broad range of careers that may seem very different, they all demand strong service-oriented skills and the ability to roll with the punches. Just ask all the travel agents and reservation agents who had to handle the 10-day crush of work that resulted from the airlines amazing fare wars in early 1992.

An Overview of Resume Preparation

- **Know what you're doing**—your resume is a personal billboard of accomplishments. It must communicate your worth to a prospective employer in specific terms.

- **Your language should be action-oriented,** full of "doing"-type words. And less is better than more—be concise and direct. Don't worry about using complete sentences.

- **Be persuasive.** In those sections that allow you the freedom to do so, don't hesitate to communicate your worth in the strongest language. This does not mean a numbing list of self-congratulatory superlatives; it does mean truthful claims about your abilities and the evidence (educational, experiential) that supports them.

- **Don't be cheap or gaudy.** Don't hesitate to spend the few extra dollars necessary to present a professional-looking resume. Do avoid outlandish (and generally ineffective) gimmicks like oversized or brightly-colored paper.

- **Find an editor.** Every good writer needs one, and you are writing your resume. At the very least, it will offer you a second set of eyes proofreading for embarrassing typos. But if you are fortunate enough to have a professional in the field—a recruiter or personnel executive—critique a draft, grab the opportunity and be immensely grateful.

- **If you're the next Michelangelo,** so multitalented that you can easily qualify for jobs in different career areas, don't hesitate to prepare two or more completely different resumes. This will enable you to change the emphasis on your education and skills according to the specific career objective on each resume, a necessary alteration that will correctly target each one.

- **Choose the proper format.** There are only three we recommend—chronological, functional, and targeted format—and it's important you use the one that's right for you.

The Records You Need

The resume-writing process begins with the assembly and organization of all the personal, educational, and employment data from which you will choose the pieces that actually end up on paper. If this information is properly organized, writing your resume will be a relatively easy task, essentially a simple process of just shifting data from a set of the worksheets to another, to your actual resume. At the end of this chapter, you'll find all the forms you need to prepare your resume, including worksheets, fill-in-the-blanks resume forms, and sample resumes.

As you will soon see, there is a great deal of information you'll need to keep track of. In order to avoid a fevered search for important information, take the time right now to designate a single location in which to store all your records. My recommendation is either a filing cabinet or an expandable pocket portfolio. The latter is less expensive, yet it will still enable you to sort your records into an unlimited number of more-manageable categories.

Losing important report cards, citations, letters, etc., is easy to do if your life's history is scattered throughout your room or, even worse, your house! While copies of many of these items may be obtainable, why put yourself through all that extra work? Making good organization a habit will ensure that all the records you need to prepare your resume will be right where you need them when you need them.

For each of the categories summarized below, designate a separate file folder in which pertinent records can be kept. Your own notes are important, but keeping actual report cards, award citations, letters, etc. is even more so. Here's what your record-keeping system should include:

Transcripts (Including GPA and Class Rank Information)

Transcripts are your school's official record of your academic history, usually available, on request, from your high school's guidance office or college registrar's office. Your college may charge you for copies and "on request" doesn't mean "whenever you want"—you may have to wait some time for your request to be processed (so **don't** wait until the last minute!).

Your school-calculated GPA (Grade Point Average) is on the transcript. Most schools calculate this by multiplying the credit hours assigned to each course times a numerical grade equivalent (e.g., "A" = 4.0, "B" = 3.0, etc.), then dividing by total credits/courses taken. Class rank is simply a listing of GPAs, from highest to lowest.

Employment Records

Details on every part-time or full-time job you've held, including:

- Each employer's name, address and telephone number
- Name of supervisor
- Exact dates worked
- Approximate numbers of hours per week
- Specific duties and responsibilities
- Specific skills utilized and developed
- Accomplishments, honors
- Copies of awards, letters of recommendation

Volunteer Activities

Just because you weren't paid for a specific job—stuffing envelopes for the local Republican candidate, running a car wash to raise money for the homeless, manning a drug hotline—doesn't mean that it wasn't significant or that you shouldn't include it on your resume.

So keep the same detailed notes on these volunteer activities as you have on the jobs you've held:

- Each organization's name, address and telephone number
- Name of supervisor
- Exact dates worked

- Approximate numbers of hours per week
- Specific duties and responsibilities
- Specific skills utilized
- Accomplishments, honors
- Copies of awards, letters of recommendation

Extracurricular Activities

List all sports, clubs, or other activities in which you've participated, either inside or outside school. For each, you should include:

- Name of activity/club/group
- Office(s) held
- Purpose of club/activity
- Specific duties/responsibilities
- Achievements, accomplishments, awards

If you were a long-standing member of a group or club, also include the dates that you were a member. This could demonstrate a high-level of commitment that could be used as a selling point.

Honors and Awards

Even if some of these honors are previously listed, specific data on every honor or award you receive should be kept, including, of course, the award itself! Keep the following information in your awards folder:

- Award name
- Date and from whom received
- What it was for
- Any pertinent details

Military Records

Complete military history, if pertinent, including:

- Dates of service
- Final rank awarded
- Duties and responsibilities
- All citations and awards
- Details on specific training and/or special schooling
- Skills developed
- Specific accomplishments

At the end of this chapter are seven **Data Input Sheets**. The first five cover employment, volunteer work, education, activities and awards and are essential to any resume. The last two—covering military service and language skills—are important if, of course, they apply to you. I've only included one copy of each but, if you need to, you can copy the forms you need or simply write up your own using these as models.

Here are some pointers on how to fill out these all-important Data Sheets:

Employment Data Input Sheet: You will need to record the basic information—employer's name, address and phone number, dates of employment and your supervisor's name—for your own files anyway. It may be an important addition to your networking list and will be necessary should you be asked to supply a reference list.

Duties should be a series of brief action statements describing what you did on this job. For example, if you worked as a hostess in a restaurant, this section might read: "Responsible for the delivery of 250 meals at dinner time and the supervision of 20 waiters and busboys. Coordinated reservations. Responsible for check and payment verification."

Skills should enumerate specific capabilities either necessary for the job or developed through it.

If you achieved *specific results*—e.g., "developed new filing system," "collected over $5,000 in previously-assumed bad debt," "instituted award-winning art program," etc.—or *received any award, citation or other honor*—"named Employee of the Month three times," "received Mayor's Citation for Innovation," etc.—make sure you list these.

Prepare one employment data sheet for each of the last three positions you have held; this is a basic guideline, but you can include more if relevant. Do not include sheets for short-term jobs (i.e., those that lasted one month or less).

Volunteer Work Data Input Sheet: Treat any volunteer work, no matter how basic or short (one day counts!), as if it were a job and record the same information. In both cases, it is especially important to note specific duties and responsibilities, skills required or developed and any accomplishments or achievements you can point to as evidence of your success.

Educational Data Input Sheet: If you're in college, omit details on high school. If you're a graduate student, list details on both graduate and undergraduate coursework. If you have not yet graduated, list your anticipated date of graduation. If more than a year away, indicate the numbers of credits earned through the most recent semester to be completed.

Activities Data Input Sheet: List your participation in the Student Government, Winter Carnival Press Committee, Math Club, Ski Patrol, etc., plus sports teams and/or any participation in community or church groups. Make sure you indicate if you were elected to any positions in clubs, groups, or on teams.

Awards and Honors Data Input Sheet: List awards and honors from your school (prestigious high school awards can still be included here, even if you're in graduate school), community groups, church groups, clubs, etc.

Military Service Data Input Sheet: Many useful skills are learned in the armed forces. A military stint often hastens the maturation process, making you a more attractive candidate. So if you have served in the military, make sure you include details in your resume. Again, include any computer skills you gained while in the service.

Language Data Input Sheet: An extremely important section for those of you with a real proficiency in a second language. And do make sure you have at least conversational fluency in the language(s) you list. One year of college French doesn't count, but if you've studied abroad, you probably are fluent or near-fluent. Such a talent could be invaluable, especially in today's increasingly international business climate.

While you should use the Data Input Sheets to summarize all of the data you have collected, do not throw away any of the specific information—report cards, transcripts, citations, etc.—just because it is recorded on these sheets. Keep all records in your files; you'll never know when you'll need them again!

Creating Your First Resume

There are many options that you can include or leave out. In general, we suggest you always include the following data:

1. Your name, address and telephone number
2. Pertinent educational history (grades, class rank, activities, etc.) Follow the grade point "rule of thumb"—mention it only if it is above 3.0.
3. Pertinent work history
4. Academic honors
5. Memberships in organizations
6. Military service history (if applicable)

You have the option of including the following:

1. Your career objective
2. Personal data
3. Hobbies
4. Summary of qualifications
5. Feelings about travel and relocation (Include this if you know in advance that the job you are applying for requires it. Often times, for future promotion, job seekers **must** be willing to relocate.

And you should never include the following:

1. Photographs or illustrations (of yourself or anything else) unless they are required by your profession—e.g., actors' composites
2. Why you left past jobs
3. References
4. Salary history or present salary objectives/requirements (if salary history is specifically requested in an ad, it may be included in your cover letter)

Special note: There is definitely a school of thought that discourages any mention of personal data—marital status, health, etc.—on a resume. While I am not vehemently opposed to including such information, I am not convinced it is particularly necessary, either.

As far as hobbies go, I would only include such information if it were in some way pertinent to the job/career you're targeting, or if it shows how well-rounded you are. Your love of reading is pertinent if, for example, you are applying for a part-time job at a library. But including details on the joys of "hiking, long walks with my dog and Isaac Asimov short stories" is nothing but filler and should be left out.

Maximizing Form and Substance

Your resume should be limited to a single page if possible. A two-page resume should be used **only** if you have an extensive work background related to a future goal. When you're laying out the resume, try to leave a reasonable amount of "white space"—generous margins all around and spacing between entries. It should be typed or printed (not Xeroxed) on 8 1/2" x 11" white, cream, or ivory stock. The ink should be black. Don't scrimp on the paper quality—use the best bond you can afford. And since printing 100 or even 200 copies will cost only a little more than 50, if you do decide to print your resume, *over*estimate your needs and opt for the highest quantity you think you may need. Prices at various "quick print" shops are not exorbitant and the quality look printing affords will leave the impression you want.

Use Power Words for Impact

Be brief. Use phrases rather than complete sentences. Your resume is a summary of your talents, not a term paper. Choose your words carefully and use "power words" whenever possible. "Organized" is more powerful than "put together;" "supervised" better than "oversaw;" "formulated" better than "thought up." Strong words like these can make the most mundane clerical work sound like a series of responsible, professional positions. And, of course, they will tend to make your resume stand out. Here's a starter list of words that you may want to use in your resume:

achieved	developed	issued	researched
administered	devised	launched	reviewed
advised	directed	lectured	revised
analyzed	established	litigated	reorganized
applied	evaluated	lobbied	regulated
arranged	executed	managed	selected
budgeted	formulated	negotiated	solved
calculated	gathered	operated	scheduled
classified	generated	organized	supervised
communicated	guided	overhauled	systematized
completed	implemented	planned	taught
computed	improved	prepared	tested
conceptualized	initiated	presented	trained
coordinated	instituted	presided	updated
critiqued	instructed	programmed	utilized
delegated	introduced	promoted	
determined	invented	recommended	

Choose the Right Format

There is not much mystery here—your background will generally lead you to the right format. For an entry-level job applicant with limited work experience, the chronological format, which organizes your educational and employment history by date (most recent first) is the obvious choice. For older or more experienced applicants, either the functional—which emphasizes the duties and responsibilities of all your jobs over the course of your career, may be more suitable. If you are applying for a specific position in one field, the targeted format is for you. While I have tended to emphasize the chronological format in this chapter, one of the other two may well be the right one for you.

A List of Do's and Don't's

In case we didn't stress them enough, here are some rules to follow :

- **Do** be brief and to the point—Two pages if absolutely necessary, one page if at all possible. Never longer!

- **Don't** be fancy. Multicolored paper and all-italic type won't impress employers, just make your resume harder to read (and easier to discard). Use plain white or ivory paper, blue or black ink and an easy-to-read standard typeface.

- **Do** forget rules about sentences. Say what you need to say in the fewest words possible; use phrases, not drawn-out sentences.

- **Do** stick to the facts. Don't talk about your dog, vacation, etc.

- **Don't** ever send a resume blind. A cover letter should always accompany a resume and that letter should always be directed to a specific person.

- **Don't** have any typos. Your resume must be perfect—proofread everything as many times as necessary to catch any misspellings, grammatical errors, strange hyphenations, or typos.

- **Do** use the spell check feature on your personal computer to find errors, and also try reading the resume backwards—you'll be surprised at how errors jump out at you when you do this. Finally, have a friend proof your resume.

- **Do** use your resume as your sales tool. It is, in many cases, as close to you as an employer will ever get. Make sure it includes the information necessary to sell yourself the way you want to be sold!

- **Do** spend the money for good printing. Soiled, tattered or poorly reproduced copies speak poorly of your own self-image. Spend the money and take the time to make sure your resume is the best presentation you've ever made.

- **Do** help the reader, by organizing your resume in a clear-cut manner so key points are easily gleaned.

- **Don't** have a cluttered resume. Leave plenty of white space, especially around headings and all four margins.

- **Do** use bullets, asterisks, or other symbols as "stop signs" that the reader's eye will be naturally drawn to.

On the following pages, I've included a "fill-in-the-blanks" resume form so you can construct your own resume right away, plus a couple of samples of well-constructed student resumes.

EMPLOYMENT DATA INPUT SHEET

Employer name:_____

Address:_____

Phone:_____ Dates of employment: _____

Hours per week:_____ Salary/Pay: _____

Supervisor's name and title:_____

Duties:_____

_____

_____

Skills utilized:_____

_____

_____

_____

Accomplishments/Honors/Awards:_____

_____

_____

_____

Other important information:_____

_____

_____

_____

VOLUNTEER WORK DATA INPUT SHEET

Organization name:_____

Address:_____

Phone:_____ Dates of activity:_____

Hours per week:_____

Supervisor's name and title:_____

Duties:_____

_____

_____

Skills utilized:_____

_____

_____

_____

Accomplishments/Honors/Awards:_____

_____

_____

_____

Other important information:_____

_____

_____

_____

HIGH SCHOOL DATA INPUT SHEET

School name:_____

Address:_____

Phone:_____   Years attended: _____

Major studies:_____

GPA/Class rank:_____

Honors:_____

Important courses:_____

_____

_____

_____

_____

OTHER SCHOOL DATA INPUT SHEET

School name:_____

Address:_____

Phone:_____   Years attended: _____

Major studies:_____

GPA/Class rank:_____

Honors:_____

Important courses:_____

_____

_____

COLLEGE DATA INPUT SHEET

College:_____

Address:_____

Phone:_____   Years attended: _____

Degrees earned:_____   Major: _____   Minor:_____

Honors:_____

Important courses:_____

_____

_____

_____

GRADUATE SCHOOL DATA INPUT SHEET

College:_____

Address:_____

Phone:_____   Years attended: _____

Degrees earned:_____   Major: _____   Minor:_____

Honors:_____

Important courses:_____

_____

_____

MILITARY SERVICE DATA INPUT SHEET

Branch:_____

Rank (at discharge):_____

Dates of service:_____

Duties and responsibilities:_____

_____

_____

_____

Special training and/or school attended:_____

_____

_____

_____

Citations or awards:_____

_____

_____

_____

Specific accomplishments:_____

_____

_____

_____

_____

ACTIVITIES DATA INPUT SHEET

Club/activity: _____ Office(s) held: _____

Description of participation: _____

_____

_____

Duties/responsibilities: _____

_____

Club/activity: _____ Office(s) held: _____

Description of participation: _____

_____

_____

Duties/responsibilities: _____

_____

Club/activity: _____ Office(s) held: _____

Description of participation: _____

_____

_____

Duties/responsibilities: _____

_____

AWARDS AND HONORS DATA INPUT SHEET

Name of Award or Citation: _____

From Whom Received: _____ Date: _____

Significance: _____

_____

Other pertinent information: _____

_____

Name of Award or Citation: _____

From Whom Received: _____ Date: _____

Significance: _____

_____

Other pertinent information: _____

_____

Name of Award or Citation: _____

From Whom Received: _____ Date: _____

Significance: _____

_____

Other pertinent information: _____

_____

LANGUAGE DATA INPUT SHEET

Language: _____

___Read   ___Write   ___Converse

Background (number of years studied, travel, etc.) _____

_____

_____

_____

_____

Language: _____

___Read   ___Write   ___Converse

Background (number of years studied, travel, etc.) _____

_____

_____

_____

Language: _____

___Read   ___Write   ___Converse

Background (number of years studied, travel, etc.) _____

_____

_____

_____

FILL-IN-THE-BLANKS RESUME OUTLINE

Name: _____

Address: _____

City, state, ZIP Code: _____

Telephone number: _____

OBJECTIVE: _____

_____

_____

_____

_____

SUMMARY OF QUALIFICATIONS: _____

_____

_____

_____

_____

EDUCATION

GRADUATE SCHOOL: _____

Address: _____

City, state, ZIP Code: _____

Expected graduation date: _____   Grade Point Average: _____

Degree earned (expected): _____   Class Rank: _____

Important classes, especially those related to your career:_____

_____

_____

_____

_____

_____

_____

═══

COLLEGE: _____

Address: _____

City, state, ZIP Code: _____

Expected graduation date: _____ Grade Point Average:_____

Class rank: _____ Major: _____ Minor:_____

Important classes, especially those related to your career:_____

_____

_____

_____

_____

_____

_____

HIGH SCHOOL: _____

Address: _____

City, state, ZIP Code: _____

Expected graduation date: _____ Grade Point Average: _____

Class rank: _____

Important classes, especially those related to your career:_____

_____

_____

_____

_____

_____

_____

_____

HOBBIES AND OTHER INTERESTS (OPTIONAL)_____

_____

_____

_____

_____

_____

_____

EXTRACURRICULAR ACTIVITIES (Activity name, dates participated, duties and responsibilities, offices held, accomplishments): ————————

———————————————————————————————————————

———————————————————————————————————————

———————————————————————————————————————

———————————————————————————————————————

———————————————————————————————————————

———————————————————————————————————————

———————————————————————————————————————

AWARDS AND HONORS (Award name, from whom and date received, significance of the award and any other pertinent details): ————————

———————————————————————————————————————

———————————————————————————————————————

———————————————————————————————————————

———————————————————————————————————————

———————————————————————————————————————

———————————————————————————————————————

———————————————————————————————————————

WORK EXPERIENCE. Include job title, name of business, address and telephone number, dates of employment, supervisor's name and title, your major responsibilities, accomplishments, and any awards won. Include volunteer experience in this category. List your experiences with the most recent dates first, even if you later decide not to use a chronological format.

_____

_____

_____

_____

_____

_____

_____

_____

_____

_____

_____

_____

_____

_____

_____

REFERENCES. Though you should *not* include references in your resume, you do need to prepare a separate list of at least three people who know you fairly well and will recommend you highly to prospective employers. For each, include job title, company name, address, and telephone number. Before you include anyone on this list, make sure you have their permission to use their name as a reference and confirm what they intend to say about you to a potential employer.

1. _____

_____

_____

_____

2. _____

_____

_____

3. _____

_____

_____

4. _____

_____

_____

5. _____

_____

_____

ELIZABETH FERNANDEZ
541 North Stebbens Avenue
Englewood, New Jersey 09876
(201) 555-5867

GOAL

An entry level position in **Hotel Sales** offering Advancement Based on

Performance.

EDUCATION

State University, Engelwood, NJ
Bachelor of Science in **Hotel Administration,** May, 1993
Grade Point Average: 3.5
Study Abroad: Oxford Program, 1990
Honors: Dean's List

ABILITIES

Adept with computerized systems, including Encore and Covia.
Effective in establishing positive relationships with patrons.
Quick problem solving skills; Successful in setting/meeting goals.
Adaptable; Able to meet quotas and work under pressure.

RELEVANT
EXPERIENCE
Summer, 1992

Assistant Steward, Hyatt Regency, Cherry Hill, NJ
Supervised 8-person crew; Assisted with scheduling and payroll
administration; Interviewed and screened prospective
employees for all operations.
Key Results: Established zero defect rate in all areas of hotel
performance.

Summer, 1991

Sales Coordinator, Grollia Publications, NY, NY
Coordinated sales department activities for all regional trade shows;
aided in scheduling speakers and events.
Key Results: Created and designed sales manual currently used
throughout company.

Summer, 1990

Salesperson, Lucky Vacuum Cleaners, Verona, NJ
Responsible for all lead generation, sales and sales follow-up in tri-
county territory.
Key Results: Established (still-standing) record for summer sales.
Winner "Best Part-Time Salesperson of the Year" Award.

ACTIVITIES

Advertising Sales Manager, *Big Red*, campus newspaper, 1990-91
Lamda Lamda Lamda Sorority, Executive Committee/Social Chair

REFERENCES

Furnished Upon Request

DAVID D. SMITH
123 North Street
Englewood, NJ 09876
(201) 555-5867

Sample Resume: Functional

OBJECTIVE   An entry-level position in the **Travel Industry**.

EDUCATION   Community College, Englewood, NJ
Associate Degree in **Travel and Tourism**, May 1993
Cumulative GPA: 2.9
Major GPA: 3.6 (Financed 75% of educational expense
by working 35 hours per week)

PUBLIC RELATIONS

* Complete responsibility for positive community relations
  efforts.
* Supported and participated in neighborhood outreach
  programs, including block parties and church socials.
* Established community sponsorship of softball team (raised
  $2,000).

COMMUNICATIONS

* Effective liaison between customers and staff.
* Ability to solve problems in scheduling staff of 20.
* Coached (volunteer) neighborhood softball team.

**COMPUTER
EXPERTISE**

* Current in computerized travel information network.
* DOS, WordPerfect 5.1
* 60 WPM (accurate)

**WORK
EXPERIENCE**

McDonalds Corporation   Englewood, NJ
9/91 - Present   Assistant Manager
6/90 - 8/91   Crew Chief
10/89 - 5/90   Crew Member

ACTIVITIES   Softball League, Organizer/Coach
Enjoy travelling and meeting new people
Avid reader, *National Geographic*

REFERENCES   Available Upon Request

AMY C. McKNIGHT

Current Address:
East Quad # 456 - State University
Detroit, MI 48221
(313) 401-8964

Permanent Address:
509 Pleasant Trail
Detroit, MI 48226
(313) 555-3468

CAREER OBJECTIVE

Entry-level position in the **Hospitality Industry**.

EDUCATION

State University, Detroit, MI
Bachelor of Science in **Hotel Management**, May 1993
Grade Point Average: 3.2

HONORS

Dean's Advisory Board
"5-Star Hotel" Simulation Award
Competitive Scholarship

EMPLOYMENT EXPERIENCE

Roma Hall
Detroit, MI
  Head Banquet Waitress   Sept. 1992 - Present
  *Organize parties of 20-100 patrons including room preparation,
    staff scheduling, and coordination with kitchen.
  *Supervise wait staff (3-8).
  *Display excellent problem solving skill during pressured situations.

  Waitress   Sept. 1991 - August 1992
  *Attended to needs of patrons.
  *Received commendation from supervisor.

Tastee Freeze
Ferndale, MI
  Counter Assistant   May 1991 - August 1991
  *Managed counter and tracked supplies.
  *Opportunity to deal with varied clientele.

INTERESTS

Residence Hall Representative, 1991-92
Intramural Soccer
Enjoy bicycling, aerobics, and swimming
Certified in CPR and First Aid

CHAPTER SIXTEEN

Writing Better Letters

Stop for a moment and review your resume draft. It is undoubtedly (by now) a near-perfect document that instantly tells the reader the kind of job you want and why you are qualified. But does it say anything personal about you? Any amplification of your talents? Any words that are ideally "you?" Any hint of the kind of person who stands behind that resume?

If you've prepared it properly, the answers should be a series of ringing "no's"—your resume should be a mere sketch of your life, a bare-bones summary of your skills, education, and experience.

To the general we must add the specific. That's what your letters must accomplish—adding the lines, colors, and shading that will help fill out your self-portrait. This chapter will cover the kinds of letters you will most often be called upon to prepare in your job search. There are essentially nine different types you will utilize again and again, based primarily on what each is trying to accomplish. I've included at least one well-written example of each at the end of this chapter.

Answer these Questions

Before you put pencil to paper to compose any letter, there are five key questions you must ask yourself:

- **Why** are you writing it?

- To **Whom**?

- **What** are you trying to accomplish?

- **Which** lead will get the reader's attention?

- **How** do you organize the letter to best accomplish your objectives?

Why?

There should be a single, easily definable reason you are writing any letter. This reason will often dictate what and how you write—the tone and flavor of the letter—as well as what you include or leave out.

Have you been asked in an ad to amplify your qualifications for a job and provide a salary history and college transcripts? Then that (minimally) is your objective in writing. Limit yourself to following instructions and do a little personal selling—but very little. Including everything asked for and a simple, adequate cover letter is better than writing a "knock 'em, sock 'em" letter and omitting the one piece of information the ad specifically asked for.

If, however, you are on a networking search, the objective of your letter is to seek out contacts who will refer you for possible informational or job interviews. In this case, getting a name and address—a referral—is your stated purpose for writing. You have to be specific and ask for this action.

You will no doubt follow up with a phone call, but be certain the letter conveys what you are after. Being vague or oblique won't help you. You are after a definite yes or no when it comes to contact assistance. The recipient of your letter should know this. As they say in the world of selling, at some point you have to ask for the order.

Who?

Using the proper "tone" in a letter is as important as the content—you wouldn't write to the owner of the local meat market using the same words and style as you would employ in a letter to the director of personnel of a major company. Properly addressing the person or persons you are writing to is as important as what you say to them.

Some hints to utilize: the recipient's job title and level, his or her hiring clout (correct title and spelling are a **must**), the kind of person they are (based on your knowledge of their area of involvement), etc. (Even if you know the letter is going through a screening stage instead of to the actual person you need to contact, don't take the easy way out. You have to sell the person doing the screening just as convincingly as you would the actual contact, or else you might get passed over instead of passed along! Don't underestimate the power of the person doing the screening.)

For example, it pays to sound technical with technical people—in other words, use the kinds of words and language which they use on the job. If you have had the opportunity to speak with them, it will be easy for you. If not, and you have formed some opinions as to their types then use these as the basis of the language you employ. The cardinal rule is to say it in words you think the recipient will be comfortable hearing, not in the words you might otherwise personally choose.

What?

What do you have to offer that company? What do you have to contribute to the job, process or work situation that is unique and/or of particular benefit to the recipient of your letter.

For example, if you were applying for a sales position and recently ranked number one in a summer sales job, then conveying this benefit is logical and desirable. It is a factor you may have left off your resume. Even if it was listed in your skills/accomplishment section of the resume, you can underscore and call attention to it in your letter. Repetition, when it is properly focused, can be a good thing.

Which?

Of all the opening sentences you can compose, which will immediately get the reader's attention? If your opening sentence is dynamic, you are already fifty percent of the way to your end objective—having your entire letter read. Don't slide into it. Know the point you are trying to make and come right to it. One word of caution: your first sentence **must** make mention of what led you to write—was it an ad, someone at the company, a story you saw on television? Be sure to give this point of reference.

How?

While a good opening is essential, how do you organize your letter so that it is easy for the recipient to read in its entirety. This is a question of *flow*—the way the words and sentences naturally lead one to another, holding the reader's interest until he or she reaches your signature.

If you have your objective clearly in mind, this task is easier than it sounds: Simply convey your message(s) in a logical sequence. End your letter by stating what the next steps are—yours and/or the reader's).

One More Time

Pay attention to the small things. Neatness still-counts. Have your letters typed. Spend a few extra dollars and have some personal stationery printed.

And most important, make certain that your correspondence goes out quickly. The general rule is to get a letter in the mail during the week in which the project comes to your attention or in which you have had some contact with the organization. I personally attempt to mail follow-up letters the same day as the contact; at worst, within 24 hours.

When to Write

- To answer an ad
- To prospect (many companies)
- To inquire about specific openings (single company)
- To obtain a referral
- To obtain an informational interview
- To obtain a job interview
- To say "thank you"
- To accept or reject a job offer
- To withdraw from consideration for a job

In some cases, the letter will accompany your resume; in others, it will need to stand alone. Each of the above circumstance is described in the pages that follow. I have included at least one sample of each type of letter at the end of this chapter.

Answering an Ad

Your eye catches an ad in the Positions Available section of the Sunday paper for a reservations clerk. It tells you that the position is at a large hotel, and that, though some experience would be desirable, it is not required. Well, you possess *those* skills. The ad asks that you send a letter and resume to a Post Office Box. No salary is indicated, no phone number given. You decide to reply.

Your purpose in writing—the objective (why?)—is to secure a job interview. Since no person is singled out for receipt of the ad, and since it is a large company, you assume it will be screened by Human Resources.

Adopt a professional, formal tone. You are answering a "blind" ad, so you have to play it safe. In your first sentence, refer to the ad, including the place and date of publication and the position outlined. (There is a chance that the hotel is running more than one ad on the same date and in the same paper, so you need to identify the one to which you are replying.) Tell the reader what (specifically) you have to offer that hotel. Include your resume, phone number, and the times it is easiest to reach you. Ask for the order—tell them you'd like to have an appointment. (A sample of this and other letter types is included at the end of this chapter.)

Blanket Prospecting Letter

In June of this year you will graduate from a four-year college with a degree in hotel management. You seek a position (internship or full-time employment) in a major hotel's creative department. You have decided to write to 50 top hotels, sending each a copy of your resume. You don't know which, if any, have job openings.

Such blanket mailings are effective given two circumstances: 1) You must have an exemplary record and a resume which reflects it; and 2) You must send out a goodly number of packages, since the response rate to such mailings is very low.

A blanket mailing doesn't mean an impersonal one—you should always be writing to a specific executive. If you have a referral, send a personalized letter to that person. If not, do not simply mail a package to the Human Resources department; identify the department head and *then* send a personalized letter. And make sure you get on the phone and follow up each letter within about ten days. Don't just sit back and wait for everyone to call you. They won't.

Just Inquiring

The inquiry letter is a step above the blanket prospecting letter; it's a "cold-calling" device with a twist. You have earmarked a company (and a person) as a possibility in your job search based on something you have read about them. Your general research tells you that it is a good place to work. Although you are not aware of any specific openings, you know that they employ entry-level personnel with your credentials.

While ostensibly inquiring about any openings, you are really just "referring yourself" to them in order to place your resume in front of the right person. This is what I would call a "why not?" attempt at securing a job interview. Its effectiveness depends on their actually having been in the news. This, after all, is your "excuse" for writing.

Networking

It's time to get out that folder marked "Contacts" and prepare a draft networking letter. The lead sentence should be very specific, referring immediately to the friend, colleague, etc. "who suggested I write you about..." Remember: Your objective is to secure an informational interview, pave the way for a job interview, and/or get referred to still other contacts.

This type of letter should not place the recipient in a position where a decision is necessary; rather, the request should be couched in terms of "career advice." The second paragraph can then inform the reader of your level of experience. Finally, be specific about seeking an appointment.

Unless you have been specifically asked by the referring person to do so, you will probably not be including a resume with such letters. So the letter itself must highlight your credentials, enabling the reader to gauge your relative level of experience. For entry-level personnel, education, of course, will be most important.

For an Informational Interview

Though the objectives of this letter are similar to those of the networking letter, they are not as personal. These are "knowledge quests" on your part and the recipient will most likely not be someone you have been referred to. The idea is to convince the reader of the sincerity of your research effort. Whatever selling you do, if you do any at all, will arise as a consequence of the meeting, not beforehand. A positive response to this type of request is in itself a good step forward. It is, after all, exposure, and amazing things can develop when people in authority agree to see you.

Thank-You Letters

Although it may not always seem so, manners do count in the job world. But what counts even more are the simple gestures that show you actually care—like writing a thank-you letter. A well-executed, timely thank-you note tells more about your personality than anything else you may have sent, and it also demonstrates excellent follow-through skills. It says something about the way you were brought up—whatever else your resume tells them, you are, at least, polite, courteous and thoughtful.

Thank-you letters may well become the beginning of an all-important dialogue that leads directly to a job. So be extra careful in composing them, and make certain that they are custom made for each occasion and person.

The following are the primary situations in which you will be called upon to write some variation of thank-you letter:

1. After a job interview

2. After an informational interview

3. Accepting a job offer

4. Responding to rejection: While optional, such a letter is appropriate if you have been among the finalists in a job search or were rejected due to limited experience. Remember: Some day you'll *have* enough experience; make the interviewer want to stay in touch.

5. Withdrawing from consideration: Used when you decide you are no longer interested in a particular position. (A variation is usable for declining an actual job offer.) Whatever the reason for writing such a letter, it's wise to do so and thus keep future lines of communication open.

IN RESPONSE TO AN AD

10 E. 89th Street
New York, NY 10028
August 10, 1992

The *New York Times*
PO Box 7520
New York, NY 10128

Dear Sir or Madam:

This letter is in response to your advertisement for a reservations clerk which appeared in the July 20th issue of the *New York Times*.

I have the qualifications you are seeking. I graduated from Emerson Junior College with a degree in Hotel Management. In addition to coursework covering all aspects of the hotel industry, I also gained experience during Emerson's semi-annual hotel exercises, in which undergraduates were responsible for running a real on-campus hotel for a month per semester.

I have worked at the Bosco Hotel as a part-time front desk clerk for the past two semesters. This position has provided me with hands-on experience in the hotel field, as well as the chance to use and hone my interpersonal skills. My resume is enclosed.

I would like to have the opportunity to meet with you personally to discuss your requirements for the position. I can be reached at (212) 555-1225 between 8:00 a.m. and 5:00 p.m. and at (212) 555-4221 after 5:00 p.m. I look forward to hearing from you.

Sincerely,

Karen Weber

Enclosure: Resume

PROSPECTING LETTER

Kim Kerr
8 Robutuck Hwy.
Hammond, IN 54054
515-555-2392

August 10, 1992

Mr. Fred Jones
Vice President--Convention Sales
Alcott Hotel Group
One Lakeshore Drive
Chicago, IL 60606

Dear Mr. Jones:

The name of Alcott Hotel Group continually pops up in our classroom discussions of outstanding marketing-driven hotel chains. Given my interest in the hotel business as a career and convention sales as a specialty, I've taken the liberty of enclosing my resume.

As you can see, I have just completed a very comprehensive four years of study at the Vernon Valley School of Hotel Administration, which included courses in all areas of hotel management, including marketing, food service, front desk, etc. Though my resume does not indicate it, I will be graduating in the top 10% of my class, with honors.

I will be in the Chicago area on August 29 and will call your office to see when it is convenient to arrange an appointment.

Sincerely yours,

Kim Kerr

INQUIRY LETTER

42 7th Street
Ski City, VT 85722
September 30, 1992

Mr. Michael Maniaci
President
Pinnacle Hotels, Inc.
521 West Elm Street
Indianapolis, IN 83230

Dear Mr. Maniaci:

I just completed reading the article in the October issue of *Fortune* on Pinnacle Hotels, Inc.

Your innovative approach to recruiting minorities is of particular interest to me because of my background in the hotel industry and minority recruitment.

I am interested in learning more about your work as well as the possibilities of joining your firm. My qualifications include:

- B.A. in Hotel Administration
- Research on minority recruitment
- Hospitality Seminar participation (Univ. of Virginia)
- Reports preparation on education, employment, and minorities

I will be in Indiana during the week of October 10 and hope your schedule will permit us to meet briefly to discuss our mutual interests. I will call your office next week to see if such a meeting can be arranged.

I appreciate your consideration.

Sincerely yours,

Ronald W. Sommerville

NETWORKING LETTER

Richard A. Starky
42 Bach St.
Musical City, IN 20202
317-555-1515

November 14, 1992

Ms. Michelle Fleming
Vice President
Freedom First Travel
42 Jenkins Avenue
Fulton, MS 23232

Dear Ms. Fleming:

Sam Kinney suggested I write you. I am interested in an entry-level position in the accounting department of a major travel agency. Sam felt it would be mutually beneficial for us to meet and talk.

I have been educated and trained as an accountant and have just over two years part-time experience in bookkeeping, accounting, auditing, and tax work.

Sam mentioned you as one of the leading experts in this growing field of tax-deferred travel. As I begin my job search during the next few months, I am certain your advice would help me. Would it be possible for us to meet briefly? My resume is enclosed.

I will call your office next week to see when your schedule would permit such a meeting.

Sincerely,

Richard A. Starky

TO OBTAIN AN INFORMATIONAL INTERVIEW

16 NW 128th Street
Raleigh, NC 75775
December 2, 1992

Mr. Johnson B. McClure
Vice President
Golden Convention Bureau
484 Smithers Road
Awkmont, NC 76857

Dear Mr. McClure:

I'm sure a good deal of the credit for your city's 23% jump in tourism last year is attributable to the highly-motivated staff you have recruited during the last three years. I hope to obtain an entry-level position for a company just as committed to growth.

I believe my summer work with the Warrenville Travel and Tourism Department, and my Bachelor's degree in public relations from American University have properly prepared me for a career in the area of convention bureaus.

As I begin my job search, I am trying to gather as much information and advice as possible before applying for positions. Could I take a few minutes of your time next week to discuss my career plans? I will call your office on Monday, December 6, to see if such a meeting can be arranged.

I appreciate your consideration and look forward to meeting you.

Sincerely,

Karen R. Burns

AFTER AN INFORMATIONAL INTERVIEW

Lazelle Wright
921 West Fourth Street
Steamboat Springs, CO 72105
303-555-3303

November 21, 1992

Mr. James R. Payne
Meeting Planner
Bradley Finch, Inc.
241 Snowridge
Ogden, UT 72108

Dear Mr. Payne:

Jinny Basten was right when she said you would be most helpful in advising me on a career in meeting planning.

I appreciated your taking the time from your busy schedule to meet with me. Your advice was most helpful and I have incorporated your suggestions into my resume. I will send you a copy next week.

Again, thanks so much for your assistance. As you suggested, I will contact Joe Simmons next week in regard to a possible opening with his company.

Sincerely,

Lazelle Wright

AFTER A JOB INTERVIEW

1497 Lilac Street
Old Adams, MA 01281
October 15, 1992

Mr. Rudy Delacort
Director of Personnel
Grace Airlines, Inc.
175 Boylston Avenue
Ribbit, MA 02857

Dear Mr. Delacort:

Thank you for the opportunity to interview yesterday for the trainee position at your Reservations Center. I enjoyed meeting with you and Cliff Stoudt and learning more about Grace.

Your organization appears to be growing in a direction which parallels my interests and goals. The interview with you and your staff confirmed my initial positive impressions of Grace, and I want to reiterate my strong interest in working for you.

I am convinced my prior experience as an intern for Worldwide Airlines, and my college training in public relations would enable me to progress steadily through your training program and become a productive member of your team.

Again, thank you for your consideration. If you need any additional information from me, please feel free to call.

Yours truly,

Harold Beaumont

cc: Mr. Cliff Stoudt
    Reservations Center.

ACCEPTING A JOB OFFER

1497 Lilac Street
Old Adams, MA 01281
October 7, 1992

Mr. Rudy Delacort
Director of Personnel
Grace Airlines, Inc.
175 Boylston Avenue
Ribbit, MA 01281

Dear Mr. Delacort:

I want to thank you and Mr. Stoudt for giving me the opportunity to work for Grace. I am very pleased to accept the position as a trainee at your Reservations Center. The position entails exactly the kind of work I want to do, and I know that I will do a good job for you.

As we discussed, I shall begin work on December 5, 1992. In the interim, I shall complete all the necessary employment forms, obtain the required physical examination and locate housing.

I plan to be in Ribbit within the next two weeks and would like to deliver the paperwork to you personally. At that time, we could handle any remaining items pertaining to my employment. I'll call next week to schedule an appointment with you.

Sincerely yours,

Harold Beaumont

cc: Mr. Cliff Stoudt
    Reservations Center

WITHDRAWING FROM CONSIDERATION

1497 Lilac Street
Old Adams, MA 01281
October 7, 1992

Mr. Rudy Delacort
Director of Personnel
Grace Airlines, Inc.
175 Boylston Avenue
Ribbit, MA 01281

Dear Mr. Delacort:

It was indeed a pleasure meeting with you and Mr. Stoudt last week to discuss your needs for a trainee at your Reservations Center. Our time together was most enjoyable and informative.

As I discussed with you during our meetings, I believe one purpose of preliminary interviews is to explore areas of mutual interest and to assess the fit between the individual and the position. After careful thought, I have decided to withdraw from consideration for the position.

My decision is based primarily upon two factors. First, the emphasis on data entry is certainly needed in your case, but I would prefer more balance in my work activities. Second, the position would require more mandatory overtime during the next three months than I am able to accept, given my other responsibilities.

I want to thank you for interviewing me and giving me the opportunity to learn about your needs. You have a fine staff and I would have enjoyed working with them.

Yours truly,

Harold Beaumont

cc: Mr. Cliff Stoudt
    Reservations Center.

IN RESPONSE TO REJECTION

1497 Lilac Street
Old Adams, MA 01281
October 7, 1992

Mr. Rudy Delacort
Director of Personnel
Grace Airlines, Inc.
175 Boylston Avenue
Ribbit, Massachusetts 01281

Dear Mr. Delacort:

Thank you for giving me the opportunity to interview for the trainee position in your Reservations Center. I appreciate your consideration and interest in me.

Although I am disappointed in not being selected for your current vacancy, I want you to know that I appreciated the courtesy and professionalism shown to me during the entire selection process. I enjoyed meeting you, Cliff Stoudt, and the other members of your staff. My meetings confirmed that Grace would be an exciting place to work and build a career.

I want to reiterate my strong interest in working for you. Please keep me in mind if a similar position becomes available in the near future.

Again, thank you for the opportunity to interview and best wishes to you and your staff.

Sincerely yours,

Harold Beaumont

cc: Mr. Cliff Stoudt
    Reservations Center

Questions for You, Questions for Them

You've finished your exhaustive research, contacted everyone you've known since kindergarten, compiled a professional-looking and sounding resume, and written brilliant letters to the dozens of companies your research has revealed are perfect matches for your own strengths, interests and abilities. Unfortunately, all of this preparatory work will be meaningless if you are unable to successfully convince one of those firms to hire you.

If you were able set up an initial meeting at one of these companies, your resume and cover letter obviously peaked someone's interest. Now you have to traverse the last minefield—the job interview itself. It's time to make all that preparation pay off.

This chapter will attempt to put the interview process in perspective, giving you the "inside story" on what to expect and how to handle the questions and circumstances that arise during the course of a normal interview—and even many of those that surface in the bizarre interview situations we have all sometimes experienced.

Why Interviews Shouldn't Scare You

Interviews shouldn't scare you. The concept of two (or more) persons meeting to determine if they are right for each other is a relatively logical idea. As important as research, resumes, letters, and phone calls are, they are inherently impersonal. The interview is your chance to really see and feel the company firsthand—"up close and personal," as Howard Cosell used to crow—so think of it as a positive opportunity, your chance to succeed.

That said, many of you will still be put off by the inherently inquisitive nature of the process. Though many questions *will* be asked, interviews are essentially experiments in chemistry. Are you right for the company? Is the company right for you? Not just on paper—*in the flesh.*

If you decide the company is right for you, your purpose is simple and clear-cut—to convince the interviewer that you are the right person for the job, that you will fit in, and that you will be an asset to the company now and in the future. The interviewer's purpose is equally simple—to decide whether he or she should buy what you're selling.

This chapter will focus on the kinds of questions you are likely to be asked, how to answer them and the questions you should be ready to ask of the interviewer. By removing the workings of the interview process from the "unknown" category, you will reduce the fear it engenders.

But all the preparation in the world won't completely eliminate your sweaty palms, unless you can convince yourself that the interview is an important, positive life experience from which you will benefit—even if you don't get the job. Approach it with enthusiasm, calm yourself, and let your personality do the rest. You will undoubtedly spend an interesting hour, one that will teach you more about yourself. It's just another step in the learning process you've undertaken.

What to Do First

Start by setting up a calendar on which you can enter and track all your scheduled appointments. When you schedule an interview with a company, ask them how much time you should allow for the appointment. Some require all new applicants to fill out numerous forms and/or complete a battery of intelligence or psychological tests—all before the first interview. If you've only allowed an hour for the interview—and scheduled another at a nearby firm ten minutes later—the first time you confront a three-hour test series will effectively destroy any schedule.

Some companies, especially if the first interview is very positive, like to keep applicants around to talk to other executives. This process may be planned or, in a lot of cases, a spontaneous decision by an interviewer who likes you and wants you to meet some other key decision makers. Other companies will tend to schedule such a series of second interviews on a separate day. Find out, if you can, how the company you're planning to visit generally operates. Otherwise, especially if you've traveled to another city to interview with a number of firms in a short period of time, a schedule that's too tight will fall apart in no time at all.

If you need to travel out-of-state to interview with a company, be sure to ask if they will be paying some or all of your travel expenses. (It's generally expected that you'll be paying your own way to firms within your home state.) If they don't offer—and you don't ask—presume you're paying the freight.

Even if the company agrees to reimburse you, make sure you have enough money to pay all the expenses yourself. While some may reimburse you immediately, the majority of firms may take from a week to a month to forward you an expense check.

Research, Research, and More Research

The research you did to find these companies is nothing compared to the research you need to do now that you're beginning to narrow your search. If you followed our detailed suggestions when you started targeting these firms in the first place, you've already amassed a great deal of information about them. If you didn't do the research then, you sure better decide to do it now. Study each company as if you were going to be tested on your detailed knowledge of their organization and operations. Here's a complete checklist of the facts you should try to know about each company you plan to visit for a job interview:

The Basics

1. The address of (and directions to) the office you're visiting

2. Headquarters location (if different)

3. Some idea of domestic and international branches

4. Relative size (compared to other similar companies)

5. Annual billings, sales and/or income (last two years)

6. Subsidiary companies; specialized divisions

7. Departments (overall structure)

8. Major accounts, products, or services

The Subtleties

1. History of the firm (specialties, honors, awards, famous names)

2. Names, titles and backgrounds of top management

3. Existence (and type) of training program

4. Relocation policy

5. Relative salaries (compared to other companies in field or by size)

6. Recent developments concerning the company and its products or services (from your trade magazine and newspaper reading)

7. Everything you can learn about the career, likes, and dislikes of the person(s) interviewing you

The amount of time and work necessary to be this well prepared for an interview is considerable. It will not be accomplished the day before the interview. You may even find some of the information you need is unavailable on short notice.

Is it really so important to do all this? Well, somebody out there is going to. And if you happen to be interviewing for the same job as that other, well-prepared, knowledgeable candidate, who do you think will impress the interviewer more?

As we've already discussed, if you give yourself enough time, most of this information is surprisingly easy to obtain. In addition to the reference sources covered in the **Career Resources** chapter, the company itself can probably supply you with a great deal of data. A firm's annual report—which all publicly-owned companies must publish yearly for their stockholders—is a virtual treasure trove of information. Write each company and request copies of their last two annual reports. A comparison of sales, income, and other data over this period may enable you to discover some interesting things about their overall financial health and growth potential. Many libraries also have collections of annual reports from major corporations.

Attempting to learn about your interviewer is hard work, the importance of which is underestimated by most applicants (who then, of course, don't bother to do it). Being one of the exceptions may get you a job. Use the biographical references covered previously. If he or she is listed in any of these sources, you'll be able to learn an awful lot about his or her background. In addition, find out if he or she has written any articles that have appeared in the trade press or, even better, books on his or her area(s) of expertise. Referring to these writings during the course of an interview, without making it too obvious a compliment, can be very effective. We all have egos and we all like people to talk about us. The interviewer is no different from the rest of us. You might also check to see if any of your networking contacts worked with him or her at his current (or a previous) company and can help "fill you in."

Selection vs. Screening Interviews

The process to which the majority of this chapter is devoted is the actual **selection interview,** usually conducted by the person to whom the new hire will be reporting. But there is another process—the **screening interview**—which many of you may have to survive first.

Screening interviews are usually conducted by a member of the personnel department. Though they may not be empowered to hire, they are in a position to screen out or eliminate those candidates they feel (based on the facts) are not qualified to handle the job. These decisions are not usually made on the basis of personality, appearance, eloquence, persuasiveness, or any other subjective criteria, but rather by clicking off yes or no answers against a checklist of skills. If you don't have the requisite number, you will be eliminated from further consideration. This may seem arbitrary, but it is a realistic and often necessary way for corporations to minimize the time and dollars involved in filling even the lowest jobs on the corporate ladder.

Remember, screening personnel are not looking for reasons to *hire* you; they're trying to find ways to *eliminate* you from the job search pack. Resumes sent blindly to the personnel department will usually be subjected to such screening; you will be eliminated without any personal contact (an excellent reason to construct a superior resume and not send out blind mailings).

If you are contacted, it will most likely be by telephone. When you are responding to such a call, keep these three things in mind: 1) It is an interview, be on your guard; 2) Answer all questions honestly; 3) Be enthusiastic; and 4) Don't offer any more information than you are asked for. Remember, this is another screening step, so don't say anything that will get you screened out before you even get in. You will get the standard questions from the interviewer—his or her attempts to "flesh out" the information included on your resume and/or cover letter. Strictly speaking, they are seeking out any negatives which may exist. If your resume is honest and factual (and it should be), you have no reason to be anxious, because you have nothing to hide.

Don't be nervous—be glad you were called and remember your objective: to get past this screening phase so you can get on to the real interview.

The Day of the Interview

On the day of the interview, wear a conservative (not funereal) business suit—*not* a sports coat, *not* a "nice" blouse and skirt. Shoes should be shined, nails cleaned, hair cut and in place. And no low-cut or tight-fitting clothes.

It's not unusual for resumes and cover letters to head in different directions when a company starts passing them around to a number of executives. If you sent them, both may even be long gone. So bring along extra copies of your resume and your own copy of the cover letter that originally accompanied it.

Whether or not you make them available, we suggest you prepare a neatly-typed list of references (including the name, title, company, address, and phone number of each person). You may want to bring along a copy of your high school or college transcript, especially if it's something to brag about. (Once you get your first job, you'll probably never use it—or be asked for it—again, so enjoy it while you can!)

On Time Means Fifteen Minutes Early

Plan to arrive fifteen minutes before your scheduled appointment. If you're in an unfamiliar city or have a long drive to their offices, allow extra time for the unexpected delays that seem to occur with mind-numbing regularity on important days.

Arriving early will give you some time to check your appearance, catch your breath, check in with the receptionist, learn how to correctly pronounce the interviewer's name, and get yourself organized and battle ready.

Arriving late does not make a sterling first impression. If you are only a few minutes late, it's probably best not to mention it or even excuse yourself. With a little luck, everybody else is behind schedule and no one will notice. However, if you're more than fifteen minutes late, have an honest (or at least serviceable) explanation ready and offer it at your first opportunity. Then drop the subject as quickly as possible and move on to the interview.

The Eyes Have It

When you meet the interviewer, shake hands firmly. People notice handshakes and often form a first impression based solely on them.

Try to maintain eye contact with the interviewer as you talk. This will indicate you're interested in what he or she has to say. Eye contact is important for another reason—it demonstrates to the interviewer that you are confident about yourself and your job skills. That's an important message to send.

Sit straight. Body language is also another important means of conveying confidence.

Should coffee or a soft drink be offered, you may accept (but should do so only if the interviewer is joining you).

Keep your voice at a comfortable level, and try to sound enthusiastic (without imitating Charleen Cheerleader). Be confident and poised, and provide direct, accurate and honest answers to the trickiest questions.

And, as you try to remember all this, just be yourself, and try to act like you're comfortable and almost enjoying this whole process!

Don't Name Drop...Conspicuously

You Don't Have to Say a Word

"Eighty percent of the initial impression you make is nonverbal," asserts Jennifer Maxwell Morris, a New York-based image consultant, quoting a University of Minnesota study. Some tips: walk tall, enter the room briskly while making eye contact with the person you're going to speak to, keep your head up, square your shoulders and keep your hand ready for a firm handshake that involves the whole hand but does not pump.

Source: *Working Woman*

A friendly relationship with other company employees may have provided you with valuable information prior to the interview, but don't flaunt such relationships. The interviewer is interested only in how you will relate to him or her and how well he or she surmises you will fit in with the rest of the staff. Name dropping may smack of favoritism. And you are in no position to know who the interviewer's favorite (or least favorite) people are.

On the other hand, if you have established a complex network of professionals through informational interviews, attending trade shows, reading trade magazines, etc., it is perfectly permissible to refer to these people, their companies, conversations you've had, whatever. It may even impress the interviewer with the extensiveness of your preparation.

Fork on the Left, Knife on the Right

Interviews are sometimes conducted over lunch, though this is not usually the case with entry-level people. If it does happen to you, though, try to order something in the middle price range, neither filet mignon nor a cheeseburger.

Do not order alcohol—ever! If your interviewer orders a carafe of wine, politely decline. You may meet another interviewer later who smells the alcohol on your breath, or your interviewer may have a drinking problem. It's just too big a risk to take after you've come so far. Just do your best to maintain your poise, and you'll do fine.

The Importance of Last Impressions

There are some things interviewers will always view with displeasure: street language, complete lack of eye contact, insufficient or vague explanations or answers, a noticeable lack of energy, poor interpersonal skills (i.e., not listening or the basic inability to carry on an intelligent conversation), and a demonstrable lack of motivation.

Every impression may count. And the very *last* impression an interviewer has may outweigh everything else. So, before you allow an interview to end, summarize why you want the job, why you are qualified, and what, in particular, you can offer their company.

Then, take some action. If the interviewer hasn't told you about the rest of the interview process and/or where you stand, ask him or her. Will you be seeing other people that day? If so, ask for some background on anyone else with whom you'll be interviewing. If there are no other meetings that day, what's the next step? When can you expect to hear from them about coming back?

Ask for a business card. This will make sure you get the person's name and title right when you write your follow-up letter. You can staple it to the company file for easy reference as you continue networking. When you return home, file all the business cards, copies of correspondence, and notes from the interview(s) with each company in the appropriate files. Finally, but most importantly, ask yourself which firms you really want to work for and which you are no longer interested in. This will quickly determine how far you want the process at each to develop before you politely tell them to stop considering you for the job.

Immediately send a thank-you letter to each executive you met. These should, of course, be neatly-typed business letters, not handwritten notes (unless you are most friendly, indeed, with the interviewer and want to stress the "informal" nature of your note). If you are still interested in pursuing a position at their company, tell them in no uncertain terms. Reiterate why you feel you're the best candidate and tell each of the executives when you hope (expect?) to hear from them.

On the Eighth Day God Created Interviewers

Though most interviews will follow a relatively standard format, there will undoubtedly be a wide disparity in the skills of the interviewers you meet. Many of these executives (with the exception of the Personnel staff) will most likely not have extensive interviewing experience, have limited knowledge of interviewing techniques, use them infrequently, be hurried by the other duties, or not even view your interview as critically important.

Rather than studying standardized test results or utilizing professional evaluation skills developed over many years of practice, these nonprofessionals react intuitively—their initial (first five minutes) impressions are often the lasting and over-riding factors they remember. So you must sell yourself—fast.

The best way to do this is to try to achieve a comfort level with your interviewer. Isn't establishing rapport—through words, gestures, appearance common interests, etc.—what you try to do in *any* social situation? It's just trying to know one another better. Against this backdrop, the questions and answers will flow in a more natural way.

The Set Sequence

Irrespective of the competence levels of the interviewer, you can anticipate an interview sequence roughly as follows:

- Greetings
- Social niceties (small talk)
- Purpose of meeting (let's get down to business)
- Broad questions/answers
- Specific questions/ answers
- In-depth discussion of company, job, and opportunity
- Summarizing information given & received
- Possible salary probe (this should only be brought up at a second interview)
- Summary/indication as to next steps

When you look at this sequence closely, it is obvious that once you have gotten past the greeting, social niceties and some explanation of the job (in the "getting down to business" section), the bulk of the interview will be questions—yours and the interviewer's. In this question and answer session, there are not necessarily any right or wrong answers, only good and bad ones. Be forewarned, however. This sequence is not written in stone, and some interviewers will deliberately **not** follow it. Some interviewers will try to fluster you by asking off-the-wall questions, while others are just eccentric by nature. Be prepared for anything once the interview has started.

A new style of interview called the "situational interview," or low-fidelity simulation, asks prospective employees what they would do in hypothetical situations, presenting illustrations that are important in the job opening. Recent research is encouraging employers to use this type of interview approach, because studies show that what people say they would do is pretty much what they will do when the real-life situation arises.

Source: *Working Woman*

It's Time to Play Q & A

You can't control the "chemistry" between you and the interviewer—do you seem to "hit it off" right from the start or never connect at all? Since you can't control such a subjective problem, it pays to focus on what you *can* control—the questions you will be asked, your answers and the questions you had better be prepared to ask.

Not surprisingly, many of the same questions pop up in interview after interview, regardless of company size, type, or location. I have chosen the 14 most common—along with appropriate hints and answers for each—for inclusion in this chapter. Remember: There are no right or wrong answers to these questions, only good and bad ones.

Substance counts more than speed when answering questions. Take your time and make sure that you listen to each question—there is nothing quite as disquieting as a lengthy, intelligent answer that is completely irrelevant to the question asked. You wind up looking like a programmed clone with stock answers to dozens of questions who has, unfortunately, pulled the wrong one out of the grab bag.

Once you have adequately answered a specific question, it is permissible to go beyond it and add more information if doing so adds something to the discussion and/or highlights a particular strength, skill, course, etc. But avoid making lengthy speeches just for the sake of sounding off. Even if the interviewer asks a question that is right up your "power alley", one you could talk about for weeks, keep your answers short. Under two minutes for any answer is a good rule of thumb.

Study the list of questions (and hints) that follow, and prepare at least one solid, concise answer for each. Practice with a friend until your answers to these most-asked questions sound intelligent, professional and, most important, unmemorized and unrehearsed.

"Why do you want to be in this field?"

Using your knowledge and understanding of the particular field, explain why you find the business exciting and where and what role you see yourself playing in it.

"Why do you think you will be successful in this business?"

Using the information from your self-evaluation and the research you did on that particular company, formulate an answer which marries your strengths to their's and to the characteristics of the position for which you're applying.

"Why did you choose our company?"

This is an excellent opportunity to explain the extensive process of education and research you've undertaken. Tell them about your strengths and how you match up with their firm. Emphasize specific things about their company that led you to seek an interview. Be a salesperson—be convincing.

"What can you do for us?"

Construct an answer that essentially lists your strengths, the experience you have which will contribute to your job performance, and any other unique qualifications that will place you at the head of the applicant pack. Use action-oriented words to tell exactly what you think you can do for the company—all your skills mean nothing if you can't use them to benefit the company you are interviewing with. Be careful: This is a question specifically designed to *eliminate* some of that pack. Sell yourself. Be one of the few called back for a second interview.

"What position here interests you?"

If you're interviewing for a specific position, answer accordingly. If you want to make sure you don't close the door on other opportunities of which you might be unaware, you can follow up with your own question: "I'm here to apply for your Analyst Training Program. Is there another position open for which you feel I'm qualified?"

If you've arranged an interview with a company without knowing of any specific openings, use the answer to this question to describe the kind of work you'd like to do and why you're qualified to do it. Avoid a specific job title, since they will tend to vary from firm to firm.

If you're on a first interview with the personnel department, just answer the question. They only want to figure out where to send you.

"What jobs have you held and why did you leave them?"

Or the direct approach: "Have you ever been fired?" Take this opportunity to expand on your resume, rather than precisely answering the question by merely recapping your job experiences. In discussing each job, point out what you liked about it, what factors led to your leaving, and how the next job added to your continuing professional education. If you have been fired, say so. It's very easy to check.

"What are your strengths and weaknesses?"

Or **"What are your hobbies (or outside interests)?"** Both questions can be easily answered using the data you gathered to complete the self-evaluation process. Be wary of being too forthcoming about your glaring faults (nobody expects you to volunteer every weakness and mistake), but do not reply, "I don't have any." They won't believe you and, what's worse, you won't believe you. After all, you did the evaluation—you know it's a lie!

Good answers to these questions are those in which the interviewer can identify benefits for him or herself. For example: "I consider myself to be an excellent planner. I am seldom caught by surprise and I prize myself on being able to anticipate problems and schedule my time to be ahead of the game. I devote a prescribed number of hours each week to this activity. I've noticed that many people just react. If you plan ahead, you should be able to cut off most problems before they arise."

You may consider disarming the interviewer by admitting a weakness, but doing it in such a way as to make it relatively unimportant to the job function. For example: "Higher mathematics has never been my strong suit. Though I am competent enough, I've always envied my friends with a more mathematical bent. In sales, though, I haven't found this a liability. I'm certainly quick enough in figuring out how close I am to monthly quotas and, of course, I keep a running record of commissions earned."

"Do you think your extracurricular activities were worth the time you devoted to them?"

This is a question often asked of entry-level candidates. One possible answer: "Very definitely. As you see from my resume, I have been quite active in the Student Government and French Club. My language fluency allowed me to spend my junior year abroad as an exchange student, and working in a functioning government gave me firsthand knowledge of what can be accomplished with people in the real world. I suspect my marks would have been somewhat higher had I not taken on so many activities outside of school, but I feel the balance they gave me contributed significantly to my overall growth as a person."

"What are your career goals?"

Interviewers are always seeking to probe the motivations of prospective employees. Nowhere is this more apparent than when the area of ambition is discussed. The high key answer to this question might be; "Given hard work, company growth, and personal initiative, I'd look forward to being in a top executive position by the time I'm 35. I believe in effort and the risk/reward system—my research on this company has shown me that it operates on the same principles. I would hope it would select its future leaders from those people who displaying such characteristics."

"At some future date would you be willing to relocate?"

Pulling up one's roots is not the easiest thing in the world to do, but it is often a fact of life in the corporate world. If you're serious about your career (and such a move often represents a step up the career ladder), you will probably not mind such a move. Tell the interviewer. If you really *don't* want to move, you may want to say so, too—though I would find out how probable or frequent such relocations would be before closing the door while still in the interview stage.

Keep in mind that as you get older, establish ties in a particular community, marry, have children, etc., you will inevitably feel less jubilation at the thought of moving once a year or even "being out on the road." So take the opportunity to experience new places and experiences while you're young. If you don't, you may never get the chance.

"How did you get along with your last supervisor?"

This question is designed to understand your relationship with (and reaction to) authority. Remember: Companies look for team players, people who will fit in with their hierarchy, their rules, their ways of doing things. An answer might be: "I prefer to work with smart, strong people who know what they want and can express themselves. I learned in the military that in order to accomplish the mission, someone has to be the leader and that person has to be given the authority to lead. Someday I aim to be that leader. I hope then my subordinates will follow me as much and as competently as I'm ready to follow now."

"What are your salary requirements?"

If they are at all interested in you, this question will probably come up, though it is more likely at a second interview. The danger, of course, is that you may price yourself too low or, even worse, right out of a job you want. Since you will have a general idea of industry figures for that position (and may even have an idea of what that company tends to pay new people for the position), why not refer to a range of salaries, such as $25,000 - $30,000?

If the interviewer doesn't bring up salary at all, it's doubtful you're being seriously considered, so you probably don't need to even bring the subject up. (If you know you aren't getting the job or aren't interested in it if offered, you may try to nail down a salary figure in order to be better prepared for the next interview.)

"Tell me about yourself"

Watch out for this one! It's often one of the first questions asked. If you falter here, the rest of the interview could quickly become a downward slide to nowhere. Be prepared, and consider it an opportunity to combine your answers to many of the previous questions into one concise description of who you are, what you want to be, and why that company should take a chance on you. Summarize your resume—briefly—

and expand on particular courses or experiences relevant to the firm or position. Do not go on about your hobbies or personal life, where you spent your summer vacation, or anything that is not relevant to securing that job. You may explain how that particular job fits in with your long-range career goals and talk specifically about what attracted you to their company in the first place.

"Do You Have Any Questions?"

It's the last fatal question on our list, often the last one an interviewer throws at you after an hour or two of grilling. Even if the interview has been very long and unusually thorough, you *should* have questions—about the job, the company, even the industry. Unfortunately, by the time this question off-handedly hits the floor, you are already looking forward to leaving and may have absolutely nothing to say.

Your Turn to Ask the Questions

1. What will my typical day be like?
2. What happened to the last person who had this job?
3. Given my attitude and qualifications, how would you estimate my chances for career advancement at your company?
4. Why did you come to work here? What keeps you here?
5. If you were I, would you start here again?
6. How would you characterize the management philosophy of your firm?
7. What characteristics do the successful employees at your company have in common?
8. What's the best (and worst) thing about working here?

Preparing yourself for an interview means more than having answers for some of the questions an interviewer may ask. It means having your own set of questions—at least five or six—for the interviewer. The interviewer is trying to find the right person for the job. You're trying to find the right job. So you should be just as curious about him or her and the company as he or she is about you. Be careful with any list of questions prepared ahead of time. Some of them were probably answered during the course of the interview, so to ask that same question at this stage would demonstrate poor listening skills. Listening well is becoming a lost art, and its importance cannot be stressed enough. (See the box on this page for a short list of questions you may consider asking on any interview).

The Not-So-Obvious Questions

Every interviewer is different and, unfortunately, there are no rules saying he or she has to use all or any of the "basic" questions covered above. But we think the odds are against his or her avoiding all of them. Whichever of these he or she includes, be assured most interviewers do like to come up with questions that are "uniquely theirs." It may be just one or a whole series—questions developed over the years that he or she feels help separate the wheat from the chaff.

You can't exactly prepare yourself for questions like, "What would you do if...(fill in the blank with some obscure occurrence)?," "What do you remember about kindergarten?," or "What's your favorite ice cream flavor?" Every interviewer we know has his or her favorites and all of these questions seem to come out of left field. Just stay relaxed, grit your teeth (quietly), and take a few seconds to frame a reasonably intelligent reply.

The Downright Illegal Questions

Some questions are more than inappropriate—they are illegal. The Civil Rights

Act of 1964 makes it illegal for a company to discriminate in its hiring on the basis of race, color, religion, sex, or national origin. It also means that any interview questions covering these topics are strictly off-limits. In addition to questions about race and color, what other types questions can't be asked? Some might surprise you:

- Any questions about marital status, number and ages of dependents, or marriage or child-bearing plans.

- Any questions about your relatives, their addresses, or their place of origin.

- Any questions about your arrest record. If security clearance is required, it can be done after hiring but before you start the job.

A Quick Quiz to Test Your Instincts

After reading the above paragraphs, read through the 10 questions below. Which ones do you think would be legal to ask at a job interview? Answers provided below.

1. Confidentially, what is your race?
2. What kind of work does your spouse do?
3. Are you single, married, or divorced?
4. What is your native language?
5. Who should we notify in case of an emergency?
6. What clubs, societies, or organizations do you belong to?
7. Do you plan to have a family?
8. Do you have any disability?
9. Do you have a good credit record?
10. What is your height and weight?

The answers? Not a single question out of the ten is legal at a job interview, because all could lead to a discrimination suit. Some of the questions would become legal once you were hired (obviously a company would need to know who to notify in an emergency), but none belong at an interview.

Now that you know what an interviewer can't ask you, what if he or she does? Well, don't lose your cool, and don't point out that the question may be outside the law—the nonprofessional interviewer may not realize such questions are illegal, and such a response might confuse, even anger, him or her.

Instead, whenever any questions are raised that you feel are outside legal boundaries, politely state that you don't understand how the question has bearing on the job opening and ask the interviewer to clarify him or herself. If the interviewer persists, you may be forced to state that you do not feel comfortable answering questions of that nature. Bring up the legal issue as a last resort, but if things reach that stage, you probably don't want to work for that company after all.

Testing and Applications

Though not part of the selection interview itself, job applications, skill tests, and psychological testing are often part of the pre-interview process. You should know something about them.

The job application is essentially a record-keeping exercise—simply the transfer of work experience and educational data from your resume to a printed application forms. Though taking the time to recopy data may seem like a waste of time, some companies simply want the information in a particular order on a standard form. One difference: Applications often require the listing of references and salary levels achieved. Be sure to bring your list of references with you to any interview (so you can transfer the pertinent information), and don't lie about salary history; it's easily checked.

Many companies now use a variety of psychological tests as additional mechanisms to screen out undesirable candidates. Although their accuracy is subject to question, the companies that use them obviously believe they are effective at identifying applicants whose personality makeups would preclude their participating positively in a given work situation, especially those at the extreme ends of the behavior spectrum.

Their usefulness in predicting job accomplishment is considered limited. If you are normal (like the rest of us), you'll have no trouble with these tests and may even find them amusing. Just don't try to outsmart them—you'll just wind up outsmarting yourself.

Stand Up and Be Counted

Your interview is over. Breathe a sigh of relief. Make your notes—you'll want to keep a file on the important things covered for use in your next interview. Some people consider one out of ten (one job offer for every ten interviews) a good score—if you're keeping score. We suggest you don't. It's virtually impossible to judge how others are judging you. Just go on to the next interview. Sooner than you think, you'll be hired. For the right job.

JOB
OPPORTUNITIES
DATABANK

CHAPTER EIGHTEEN

Job Opportunities Databank

The Job Opportunities Databank contains listings for more than 400 hotels and hotel chains, airlines, cruise lines, travel agencies, convention and visitor bureaus, tourist boards, amusement parks and resorts, and car rental firms that offer entry-level hiring and/or internships. It is divided into two sections: Entry-Level Job and Internship Listings, which provides full descriptive entries for companies in the United States; and Companies Supplying No Further Information, which includes name, address, and telephone information only for companies that did not respond to our inquiries. For complete details on the information provided in this chapter, please consult the introductory material at the front of this directory.

Entry-Level Job and Internship Listings

ACCOR North America
2 Overhill, Ste. 420
Scarsdale, NY 10583
Phone: (914)725-5055

Business Description: The company has 15 properties.

Opportunities: Graduates with a hotel management degree are eligible for assistant manager positions in restaurant or front office. Inexperienced people are hired as guest service agents in the front office. Good potential for advancement—ACCOR promotes from within. "The hotel industry has weird hours and a lot of pressure—it's not for everyone."

Human Resources: David Newton, Human Resources Dir.

Application Procedures: Send resume and cover letter, no applications given until after interview.

Aeromexico
13405 Northwest Fwy., Ste. 240
Houston, TX 77040
Phone: (713)744-8415

Employees: 60.

Average Entry-Level Hiring: 10-20.

Opportunities: Opportunities include reservation agents—not necessarily college graduates. Chance for promotion to reservation supervisor. Tourism experience helpful. Need bilingual people.

Human Resources: Janie Esconbedo, Personnel Dept.

Application Procedures: Send resume and cover letter. Applications and/or resumes kept on file for one year.

▶ **Internships**

Type: The company does not offer an internship program.

Airlines are starting to manage for quality. It costs more up front, but the payoff in brand loyalty might be crucial to improving the industry's profit margins. Advertising spiels about service didn't build brand loyalty, and frequent-flier programs were undermined by discounting. Lower fares spurred costcutting hub-and-spoke systems that alienate customers. "The minute the operation begins to rule decisions, you'll lose customers," warns George L. Mueller, senior vice-president for customer services with American Airlines.

Source: *Business Week*

Air Canada
1166 Avenue of the Americas
New York, NY 10036
Phone: (212)869-8840

Employees: 24,000. (The number listed above reflects international employment.).

Opportunities: Opportunities include customer service agents and some clerical personnel. Must pass typing, entry-level math, and vocabulary tests. College degree a plus. Bilingual people needed.

Human Resources: Valerie Ravenhill, Human Resources Representative.

Application Procedures: Applications will be mailed upon request. Call the company and leave name and address on the voice mail system.

Airlines Travel & Ticket Service
4517 Emery Industrial Pkwy.
Warrensville Heights, OH 44128
Phone: (216)831-9700

Employees: 14.

Opportunities: Sales, promotions, marketing, and many other positions are available to anyone showing sincere interest and demonstrating the necessary intelligence. The company is prepared to fully train new employees.

Human Resources: Harold Rubin, Vice Pres.

Application Procedures: Send resume and cover letter.

▶ **Internships**

Type: College credit internships available.
Number Available Annually: 3-5.

Duties: Interns will be trained in various aspects of the industry (sales, marketing, etc.).

Application Procedure: Contact the company for more information, or send resume and cover letter.

Application Deadline: Open.

Alaska Airlines Inc.
PO Box 68900
Seattle, WA 98168
Phone: (206)433-3200

Business Description: Provider of regularly-scheduled air transportation.

Officers: Bruce R. Kennedy, Pres. & Chairman of the Board; Willie G. McKnight Jr., VP of Mktg.; Doug Verstock, VP of Admin.; J. Ray Vingo, VP of Finance.

Employees: 5,663.

Human Resources: Charles Loughran, VP of Human Resources.

Albuquerque Convention & Visitors Bureau
PO Box 26866
Albuquerque, NM 87125
Phone: (505)243-3696

Employees: 32.

Average Entry-Level Hiring: Unknown.

Opportunities: Most positions require a degree in public relations or sales. No degree needed for clerical positions. The company promotes from within.

Human Resources: Thunnae Love, Human Resources Technician.

Application Procedures: Openings are posted internally for five days and externally for twenty days. Minority agencies circulate job descriptions. Send resume and cover letter.

Applications and/or resumes kept on file for six months.

▶ Internships

Contact: Paris Thomas.

Type: Offers a college internship program. Internships last for five months during the academic year. Applicants tend to be from the business school.

America West Airlines Inc.
51 W. 3rd St.
Tempe, AZ 85281
Phone: (602)894-0800

Business Description: An airline carrier with a fleet of approximately 100 aircraft. The company flies to 54 destinations in the continental United States, Hawaii, and Canada and works primarily through its hubs in Phoenix and Las Vegas. The company has also filed to gain route authority to Japan and Australia and has gained access to New York's LaGuardia and Washington's National airport. The airline is #1 in on-time performance and holds the on-time championship for 1988-1989.

Officers: Edward R. Beauvais, CEO & Chairman of the Board; Mark J. Coleman, Sr. VP of Sales & Product Development; Michael J. Conway, President & COO; Alphonse E. Frei, CFO.

Employees: 12,494.

Benefits: Benefits include medical insurance, life insurance, a 401(K) plan, a child care program, an employee assistance program, a medical facility, an employee stock ownership plan , and liberal travel benefits. The company also offers an employee cross-utilization program to provide expanded opportunities for advancement and job enrichment. Employee advisory boards also participate in management goals dealing with work-related issues and cost cutting and operations improvement ideas.

Application Procedures: Contact the company for more information.

American Airlines Inc.
4333 Amon Carter Blvd.
Fort Worth, TX 75261-9616
Phone: (817)963-1234

Business Description: Engages in air transportation of passengers and cargo, and provides food and other related services to the air transport industries.

Officers: Donald J. Carty, Sr. VP & Finance Officer; Robert L. Crandall, CEO & Pres.; Michael W. Gunn, Sr. VP of Mktg.; Max D. Hopper, Sr. VP of Info. Systems.

Employees: 77,000.

Average Entry-Level Hiring: 2,000 flight attendants.

Opportunities: Analysts in finance, marketing, information systems, operations, and research—M.B.A.s. Engineers—Master's and Ph.D. degrees required. Reservation positions in Hartford, Cincinnati, Los Angeles, Raleigh/Durham, and Dallas (other areas may be available at other times). Flight attendants, baggage handlers, and ramp attendants needed nationally. Airplane pilots.

Benefits: Non-union employees and employees represented by the Transport Workers Union make contributions toward funding a portion of the cost of their retiree health care benefits.

Human Resources: Jerry Teate, Human Resources Mgr.

Application Procedures: Airplane pilot positions available, send resume and cover letter to American Airlines, Pilot Recruitment, PO Box 619625, mail drop 4145, Fort Worth, TX or telephone (817) 261-9625.

American Eagle Inc.
900 N. Franklin St.
Chicago, IL 60610
Phone: (312)280-8222

Business Description: Provider of regularly-scheduled air transportation.

Officers: T.J. Lafin, VP & Controller; Peter Piper, President.

Employees: 1,800.

Human Resources: H.J. Londeau, VP of Human Resources.

American Express Travel Service
120 N. 44th St.
Phoenix, AZ 85034
Phone: (602)244-2660

Employees: 150.

Average Entry-Level Hiring: 2.

Opportunities: College or travel school graduate (or candidate with some experience) will start in the Processing Department and will be trained to use computers for ticket handling and processing. Opportunity for promotion to travel agent after some experience in ticket processing. Those wishing to enter as travel agents must have worked for an agency previously. Accounting—no degree required. Administrative—typing and shorthand skills required. More experienced agents train new ones. Orientation program gives all new hires an overview of the company.

Human Resources: Sheri Hedger, Employment Representative.

Application Procedures: Send resume and cover letter expressing area of interest. Accepts walk-in applicants.

American International Rent-A-Car

1 Harborside Dr.
East Boston, MA 02128
Phone: (617)561-1000

Average Entry-Level Hiring: 4.

Human Resources: Cheryl Tarrant, Manager.

Application Procedures: Apply in person, or send resume and cover letter.

Americana Congress Hotel

520 S. Michigan Ave.
Chicago, IL 60605
Phone: (312)427-3800

Employees: 350.

Average Entry-Level Hiring: As needed.

Opportunities: People with no experience start as front desk clerks.

Human Resources: Marta Maso, Human Resources Dir.

Application Procedures: Applications are accepted Monday through Friday from 9:00 A.M. to 12 noon, or send resume and cover letter.

▶ **Internships**

Type: The company does not offer an internship program.

ARA Services Inc.

1101 Market St.
Philadelphia, PA 19107
Phone: (215)238-3000
Fax: (215)238-3333

Business Description: Provides food service, including vending machines, cafeterias, dining rooms, concession stands, and coffee to businesses, correctional facilities, hospitals, universities, schools, parks, resorts, stadiums, and convention centers. The company also has food service operations in Canada, Europe, and Japan.

Officers: James E. Ksansnak, Sr. VP & CFO; Joseph Neubauer, Pres. & Chairman of the Board; Martin Spector, Exec. VP of Mktg. & Sales.

Employees: 125,000.

Average Entry-Level Hiring: 6-9.

Opportunities: Opportunities include associate programmers, accounting tax asset management, accounts receivable management, credit representatives, and auditors. Computer or MIS degree required.

Human Resources: Kim Meyerson, Human Resources Specialist; Lisa Staley, Human Resources Specialist; Diane Weltman, Human Resources.

Application Procedures: Places newspaper advertisements for certain openings. Some hiring is done through an employment agency. Send resume and cover letter to the attention of Human Resource Department.

Arizona Biltmore

24th and Missouri
Phoenix, AZ 85032
Phone: (602)955-6600

Employees: 600.

Opportunities: Entry-level employees must start in restaurant, front desk, reservations, or telecommunications departments. After six months, the employee may apply to the management training program.

Human Resources: Wendy Smith, Employment.

Application Procedures: Maintains a job hotline at 954-2547. Apply in person Monday through Wednesday between 9:00 A.M. and 12:00 P.M., or contact the company for more information.

Arrington Travel Center, Inc.
55 W. Monroe St., Ste. 2450
Chicago, IL 60603
Phone: (312)726-4900
Fax: (312)726-1447

Average Entry-Level Hiring: 6.

Human Resources: Mimi Riebe, Mgr. of Admin. Services.

Application Procedures: Send resume and cover letter.

Atlanta Hilton & Towers
255 Courtland St.
Atlanta, GA 30303
Phone: (404)659-2000

Employees: 976.

Average Entry-Level Hiring: 40-50.

Opportunities: Opportunities available for bilingual concierges (preferably French or Spanish) and front desk personnel. A management training program is available through the corporate office.

Human Resources: Jilly Algora, Employment Mgr.

Application Procedures: Apply in person Monday or Wednesday between 9:00 A.M. and 1:00 P.M., or send resume and cover letter to the attention of Employment Manager.

▶ **Internships**

Type: Internship program offered through the corporate office.

Application Procedure: For further information, contact the Los Angeles corporate office at (213)278-4321.

Atlanta Marriott Marquis
265 Peachtree Center Ave., NE
Atlanta, GA 30308
Phone: (404)521-0000

Employees: 1,300.

Opportunities: Entry-level positions in front desk, reservations, administration, restaurant, housekeeping, and kitchen. Entry-level management personnel hired through Marriott's corporate office.

Human Resources: Rosemary Strong, Personnel Dir.

Application Procedures: Apply in person Monday, Tuesday, and Wednesday between 9:00 A.M. and 12:00 P.M. and Monday between 3:30 and 5:30 P.M., or call the Job Hotline at (404)586-6240, updated after 3:00 P.M. on Friday. Contact the company for more information at (404)586-6144.

▶ **Internships**

Duties: All hiring is done through the corporate office. Contact the company for more information at (301)380-9000.

Looking for a job is largely a mind game—you're the one who defines the goal and how to get there—and flexibility has to be part of the strategy. For instance, announcements of many openings never turn up outside the employer's offices, since most companies prefer to hire from within. The trick, then, is to get inside. One way is to put your ego on hold and take a job as a clerical worker. "You need to gain employment first," says L. Patrick Sheetz, director of Michigan State University's Collegiate Employment Research Institute. "You gain promotion from there."

Source: *U.S. News & World Report*

Atlas Hotels Inc.
PO Box 85098
San Diego, CA 92186
Phone: (619)297-2597
Fax: (619)294-5957

Business Description: Operates 10 hotels including nine in the United States and one in Mexico.

Officers: Robert Dabaghian, Dir. of Data Processing; Jim Oddo, VP of Mktg.; J. Phillips, VP of Finance; R.L. Richards, President.

Employees: 2,900.

Opportunities: Positions are available for people-oriented, entry-level candidates in the Restaurant department. Clerical positions are also open.

Human Resources: Alma Gonzales, VP of Admin.

Application Procedures: Students interested in employment opportunites at Atlas's four San Diego properties (which employ a total of 1,500 people) should call the number listed above, ext. 3860, or call the hotline at (619)299-2254. Other hotels in the chain hire independently. The personnel director at each hotel is available for further information.

Austin Travel Corp.
219 S. Service Rd.
Plainview, NY 11803
Phone: (516)752-9100

Employees: 150.

Average Entry-Level Hiring: 0-5, extremely limited; experience is required.

Opportunities: Experience (but not college) required for all agent positions. Training is comprised of classes and in-house training on computers.

Human Resources: Nan Linzner, Human Resources Coordinator.

Application Procedures: Send resume and cover letter.

▶ **Internships**

Type: The company may offer an internship program.

Australian Tourist Commission
2121 Avenue of the Stars, Ste. 1200
Los Angeles, CA 10067
Phone: (213)552-1988

Employees: 10. (The number listed above is for the Los Angeles office only.).

Average Entry-Level Hiring: 1.

Opportunities: Entry-level candidates must have a college degree and extensive experience in marketing in the United States and/or travel.

Human Resources: Susan, Office Mgr.

Application Procedures: Send resume and cover letter. Applications and/or resumes kept on file for two years.

▶ **Internships**

Type: The company does not offer an internship program.

Avis Inc.
900 Old Country Rd.
Garden City, NY 11530
Phone: (516)222-3000

Business Description: Operates car rental services.

Officers: Joseph V. Vittoria, CEO.

Employees: 13,000.

Average Entry-Level Hiring: Unknown.

Opportunities: Opportunities include computer programmer, electrical engineering, and customer service trainees. Call the Marketing Department to inquire about other opportunities.

Human Resources: Thomas Turbyne, Human Resources Representative.

Application Procedures: Accepts unsolicited resumes. Applications can be filled out on site, or send resume and cover letter to the attention of Employment Department. Advertises in local newspapers. For operations management positions, send resume and cover letter to the attention of Thomas Turbyne, Human Resources Representative, 4805 Grand Ave., Maspach, NY 11375.

▶ **Internships**

Type: Salaried, year-round internships available. Departments include personnel, marketing, accounting, and technical support. **Number Available Annually:** Unknown.

Qualifications: Education or experience in area preferred, but candidates can always be taught on-the-job.

Application Procedure: Send resume and cover letter to the contact stating the type of internship in which you are interested. The company also participates in college recruiting. Company always interested in hiring interns after graduation.

Application Deadline: Ongoing. **Decision Date:** Two weeks to one month after resume is received.

Bahamas Tourist Office
150 E. 52nd St., 28th Fl.
New York, NY 10022
Phone: (212)758-2777

Employees: 15.

Average Entry-Level Hiring: Unknown.

Human Resources: Sonia Murphy, Supervisor.

Application Procedures: Resumes and applications accepted.

▶ **Internships**

Type: The company does not offer an internship program.

Bermuda Department of Tourism
310 Madison Ave., Ste. 201
New York, NY 10017
Phone: 800-223-6106

Human Resources: Jane Simmons, Admin. Sec.

Application Procedures: Personnel hired through the Bermuda office only. Applications accepted for openings only.

Best Western International
PO Box 10203
Phoenix, AZ 85064
Phone: (602)957-4200

Officers: K. Barlow, VP of Info. Systems; Clay Carpenter, VP of Finance; B. Derasmo, VP of Mktg.; R. Evans, CEO.

Employees: 1,000.

Human Resources: Judy Nelson, Personnel Mgr.

Beverly Hills Hotel
9641 Sunset Blvd.
Beverly Hills, CA 90210
Phone: (213)276-2251

Employees: 550.

Average Entry-Level Hiring: 30-40.

Opportunities: Front desk clerks. There is growth potential from this position, but little turnover—management positions rarely open.

Human Resources: Barbara Wardell, Personnel Mgr.

Application Procedures: Send resume and cover letter.

▶ **Internships**

Type: The company does not offer an internship program.

The Biltmore Hotel
506 Grand St.
Los Angeles, CA 90071
Phone: (213)624-1011

Employees: 680.

Average Entry-Level Hiring: Unknown.

Opportunities: Front desk clerk, sales secretary, catering secretary. The company promotes from within.

Human Resources: Fran Smith, Employment Mgr.

Application Procedures: Walk-ins can apply Monday and Wednesday between 9:00 A.M. and 11:30 A.M. A hotline number, (213)612-1585 will tell which jobs have openings. Send resume and cover letter or contact the company for more information at (213)624-1011, ext. 1271.

▶ **Internships**

Type: The company does not offer an internship program.

Bloomington Convention & Visitors Bureau
9801 Dupont Ave. S., Ste. 120
Bloomington, MN 55431
Phone: (612)888-8810

Employees: 14.

Average Entry-Level Hiring: Unknown.

Opportunities: Clerical and sales—college preferred but not required. Training includes classroom and on-the-job instruction.

Human Resources: Jan Kroells, Promotional Mgr.

Application Procedures: Applications accepted for openings only. Applications and/or resumes kept on file for one year.

▶ **Internships**

Type: Nonpaid. Offers internships through the local college.

Boston Park Plaza Hotel & Towers
64 Arlington St.
Boston, MA 02116-3912
Phone: (617)457-2253

Employees: 750.

Average Entry-Level Hiring: 100-500.

Opportunities: Opportunities include assistant manager or supervisor—hotel degree and experience preferred.

Human Resources: Mary Applegate, Employment Mgr.

Application Procedures: Apply in person Monday through Wednesday between 9:30 and 11:30 A.M. Interview to follow.

Boyd Group
3000 Las Vegas Blvd. S.
Las Vegas, NV 89109
Phone: (702)732-6111

Business Description: Operator of hotels and/or motels.

Officers: William Boyd, CEO & Chairman of the Board; Ralph Brown, VP & CFO.

Employees: 8,000.

Application Procedures: Contact the company for more information.

D uring a decade of airline deregulation, service took a middle seat to growth, mergers, and competition. Now airlines are working to repair the damage. This effort will become crucial as U.S. airlines push into global markets and take on high-class foreign competitors. The problem is how to make money in an extraordinarily complex, capital-intensive business and still provide the kind of service offered by such carriers as Singapore Airlines and British Airways. The answer is maddeningly simple: airlines must learn to manage for quality.

Source: *Business Week*

Boykin Management Co.
700 Terminal Tower
Cleveland, OH 44113
Phone: (216)241-6375
Fax: (216)241-1329

Business Description: Engaged in hotel management.

Officers: Robert W. Boykin, President; Raymond P. Heitland, VP & Treasurer.

Employees: 3,000.

Benefits: Benefits include medical insurance, dental insurance, life insurance, long-term disability, tuition assistance, smoke-free environment, subsidized cafeteria, and free property rooms at the hotel after a required time of employment.

Human Resources: Kathleen Matthews, VP of Human Resources; Nancy Poling, Human Resources Dir.

Application Procedures: Advertises in the *Cleveland Plain Dealer*. Apply in person at Property Human Resources offices between 9:00

AM and 5:00 PM, or applications will be mailed upon request. Faxed resumes are accepted. Send resume and cover letter to the attention of Kathleen Mathews, VP of Human Resources.

British Airways
75-20 Astoria Rd.
Jackson Heights, NY 11370
Phone: (718)397-4000

Employees: 1,700. (This number reflects employment in the United States only.).

Average Entry-Level Hiring: Unknown.

Opportunities: Opportunities include reservation sales, customer service, and marketing. Educational requirements were not specified by the company. Employees are promoted from within. Training includes six weeks of paid classroom instruction.

Application Procedures: Applications will be mailed upon request, or send resume and cover letter to the attention of Human Resources. Applications and/or resumes kept on file for two years.

British Tourist Authority
40 W. 57th St.
New York, NY 10019
Phone: (212)581-4708

Employees: 29.

Average Entry-Level Hiring: Unknown.

Opportunities: Only British citizens are hired. Authority is responsible for promoting travel to England, Scotland, Wales, and Northern Ireland.

Human Resources: Maria Valle, Admin. Asst.

Application Procedures: Send resume and cover letter. Applications and/or resumes kept on file indefinitely.

Budget Rent a Car Corp.
200 N. Michigan Ave.
Chicago, IL 60601
Phone: (312)580-5000

Business Description: Franchises and operates the third-largest passenger car rental system in the United States.

Officers: Morris Belzberg, President; Clifton E. Haley, CEO.

Employees: 5,540.

Average Entry-Level Hiring: 30.

Opportunities: Customer service representatives—six months experience in any customer-contact position, interpersonal skills, and computer literacy. Post-high school training of some kind is required; travel school is a big plus. Truck representatives—college degree required.

Human Resources: Lisa Saliano, Human Resources Representative.

Application Procedures: Places newspaper advertisements for certain openings. Apply in person, or send resume and cover letter to the attention of Human Resources Department.

▶ **Internships**

Number Available Annually: 6.

Duties: Duties include working on special project assignments based on the needs of the department.

Qualifications: Qualifications vary according to departments.

Application Procedure: Call or send resume and cover letter to the attention of Lisa Saliano.

Application Deadline: April-June. **Decision Date:** Will interview candidates after June and then make their decision.

BWIA International
118-35 Queens Blvd.
Forest Hills, NY 11375
Phone: (718)520-8100

Employees: 35,000.

Average Entry-Level Hiring: Unknown.

Human Resources: Pam Campell, Human Resources Dir.

Application Procedures: Send resume and cover letter, or applications will be mailed upon request.

Caesars New Jersey Inc.
1801 Century Park E., Ste. 2600
Los Angeles, CA 90067
Phone: (213)552-2711

Business Description: Ceasars New Jersey Inc. is the major link in a chain of resort entertainment hotels.

Officers: Henry Gluck, CEO & Chairman of the Board; Roger Lee, Sr. VP & Finance Officer.

Employees: 3,568.

Human Resources: Janet Bussiere, Human Resources Dir.

Application Procedures: Send resume and cover letter.

Caesars Palace Inc.
3570 Las Vegas Blvd. S
Las Vegas, NV 89109
Phone: (702)731-7110

Business Description: Operator of hotels and/or motels. Operator of miscellaneous sports, amusement or recreation establishments.

Officers: Lyle Bell, Dir. of Systems; Anthony Brolick, VP & CFO; Don Guglielmino, VP of Business Development; W. Dan Reichartz, President.

Employees: 4,500.

Human Resources: Brian Menzel, VP of Human Resources.

Canadian Pacific Hotels Corp.
1 University Ave., Ste. 1400
Toronto, ON, Canada M5J 2P1
Phone: (416)367-7111
Fax: (416)863-6079

Business Description: The company has 27 properties, all in Canada.

Average Entry-Level Hiring: 50-100.

Opportunities: Canadian Pacific offers a one-year hotel management and development program, which places several graduates in each hotel. Candidates choose an area of concentration, but may also rotate through various departments. After completing the program, the trainees are hired as junior or assistant managers.

Human Resources: Bonnie Holbrook, Dir. of Corp. Human Resource Services.

Application Procedures: Apply in person or send resume and cover letter. "All properties are located in Canada. American students are ineligible to work in Canada."

▶ **Internships**

Type: The company does not offer an internship program.

Caribbean Tourist Organization

20 E. 46th St.
New York, NY 10017
Phone: (212)682-0435

Employees: 12.

Average Entry-Level Hiring: Unknown.

Human Resources: Sylma Brown, Placement Mgr.

Application Procedures: Send resume and cover letter. Applications and/or resumes kept on file for six months.

▶ Internships

Type: Restricted.

Application Procedure: Contact the company for more information.

Jeffrey A. Sonnenfeld, an Emory University management professor, divides U.S. corporations into 4 categories: the Baseball Team—advertising, entertainment, investment banking, software, biotech research, and other industries based on fad, fashion, new technologies, and novelty; the Club—utilities, government agencies, airlines, banks, and other organizations that tend to produce strong generalists; the Academy—manufacturers in electronics, pharmaceuticals, office products, autos, and consumer products; and the Fortress—companies in fields such as publishing, hotels, retailing, textiles, and natural resources.

Source: *Fortune*

Carlson Companies Inc.

PO Box 59159
Minneapolis, MN 55489
Phone: (612)540-5000

Business Description: Operates, franchises, and manages hotels and resorts by the names of Radisson Hotels International, Colony Hotels and Resorts, and Country Inns by Carlson. It also owns TGI Friday's and Country Kitchen restaurants.

Officers: Terry Ashwill, VP of Finance; Edwin Gage, CEO & Pres.; James Kinney, VP of Info. Systems; J.K. Pfleider, Exec. VP of Mktg.

Employees: 63,000.

Human Resources: T.M. Butorac, VP of Human Resources; Tom Dybsky, Human Resources Dir.

Application Procedures: Places newspaper advertisements for certain openings. Accepts unsolicited resumes. Applications can be filled out on site, or send resume and cover letter to the attention of Human Resources Department.

Carlson Tours & Incentive Travel, Ltd.

Cronquist Park, Ste. 9
5580 45th St.
Red Deer, AB, Canada T4N 1L1
Phone: (403)340-8687

Employees: 15.

Average Entry-Level Hiring: 1-2.

Opportunities: Travel agent—one year of experience required.

Human Resources: Randy Thorsteinson, Operations Dir.

Application Procedures: Send resume and cover letter. Accepts walk-in applicants in some instances.

▶ Internships

Type: The company may offer an internship program.

Carlson Travel Service

757 3rd Ave., 11th Fl.
New York, NY 10017
Phone: (212)752-8980

Employees: 720.

Average Entry-Level Hiring: 3-5.

Opportunities: Travel school and/or experience required. 85 percent of those hired with these credentials become travel counselors, handling accounts from beginning to end. Non-college graduates may enter in clerical positions—packaging tickets, answering phones, typing, and filing. Training includes a six-week, in-house training program, after which candidates start as a branch training travel counselor under the guidance of a more experienced employee. Training travel counselors generally start to handle their own accounts after six months.

▶ Internships

Type: The company does not offer an internship program.

Carrier Travel

1040 Avenue of the Americas
New York, NY 10018
Phone: (212)764-4343

Employees: 70.

Opportunities: Opportunities include travel agents, messengers, clerical personnel, and receptionists.

Charlotte Convention & Visitors Bureau

122 E. Stonewall Rd.
Charlotte, NC 28202-1838
Phone: 800-231-4646

Employees: 20.

Average Entry-Level Hiring: Unknown.

Opportunities: Tourism sales and convention sales managers—experience required. Visitor information specialist—college preferred.

Human Resources: Jerry, Manager.

Application Procedures: Places newspaper advertisements for certain openings. Some hiring is done through networking or employee referrals and employment agencies. Apply in person, or send resume and cover letter. Applications and/or resumes kept on file for two years.

Chicago Convention & Tourism Bureau

2301 S. Lakeshore Dr.
Chicago, IL 60616
Phone: (312)567-8482

Employees: 300. Consists of 50 full-time and 250 part-time employees.

Average Entry-Level Hiring: 11-17, (support 3-4; finance 1-2; housing 1-2; membership 1-2; marketing 1; sales 1-2; publications 1; registration 1; and office services 1-2.).

Opportunities: Seretarial support—computer (mainframe, not PC), typing (65 wpm), and dictaphone experience required. Clerical—same as secretarial but no dictaphone. Publications—printing background, college preferred. Finance, membership, and sales—college required, background on PC (knowledge of WordPerfect 5.1 preferred), and mainframe experience preferred. Experience in sales and hotels or a bureau is necessary for sales positions.

Human Resources: Patti Evans, Office Mgr.

Application Procedures: Send resume and cover letter. Applications and/or resumes kept on file indefinitely.

▶ Internships

Type: Offers a college internship program.

Chicago Hilton and Towers

720 S. Michigan
Chicago, IL 60605
Phone: (312)922-4400

Employees: 1,500.

Average Entry-Level Hiring: Unknown.

Opportunities: Entry-level personnel start in the front office or reservations areas, which offer inexperienced people a good overview of the hotel operation. Summer internships are offered through the corporate office. Contact Hilton Hotels Corp. for further information (9336 Civic Center Dr., PO Box 5587, Beverly Hills, CA 90201 213-278-4321)

Human Resources: Gerre Smith, Employment Mgr.

Application Procedures: Apply Tuesdays between 9:00 A.M. and 12:00 P.M. for screening and interviews.

Chicago O'Hare Marriott

8535 W. Higgins Rd.
Chicago, IL 60631
Phone: (312)693-4444

Employees: 650.

Average Entry-Level Hiring: 150.

Opportunities: Sectional or lobby housekeeper—high school diploma and hospitality skills required. Bellstand, driver, dispatcher, bellstaff, greeter—good hospitality and communication skills and high school diploma required. Front desk clerks—professional appearance and attitude, organized work habits, ability to handle pressure of guest interaction and excellent hospitality skills required, as well as a high school diploma or some college. Reservations clerk—good phone etiquette and typing skills; high school diploma or some college required. Gift shop clerk—cash handling and customer service abilities; and high school diploma necessary. Cook—culinary training and food production experience. Sales catering representative, secretary, receptionist, administrative assistant—typing, WordPerfect, phone and communication skills; college degree or business experience needed. Security—emergency first aid, fire procedure, federal and state law compliance, and experience in hospitality industry. Accounts receivable/payable clerk, accounting clerk, credit card clerk—college degree in accounting required. Engineering—general maintenance skills. Room service server, attendant, telephone operator/cashier—excellent hospitality and communication skills; high school diploma required. Restaurant host/hostess, server, service attendant—good hospitality and communication skills; high school diploma or past work experience. Banquet server, bartender, attendants—good hospitality and communication skills; bartender school. "Every department manager will help the employees in his or her department in terms of on-the-job duties and safety factors. Generally, entry-level people learn through hands-on experience. There is a hospitality training class (one day) that teaches new hirees the importance of our industry."

Human Resources: Kristen Whisnant, Employment Contact.

Application Procedures: Send resume and cover letter to the attention of Employment Manager.

▶ **Internships**

Contact: Michael Yonker, Dir. of Employment.

Type: Offers internships in human resources that may or may not be paid; culinary internships in food and beverage that last three months, nonpaid internships in accounting and in sales, and one paid position in the health club. College credit can be earned through nonpaid internships. Program duration is one summer or semester. **Number Available Annually:** 6.

Duties: Interns will be trained in all of the positions of the department they are hired for and will spend a day in every department of the hotel to understand how they all work together. They will also complete a task book to gain further knowledge on how a hotel operates and will attend some of the management meetings to experience management and executive interaction.

Application Procedure: Send resume and cover letter to the attention of Employment Director and contact the internship office at your college or university. The company interviews candidates on Mondays and Wednesdays

between 9:00 A.M. and 12:30 P.M., and on Tuedays between 12:30 P.M. and 6:00 P.M.

Application Deadline: None. **Decision Date:** One to two months before internship start date.

Clarion Hotel
141 W. 6th St.
Cincinnati, OH 45202
Phone: (513)352-2100

Employees: 500.

Average Entry-Level Hiring: 50-100.

Opportunities: Assistant restaurant manager and restaurant manager—limited experience required (e.g., waiter/waitress). Front desk supervisor. The company promotes from within after six months on the job. Phone operator is training ground for front desk position. Accounting clerks—math skills preferred, but accounting degree is not required.

Human Resources: Melissa Schmidt, Dir. of Employment.

▶ **Internships**

Type: Paid (beginning at $5.20/hour) or college credit. Internships available for front desk positions.

Application Procedure: Apply in person Tuesday through Friday between 9:00 A.M. and 12:00 P.M. or send resume and cover letter to the attention of Employment Director.

Application Deadline: Anytime; Summer—one month ahead of start time.

Clipper Cruise Line
7711 Bonhomme Ave.
St. Louis, MO 63105
Phone: (314)727-2929
Fax: (314)727-6576

Average Entry-Level Hiring: 24.

Opportunities: The only entry-level positions offered by the company are deck hands and stewardesses.

Human Resources: Mary Hasenmueller, Administrator.

Application Procedures: Send resume and cover letter along with a picture of yourself. The company may then send you an application, or you can call them for one.

▶ **Internships**

Contact: Kristen Deeg.

Commodore Cruiseline

800 Douglas Rd.
Coral Gables, FL 33134
Phone: (305)529-3000

Employees: 5.

Average Entry-Level Hiring: Unknown.

Application Procedures: Submit a resume with work history and references. Include a day and night telephone number and home address. Interviews by appointment only. Send resume and cover letter to the attention of Personnel. PO Box 143078, Coral Gables, FL 33114.

Connecticut Travel Services Inc.

1 Central Park Plaza
PO Box 850
New Britain, CT 06050
Phone: (203)255-9491

Employees: 130.

Average Entry-Level Hiring: 2.

Opportunities: After completing the training period and a month of on-the-job activity (mainly legwork, clerical, filing, answering phones, etc.), new hires will handle their own calls and accounts. You must have completed an internship from a travel-related college curriculum in order to be a candidate for any position. Training includes one to three months in computer school, which will teach you to process a booking from beginning to end. This period of training is supervised by a personal trainer/manager.

Human Resources: Charissa Bafumo, Employment.

Application Procedures: Applications can be filled out on site, or send resume and cover letter.

Consolidated Freightways Corp.

3240 Hillview Ave.
Palo Alto, CA 94304
Phone: (415)494-2900

Business Description: Transportation services company engaged in long-haul and regional next-day trucking, worldwide air freight, intermodal truckload, customs brokerage, and ocean freight services. ("Consolidated Freightways Opens New Columbus, Ohio, Consolidation Center." *Business Wire.* 8 May 1990.)

Officers: Peter Boulais, VP of Sales; Ted Coleman, VP of Finance; Robert Lawrence, President; Phillip Seeley, Dir. of Systems.

Employees: 19,600.

Application Procedures: Send resume and cover letter to the attention of Personnel Department.

Consolidated Freightways Inc.

175 Linfield Dr.
Menlo Park, CA 94025
Phone: (415)326-1700
Fax: (415)321-1741

Business Description: Diversified transportation company specializing in commercial and industrial freight shipments. Principal operating companies are CF Motor Freight, Con-Way Transportation Services, and Emery Worldwide. The company also operates related businesses in customs brokerage, trailer manufacturing, and equipment supply. The company has 11 independent businesses, 1400 service locations, 55,000 pieces of city pick-up and road equipment, and 98 cargo aircraft. In 1989, CF companies handled almost 40-million shipments for more than 500,000 customers.

Officers: N.R. Benke, VP of Finance; W.R. Curry, VP of Mktg.; R.F. O'Brien, Pres. & Chairman of the Board; Larry R. Scott, CEO & Pres.

Employees: 41,000.

Average Entry-Level Hiring: Unknown.

Human Resources: Brian J. Tierney, Human Resources Dir.

Application Procedures: Send resume and cover letter to the attention of Mr. Tierney.

Continental Airlines Inc.
PO Box 4607
Houston, TX 77210-4607
Phone: (713)834-5000

Business Description: Provider of regularly-scheduled air transportation.

Officers: D. Joseph Corr, CEO & Chairman of the Board; John W. Nelson, Exec. VP of Mktg.; Robert Pickering, VP, Treasurer & Chief Acctg. Officer; Richard H. Shuyler, VP & CFO.

Employees: 35,649.

Human Resources: Robert F. Allen, Sr. VP of Human Resources.

Convention & Visitors Bureau of Greater Cleveland
3100 Tower City Ctr.
Cleveland, OH 44113
Phone: (216)621-4110
Toll-free: 800-321-1001

Employees: 21.

Average Entry-Level Hiring: 1.

Opportunities: Looking for experienced people only. Some clerical positions are open, but do not necessarily offer any growth potential. If you have required experience, initial positions in sales and travel and tourism are promotable.

Human Resources: Joe Zion, Human Resources Representative.

Application Procedures: Send resume and cover letter to the attention of Joe Zion for sales and marketing positions, or to the attention of Joe Ivan for clerical positions.

▶ **Internships**

Type: Offers internships for college credit in its public relations, communications, and travel and tourism departments. Provides a small stipend for transportation expenses. **Number Available Annually:** 6-8.

Duties: Public relations, communications—writing news releases and helping with in-house publications. Travel and tourism—communicating with local restaurants and tourist attractions; compiling information.

Application Procedure: Send resume and cover letter.

Application Deadline: None.

Convention & Visitors Bureau of Greater Kansas City
1100 Main St., Ste. 2550
Kansas, MO 64105
Phone: (816)221-5242

Employees: 34.

Average Entry-Level Hiring: 4.

Opportunities: "The travel business is a labor-intensive service industry.One entry-level position within the bureau is an information coordinator. This individual fulfills written and phone requests for information, compiles surveys and must be computer literate. This position lends itself to promotion from within." Training is always on the job. No formal programs are given.

Human Resources: Janet Ziegler, Dir. of Admin.

Application Procedures: Send resume and cover letter to the attention of Janet Ziegler, Dir. of Admin.

▶ **Internships**

Type: The company offers an internship program. Contact the company for more information.

Thomas Cook Travel
100 Cambridge Park Dr.
PO Box 9104
Cambridge, MA 02140
Phone: (617)868-9800
Fax: (617)349-1081

Business Description: Operates more than 300 offices throughout the United States. The company was formed by the merger of Thomas Cook Travel with Heritage Travel, Inc.

Employees: 3,000.

Average Entry-Level Hiring: 100+.

Opportunities: Entry-level opportunities include leisure agents, support agents, office and administrative assistants, accounting clerks, couriers, and related positions. Opportunities for experienced candidates include senior leisure and corporate agents, meeting planners, floaters, and branch supervisory/management positions. Opportunities at corporate and regional headquarters include positions in MIS, Finance, Sales, Marketing, Operations, and

Administration. Training includes advanced CRS (SABRE and APOLLO) skills, destination knowledge, product fluency, and general agent skill development. Additional courses focus on quality control and MIS/automation innovations.

Application Procedures: For more information, contact the Human Resources Representative in the appropriate region: New England Region (617)868-9800; Southern States (214)458-2882; Eastern States (201)507-3435; Midwestern States (708)531-8443; Central States (313)323-4374; Western States (714)553-5524.

▶ **Internships**

Type: Offers an internship program.

Corporate Travel Services Inc.

300 Lakeside Dr., Ste. 250
Oakland, CA 94612
Phone: (510)832-0779

Employees: 250.

Average Entry-Level Hiring: 25.

Opportunities: Opportunities available for travel agents with two or three years of experience plus knowledge of the Apollo reservation program (developed by United Airlines) required. Training includes a two week introductory period.

Human Resources: Sue Lazada, Employment.

Application Procedures: Send resume and cover letter.

Corporate Travel Twin Cities

1401 W. 76th St.
Minneapolis, MN 55423
Phone: (612)861-4443

Employees: 100.

Average Entry-Level Hiring: 4-5.

Opportunities: Opportunities available for travel agents and accounting personnel. Candidates must be graduates from an airline school or have taken a travel-related program in college. Training includes an extensive program within the company.

Human Resources: Irene Fillmore, Vacation Department Manager.

Application Procedures: Hires from resumes on file or advertises in the paper for new resumes/cover letters.

Costa Cruise, Inc.

80 SW 8th St.
Miami, FL 33130
Phone: (305)358-7325

Employees: 80.

Average Entry-Level Hiring: Unknown.

Human Resources: Sherry Carly, Admin. Mgr.

Application Procedures: For land-based positions, send resume and cover letter to the address shown above. For shipboard positions, send resume and cover letter to the attention of 1 Bayfront Plaza, 100 Biscayne Blvd., Miami, FL 33131.

> **"A**ssessing one's own skills is one of the most difficult things in the world," says Kenneth Taylor, a partner at Egon Zehnder International Inc., one of the world's largest executive-search firms. "People usually have latent skills that are not obvious."
>
> Source: *Business Week*

Courtyard by Marriott

1 Marriott Dr.
Washington, DC 20058
Phone: (301)380-9000
Fax: (301)380-2680

Average Entry-Level Hiring: Unknown.

Human Resources: Chuck Lamotte, Regional Human Resources Mgr.

Application Procedures: Send resume and cover letter; resumes are forwarded to the appropriate regional director.

▶ **Internships**

Contact: Chuck Lamotte, Regional Human Resources Mgr.

Type: Interns receive an hourly wage. Internship duration is three to four months. Corporate-level internships are offered in food and beverage, personnel, accounting, room operations, and sales and marketing. **Number Available Annually:** Varies.

Application Procedure: Send resume and cover letter to the attention of Chuck Lamotte.

Application Deadline: None.

Courtyard by Marriott

9631 N. Black Canyon Fwy.
Phoenix, AZ 85021
Phone: (602)944-7373

Employees: 48.

Average Entry-Level Hiring: Varies.

Opportunities: Entry-level opportunities available in the front office, housekeeping, restaurant, and all other departments of the hotel.

Human Resources: Bob, Front Desk Supervisor.

Application Procedures: Applications are accepted 24-hours-a-day and kept on file for six months.

▶ **Internships**

Type: The company does not offer an internship program.

---

ruise lines are now selling theme cruises in addition to their general fare. These include chocolate fantasy outings, a Scottish festival complete with bagpipers, smoke-free cruises, ecology tours, sports weeks, jazz and big-band cruises, film festivals, comedy weeks, and murder-mystery cruises. The theme cruises take advantage of off-season rates and group discounts to fill ships during less-popular months. Cruise specialists Landry & King have compiled a list of more than 70 theme cruises and can be reached at 1-800-223-2026.

Source: *Business Week*

Coventry Hotel Associates

50 Kenney Pl.
PO Box 1912
Saddlebrook, NJ 07662
Phone: (201)845-6200

Business Description: The company has 8 properties, all on the East Coast.

Average Entry-Level Hiring: Varies.

Opportunities: Each hotel has a management training program.

Human Resources: Ilene Kennedy, Personnel Dir.

Application Procedures: Send resume and cover letter. Connecticut corporate office (203)627-7733.

▶ **Internships**

Type: The company does not offer an internship program.

Cunard Hotels & Resorts

555 5th Ave.
New York, NY 10017
Phone: (212)880-7500

Business Description: The company has two properties, one each in Philadelphia and Washington, DC.

Average Entry-Level Hiring: Unknown.

Application Procedures: Send resume and cover letter.

▶ **Internships**

Type: The company does not offer an internship program.

Cunard Line, Ltd.

555 5th Ave.
New York, NY 10017
Phone: (212)880-7362
Fax: (212)949-0915

Average Entry-Level Hiring: Unknown.

Application Procedures: Call (212)880-7423 for application procedures for social staff or entertainment positions. For office positions, send resume and cover letter. The company will contact applicants in whom it is interested. For shipboard opportunities, send a resume and a cover letter indicating interests to: Southwest House, Canute Rd., Southhampton S09 12A, England. Phone: 70 3229933.

Curacao Tourist Board

400 Madison Ave., Ste. 311
New York, NY 10017
Phone: (212)751-8266

Employees: 5.

Average Entry-Level Hiring: None.

Human Resources: Wheel, Sales Mgr.

Application Procedures: Send resume and cover letter.

Dallas Convention & Visitors Bureau

1201 Elm St., Ste. 2000
Dallas, TX 75270
Phone: (214)746-6677

Employees: 120.

Average Entry-Level Hiring: Unknown.

Human Resources: Linda Hilbreth, Human Resources Dir.

Application Procedures: Send resume and cover letter.

▶ **Internships**

Contact: Patty Marshall.

Type: Offers internships for college credit. **Number Available Annually:** Approximately 4.

Duties: Duties vary according to project.

Application Procedure: Send resume and cover letter to the attention of Mrs. Marshall.

Application Deadline: None.

Days Inns of America Inc.

2751 Buford Hwy., NE
Atlanta, GA 30324
Phone: (404)329-7466

Business Description: Chain of 857 hotels.

Officers: Greg Casserly, Exec. VP; John D. Snodgrass, Pres. & Chairman of the Board; Mel Wilinsky, CFO.

Employees: 1,200.

Average Entry-Level Hiring: Unknown.

Opportunities: Assistant managers are hired for a variety of departments, including food and beverage and front desk. Positions in food and beverage and front desk are available in the corporate office. Properties also hire independently.

Human Resources: Susan Brew, Human Resources Representative; Richard A. Smith, VP of Human Resources.

▶ **Internships**

Contact: Luci Lindsey.

Type: Non-salaried, summer internships are available in marketing and franchise. **Number Available Annually:** 3.

Duties: Duties include assisting in the department and working on projects.

Qualifications: Most recruiting done through local universities.

Delta Air Lines Inc.

General Offices
Hartsfield Atlanta International Airport
Atlanta, GA 30320
Phone: (404)715-2600

Business Description: An air carrier providing scheduled air service for passengers, freight, and mail throughout the United States and abroad. Delta, along with Northwest Airlines Inc. and Trans World Airlines Inc. formed WORLDSPAN in February of 1990. WORLDSPAN is a limited partnership created to develop, operate, and market a computer reservations system for the travel industry.

Officers: Ronald W. Allen, CEO & Chairman of the Board; W. Whitley Hawkins, Sr. VP of Mktg.; Thomas J. Roeck Jr., Sr. VP & CFO.

Employees: 61,675.

Opportunities: Opportunties include reservations, automation services, accounting, and personnel—college education required. Six weeks of classroom training is provided.

Human Resources: Russell H. Heil; Maurice W. Worth, VP of Human Resources.

Application Procedures: Applications may be picked up at the airport or a Delta ticket office in your city. Contact the company for more information in Atlanta at (404)715-2501.

Delta Hotels

557 Church St.
Toronto, ON, Canada M4Y 2E2
Phone: (416)926-7800

Business Description: The company has 14 properties.

Average Entry-Level Hiring: Unknown.

Opportunities: The company has a management training program—no details available.

Human Resources: William Pallett, VP of Human Resources.

Application Procedures: Send resume and cover letter, the company will contact you if interested.

▶ **Internships**

Type: The company does not offer an internship program.

Disneyland
1313 Harbor Blvd.
Anaheim, CA 92803
Phone: (714)490-3272

Employees: 10,000.

Average Entry-Level Hiring: Varies.

Opportunities: College graduates start as seasonal employees working in the park. If a position opens, they can then go into advertising, finance, accounting, marketing, or public relations. Employee supply, however, is always greater than demand, so it may take over a year to get into a professional position. Advancement depends on availability of particular openings, demand, and the individual's potential. One year in-the-park training.

Human Resources: Jay Scott, Supervisor.

Application Procedures: Recruits at college campuses. Apply in person between 8:30 A.M. and 5:00 P.M., or send resume and cover letter.

▶ Internships

Type: Internships are only offered to employees.

A ccording to the Minneapolis-based consulting firm Personnel Decisions, women managers are slightly less satisfied with the nature of their work than men, are more likely to be critical of the way promotions are determined, and are more pessimistic than men about moving up. In addition, while 63% of men at the executive level think they work for top-notch managers, only 42% of women at the same level agreed.

Source: *Working Woman*

Dollar Rent-A-Car System
6141 W. Century Blvd., Box 45048
Los Angeles, CA 90045
Phone: (213)776-8100

Employees: 500.

Opportunities: Reservations agents—no experience necessary. Accounting—college or vocational attendance. Training includes two weeks on a computer.

Human Resources: Olivia Salinas, Admin. Asst.

Application Procedures: Applications can be filled out on site Monday through Thursday between 9:00 A.M. and 2:00 P.M.

▶ Internships

Type: The company does not offer an internship program.

Doral Hotels and Resorts
600 Madison Ave., 10th Fl.
New York, NY 10022
Phone: (212)752-5700

Average Entry-Level Hiring: Unknown.

Opportunities: Individuals may obtain entry-level positions as guest service agents, reservations agents, housekeeping supervisors, secretaries, receptionists, food service managers, and accountants.

Human Resources: Kathleen Oschella, Human Resources Dir.

Application Procedures: Send resume and cover letter or fill out an application at Tuscany Hotel, 120 E. 39th St., New York, NY 10016. Contact the hotel for more information at (212) 686-1600.

▶ Internships

Type: The company does not offer an internship program.

Doubletree Clubs
410 N. 44th St., Ste. 700
Phoenix, AZ 85008
Phone: (602)220-6673
Fax: (602)220-6953

Average Entry-Level Hiring: 40-50.

Human Resources: William C. Barnett, VP of Human Resources.

Application Procedures: Send resume and cover letter or apply in person. For more information, contact Human Resources at (602)220-6673, extension 6670.

▶ Internships

Type: The company does not offer an internship program.

Doubletree Hotel At Post Oak
2001 Post Oak Blvd.
Houston, TX 77057
Phone: (713)961-9300
Fax: (713)623-6685

Average Entry-Level Hiring: Unknown.

Application Procedures: Applications taken depending on positions. Applicants are interviewed as positions become available. Applications remain on file one year. For more information, contact the Assistant Director of Human Resources.

Doubletree Inc.

410 N. 44th St., Ste. 700
Phoenix, AZ 85008
Phone: (602)220-6666

Business Description: Operates a chain of 60 hotels.

Officers: G. Peter Bidstrup, CEO & Chairman of the Board; Paul Blanchard, VP of Finance; Ted Pritchard, VP of Mktg.

Employees: 10,000.

Opportunities: The company has a "learner controlled" management training program that lasts six months. The first three months are spent on general overview of the hotel business and company, the second six months in an area of concentration. Potential areas include housekeeping, purchasing, catering, restaurants, and banquets. Candidates must be self-motivated individuals and either recent college graduates (hotel degree preferred but not required) or current employees. Knowledge of industry helpful. Inexperienced candidates should consider starting "at the bottom" and working their way up.

Human Resources: William C. Barnett, VP of Human Resources; Tracy DeLater.

Application Procedures: Contact one of the human resource contacts listed above, or contact the individual hotel of choice.

Embassy Suites

222 Las Colinas, Ste. 1700
Irving, TX 75030
Phone: (214)556-1133
Fax: (214)869-6628

Average Entry-Level Hiring: Unknown.

Human Resources: Susan Steinbrecker, Human Resources Mgr.

Application Procedures: The company recommends that candidates apply in person at corporate headquarters, although the company accepts unsolicited resumes. At this writing, Embassy Suites is in the process of relocating.

▶ **Internships**

Type: The company does not offer an internship program.

Enterprise Rent-A-Car Co.

8850 Ladue Rd.
St. Louis, MO 63124
Phone: (314)863-7000

Business Description: Engaged in renting and leasing cars. The company has over 600 offices nationwide and over 75,000 cars. It operates in most of the top 100 markets in the United States, and plans to expand into the remainder of the top 100. The company's non-automotive operations include distributing food and personal care products to correctional institutions; a coffee service; distributing cellular phone equipment; and producing chocolate mints.

Officers: Ernest C. Behnke, Vice Pres.; Douglas S. Brown, Exec. VP; Marcus T. Cohn, VP of Info. Systems; Wayne C. Kaufman, Vice Pres.; Warren C. Knaup, Sr. VP & CFO; Donald L. Ross, Sr. VP of Operations; Richard V. Snyder, Vice Pres.; Andrew Taylor, President; Jack C. Taylor, CEO & Chairman of the Board.

Employees: 5,000.

Benefits: Benefits include training programs and comprehensive benefits.

Human Resources: Sherry Brannum, Human Resources Dir.

Application Procedures: Actively recruits college graduates for management trainees; recruits at the Michigan Collegiate Job Fair. All majors welcome. Those interested can also apply in person at the company's headquarters.

▶ **Internships**

Contact: Sherry Brannum, Human Resources Dir.

Type: Salaried, year-round internships available with flexible duration in management, marketing, and administrative work. **Number Available Annually:** Unknown.

Qualifications: Must be at least 21 years old and have a clean driving record.

Application Procedure: Send resume and cover letter.

Application Deadline: Ongoing. **Decision Date:** Within two weeks of receipt of resume.

L'Ermitage Hotels
1020 N. San Vicente Blvd.
West Hollywood, CA 90069

Business Description: Operates nine hotels in California.

Human Resources: Ilse Spivack, Personnel Dir.

Application Procedures: Send resume and cover letter.

The Fairmont Hotel
170 S. Market St.
San Jose, CA 95113
Phone: (408)998-1900

Average Entry-Level Hiring: Unknown.

Human Resources: Lori Essary, Human Resources Asst.

Application Procedures: Apply in person Monday, Wednesday, or Friday between 9:00 A.M. and 12:00 P.M., or send resume and cover letter. Applications and/or resumes kept on file for one year.

▶ **Internships**

Type: The company does not offer an internship program.

Fairmont Hotels
950 Mason St.
San Francisco, CA 94108
Phone: (415)772-5000

Average Entry-Level Hiring: Three to five.

Human Resources: Noel Lopez, Human Resources Dir.

Application Procedures: Apply in person on Tuesdays or Thursdays between 10:00 and 2:00, or send resume and cover letter to the attention of Human Resources Department.

▶ **Internships**

Type: The company offers internships at the corporate level. **Number Available Annually:** Varies every year.

FINNAir
10 E. 40th St.
New York, NY 10016
Phone: (212)689-9300

Employees: 200. (The number listed above reflects United States employment only.).

Average Entry-Level Hiring: Hiring freeze.

Opportunities: Opportunities include reservation agents and junior accountants—experience and/or college graduates preferred. Flight attendants, pilots, and mechanics hired through Helsinki headquarters. Classroom training for sales and upper management.

Human Resources: Maureen Baxter, Human Resources Representative.

Application Procedures: Send resume and cover letter.

Fort Worth Convention & Visitors Bureau
100 E. 15th St., Ste. 400
Fort Worth, TX 76102
Phone: (817)336-8791

Employees: 20.

Average Entry-Level Hiring: 1.

Opportunities: Opportunities available for administrative assistants—college degree preferred but not required.

Human Resources: Malory Proscia.

Application Procedures: Send resume and cover letter.

Forte Hotels Inc.
1973 Friendship Dr.
El Cajon, CA 92020
Phone: (619)448-1884

Business Description: Trusthouse Forte is the parent company of TraveLodge, Viscount Hotels, and several individual hotels.

Officers: Barry L. Conrad, CEO; William J. Hanley, Exec. VP of Mktg. & Sales; Rick Meza, CFO; Eric Unruh, Dir. of Info. Systems.

Employees: 1,400.

Opportunities: The company offers a management training program.

Human Resources: Barbara Radcliffe, Human Resources Representative; Nancy Weisman, Sr. VP of Human Resources.

Forum Hotels International Inter-Continental Hotels
1120 Avenue of the Americas
New York, NY 10036
Phone: (212)852-6400

Business Description: Operates 105 hotels in 48 countries.

Average Entry-Level Hiring: Unknown.

Opportunities: Some (but not all) properties have management training programs.

Human Resources: Jim Manley, Human Resources Dir. North Americas.

Application Procedures: Send resume and cover letter to the attention of Director of Human Resources.

▶ **Internships**

Type: The company does not offer an internship program.

Four Seasons Hotels Ltd.
Four Season's Olympic Hotel

411 University St.
Seattle, WA 98101
Phone: (206)621-1700

Business Description: Engaged in the operation of eating establishments. Operator of hotels and/or motels.

Human Resources: Debbie Brown, Personnel Dir.

Four Seasons Inn on the Park
Omni Houston Hotel

4 Riverway
Houston, TX 77056
Phone: (713)871-8181
Fax: (713)871-8116

Application Procedures: Send resume and cover letter to the attention of Personnel Director.

French Government Tourist Office
Business Travel Div.

645 N. Michigan Ave., Ste. 630
Chicago, IL 60611
Phone: (312)751-7800

Employees: 4.

Average Entry-Level Hiring: "Entry level positions available only if one of these four people leaves, which happens once every four or five years.".

▶ **Internships**

Type: The company does not offer an internship program.

Gal-Tex Corp.

23rd and Post Office, Ste. 500
Galveston, TX 77550
Phone: (409)763-8536

Business Description: Operates 17 hotels.

Average Entry-Level Hiring: Unknown.

Opportunities: Entry-level positions are available in the front office and food and catering.

Human Resources: Mike Riley, VP of Operations.

Application Procedures: Apply in person, or send resume and cover letter to the attention of Mr. Mike Riley.

▶ **Internships**

Type: The company does not offer an internship program.

Busiest airports in the U.S.

1. O'Hare International, Chicago, IL
2. Dallas-Fort Worth, TX
3. Los Angeles International Airport, CA
4. Hartsfield International, Atlanta, GA
5. J. F. Kennedy International, New York, NY
6. San Francisco International Airport, CA
7. Stapleton International, Denver, CO
8. Miami International, FL
9. La Guardia, New York, NY
10. Honolulu International, HI

Source: *Successful Meetings*

Garber Travel Service Inc.

1047 Commonwealth
Boston, MA 02215
Phone: (617)787-0600

Employees: 350.

Average Entry-Level Hiring: 35-50.

Opportunities: Travel-related degree or attendance at a travel school necessary. Entry-level jobs are ticket control office assistants, which last three to six months, supporting experienced agents. After this probationary period, these assistants become travel agents. The company's travel school graduates 10-30 people every three months. Tuition is $2,600 for a three-month certified travel agent program, which includes teaching the travel reservation system. No experience or college education is necessary to attend.

Human Resources: Susanne Lind, Human Resources.

Application Procedures: Send resume and cover letter.

German National Tourist Office
122 E. 42nd St., 32nd Fl.
New York, NY 10168-0072
Phone: (212)308-3300

Employees: 19. Employees are temporary.

Human Resources: Wuerz, Personnel Representative.

Application Procedures: Send resume and cover letter.

▶ **Internships**

Type: The company does not offer an internship program.

Americans beginning their careers in the 1990s will probably work in 10 or more jobs for five or more employers before retiring, according to Henry Conn and Joseph Boyett, authors of *Workplace 2000: The Revolution Reshaping American Business*. That means it's up to the individual to manage her or his own career.

Source: *Working Woman*

Golden Tulip Hotels
437 Madison Ave.
New York, NY 10022
Phone: (212)838-5022

Business Description: Operates 3,000 hotels around the world.

Average Entry-Level Hiring: Unknown.

Application Procedures: Send resume and cover letter.

Grand Hyatt New York
Park Avenue at Grand Central
New York, NY 10017
Phone: (212)883-1234

Employees: 1,400.

Average Entry-Level Hiring: 110.

Opportunities: Entry-level positions include

but are not limited to the following: front office clerks, greeters (in restaurants), housekeeping team leaders, concierge, reservations, operators, and assistant food and beverage managers. Training includes programs for food and beverage, front office supervisors (9-12 months), rooms (one year covering housekeeping, front desk and reservations), and other positions as needed.

Human Resources: Pam, Employee Relations.

Application Procedures: Maintains a job hotline Monday through Wednesday between 10:00 A.M. and 2:00 P.M. Applications and/or resumes kept on file for one year.

▶ **Internships**

Type: Contact Employee Relations for internship information.

Grand Hyatt Washington
1000 H St., NW
Washington, DC 20001
Phone: (202)582-1234

Employees: 900.

Average Entry-Level Hiring: 100.

Opportunities: Opportunities include front office clerks, receptionists, cashiers, housekeeping team leaders, and assistant managers.

Human Resources: Lennie Moore, Human Resources Representative.

Application Procedures: Applications accepted by appointment only, when position is posted. Applications are kept on file for six months.

▶ **Internships**

Type: The company does not offer an internship program.

Greater Birmingham Convention & Visitors Bureau
2200 9th Ave., N.
Birmingham, AL 35203
Phone: (205)252-9825

Employees: 22.

Average Entry-Level Hiring: Unknown.

Opportunities: Secretarial positions are entry-level. Experience is mandatory for any other position.

Human Resources: Doris Crumpton, Finance Officer.

Application Procedures: Accepts unsolicited resumes. Applications and/or resumes kept on file for one year.

▶ Internships

Type: The company does not offer an internship program.

Greater Boston Convention & Visitors Bureau, Inc.

Prudential Tower, Ste. 400
PO Box 490
Boston, MA 02199
Phone: (617)536-4100

Employees: 38.

Average Entry-Level Hiring: 2.

Opportunities: Convention sales and services—college degree required. For all entry-level positions, on-the-job training is provided.

Human Resources: Toni Serafini, Operations Admin.

Application Procedures: Company hires through agencies. Openings are normally filled from within. For more information, contact Christine, the bureau's operator.

▶ Internships

Type: Offers an unpaid, for course credit only, internship program, working three days a week in the public affairs, visitor services, publications, marketing, and tourism departments.

Greater Buffalo Convention & Visitors Bureau

107 Delaware Ave.
Buffalo, NY 14202
Phone: (716)852-7100

Employees: 19.

Average Entry-Level Hiring: Unknown.

Opportunities: Tourism, information clerk, and reception—no educational requirements specified by the company. Administrative assistants—college preferred. Sales and convention sales and service—college degree required.

Human Resources: Donna Devine, Office Mgr.

Application Procedures: Recruits at college campuses. Hires through employment agencies as a last resort.

▶ Internships

Type: Non-salaried, summer and/or semester internships available for the following departments: communications, tourism, conventions, and special projects.

Duties: Tourism—calling for sponsors, answering questions, and conducting mailings. Communications—writing copy for brochures and press releases.

Application Procedure: Send resume and cover letter.

Greater Cincinnati Convention & Visitors Bureau

300 W. 6th St.
Cincinnati, OH 45202
Phone: (513)621-2142

Employees: 25.

Average Entry-Level Hiring: Very low turnover.

Opportunities: Opportunities include secretarial positions and part-time visitor information clerks. Experience in sales and hotels or at a bureau is necessary for sales positions.

Application Procedures: Send resume and cover letter.

▶ Internships

Type: The company does not offer an internship program.

Greater Columbus Convention & Visitors Bureau

10 W. Broad St., Ste. 1300
Columbus, OH 43215
Phone: (614)221-6623
Toll-free: 800-821-5784

Employees: 32.

Average Entry-Level Hiring: 1.

Opportunities: Secretarial—growth potential; college is not required. Sales—college (preferred); experience necessary. On occasion, positions may also be open in visitor information, membership, or tourism.

Human Resources: Seymour Raiz, Dir. of Communications.

Application Procedures: Send resume and cover letter.

▶ **Internships**

Type: Nonpaid. **Number Available Annually:** As needed.

Duties: Responsibilities include entry-level duties related to job interest.

Application Procedure: Contact the company for more information.

Application Deadline: None.

Typically, British travelers to the U.S. head for Florida's beaches, the Japanese prefer Hawaii and Southern California, Germans tend to rent a car and drive across country, and Scandinavians opt for culture and shopping on the East Coast. Some Germans and French, having formed "cowboy and Indian" clubs, travel to Native American reservations during their visits to the U.S.

Source: *Business Week*

Greater Houston Convention & Visitors Bureau

3300 Main St.
Houston, TX 77002-9396
Phone: (713)523-5050

Employees: 47.

Opportunities: Secretarial—experience preferred. Sale and management—experience required.

Human Resources: Ron Hartlett, Dir. Office Support Service.

Application Procedures: Send resume and cover letter.

▶ **Internships**

Type: The company is currently restructuring its internship program.

Application Procedure: Contact the company for more information.

Greater Los Angeles Convention & Visitors Bureau

515 S. Figueroa St., Ste. 1100
Los Angeles, CA 90071
Phone: (213)624-7300

Employees: 55.

Average Entry-Level Hiring: Low.

Opportunities: Clerical—growth potential.

Sales positions available periodically. College preferred for most positions, required for some. Company promotes from within.

Human Resources: Anna Belle Reyes, Personnel Coordinator.

Application Procedures: Send resume and cover letter.

Greater Miami Convention & Visitors Bureau

701 Brickell Ave., Ste. 2700
Miami, FL 33131
Phone: (305)539-3000

Employees: 65.

Average Entry-Level Hiring: 3-4.

Opportunities: Support staff and clerical positions have a potential for growth. Most other positions require a college degree and experience.

Human Resources: Marina Demaio, Human Resources Dir.

Application Procedures: Apply in person, or send resume and cover letter.

▶ **Internships**

Contact: Ms. Marina Demaio, Human Resources Dir.

Type: Paid. **Number Available Annually:** 1.

Duties: Interns are rotated through the company's four major divisions.

Application Procedure: Send resume and cover letter.

Application Deadline: May 31.

Greater Milwaukee Convention & Visitors Bureau

510 W. Kilbourne Ave.
Milwaukee, WI 53202
Phone: (414)273-3950

Employees: 20.

Average Entry-Level Hiring: 1.

Opportunities: Opportunities include clerical, sales, personnel, communications, public relations, and tourism assistants.

▶ **Internships**

Contact: Judy Widlowski.

Type: Summer internships available in the communication and public relations departments. Internships last for one or two semesters. **Number Available Annually:** 2. **Applications Received:** 12.

Duties: Assisting with press releases, conferences, and telephone work. The intern will also work on computers.

Application Procedure: Send resume and cover letter.

Application Deadline: Semester prior to the planned working semester. **Decision Date:** Notification will be less than a month after receiving resume.

Greater Minneapolis Convention & Visitors Association

1219 Marquette
Minneapolis, MN 55403
Phone: (312)348-4313

Employees: 24.

Average Entry-Level Hiring: None.

Opportunities: Sales—experience required. Tourism—college required; experience helpful.

Human Resources: Roger Toussaint, Exec. VP.

Application Procedures: Send resume and cover letter.

Greater New Orleans Tourist & Convention Commission

1520 Sugar Bowl Dr.
New Orleans, LA 70112
Phone: (504)566-5011

Employees: 48.

Average Entry-Level Hiring: 10-15.

Opportunities: Clerical, Associate sales manager—college preferred but not required.

Human Resources: Cindy Collata, Dir. of Finance.

Application Procedures: Send resume and cover letter or contact the company for more information at (504)566-5030.

▶ **Internships**

Type: The company does not offer an internship program.

Greater Portland Convention and Visitors Association

26 SW Salmon
Portland, OR 97204
Phone: (503)222-2223

Employees: 37.

Average Entry-Level Hiring: Unknown.

Human Resources: Carol Lentz, Dir. of Finance.

Application Procedures: Call the switchboard between 8:30 A.M. and 5:00 P.M. to reach the appropriate departmental contacts. The switchboard number is 503/275-9750. Appropriate departments are: public affairs, convention sales and services, tourism, and membership.

▶ **Internships**

Contact: Carol Lentz, Dir. of Finance & Admin.

Type: Non-salaried, summer co-ops available for one semester in tourism and public relations. **Number Available Annually:** 4. **Applications Received:** 5.

Duties: Interns will work in the department as support staff.

Application Procedure: Contact the company for more information.

Greyhound Lines Inc.

901 Main St., Ste. 2500
Dallas, TX 75202
Phone: (214)744-6500

Business Description: Provider of regularly-scheduled intercity or interstate bus transportation.

Officers: Fred Currey, CEO & Chairman of the Board; Mike Doyle, VP of Finance; Frank Schmieder, President.

Employees: 11,000.

Application Procedures: Contact the company for more information.

Guest Quarters Suite Hotels

30 Rowes Wharf
Boston, MA 02110
Phone: (617)330-1440
Fax: (617)737-8752

Average Entry-Level Hiring: 300-500.

Opportunities: The training program for the corporate level is currently on hold. However, hiring for management positions continues at individual hotels.

Application Procedures: Send resume and cover letter to the attention of Personnel Director.

Hampton Inns Inc.

6800 Poplar Ave., Ste. 200
Memphis, TN 38138
Phone: (901)758-3100
Fax: (901)756-9479

Average Entry-Level Hiring: Unknown.

Application Procedures: Apply in person at individual hotels Monday through Thursday between 7:30 A.M. and 5:30 P.M. or Friday between 7:30 and 11:30 A.M. Or, send resume and cover letter.

A new study by the outplacement firm Drake Beam Morin shows that job seekers who were willing to relocate saw a 6 percent increase in compensation during 1990 and 1991, compared with a 1 percent decrease for those who stayed in place.

Source: *U.S. News & World Report*

Harvey Hotels

14400 N. Dallas Pkwy., Ste. 400
Dallas, TX 75240
Phone: (214)980-4170

Opportunities: Managerial positions are available in front office, housekeeping, kitchen, restaurant/bar, banquet/catering, and personnel. There is a required three-month training program for all entry-level positions, which includes rotation through each department of the hotel. Entry-level opportunities include assistant front desk manager, reservation manager, guest service manager, assistant director of housekeeping, sous chef, executive steward, assistant kitchen manager, assistant restaurant manager, room service manager, assistant banquet manager, and personnel assistant/clerk.

Human Resources: Sandy Beckett, Human Resources Mgr.

Application Procedures: Send resume and cover letter.

▶ Internships

Contact: Sandy Beckert.
Type: Paid internships available for the follow-

ing departments: front office, housekeeping, kitchen, restaurant, accounting, and sales.

Duties: Responsibilities depend on the trainee's skills. Some may handle supervisory-type positions.

Application Procedure: The company normally recruits from hospitality/restaurant schools. Resumes are considered, even if the applicant does not have a hospitality background.

Application Deadline: December through January (for summer employment).

HBR Hotels

999 Sutter
San Francisco, CA 94109
Phone: (415)441-1230

Business Description: Operates five hotels in San Francisco.

Employees: 250.

Opportunities: Entry-level positions are available as desk clerks and night auditors. There is good potential for advancement, as HBR promotes from within.

Application Procedures: Contact the company for more information.

▶ Internships

Type: Non-salaried internships available for the following positions: front desk and housekeeping.

Herrick Development Economy Inns of America

755 Raintree Dr., No. 200
Carlsbad, CA 92009
Phone: (619)438-6661

Business Description: The company has 22 properties.

Average Entry-Level Hiring: 1-3.

Human Resources: Carol Sanders, Human Resources.

Application Procedures: Send resume and cover letter, or applications can be filled out on site.

▶ Internships

Type: The company does not offer an internship program.

Duties: Management trainees are hired in pairs (i.e. married couples or siblings) to live on premises—99 percent of them are experienced graduates from schools of hotel management. There is little upward mobility from these individual managerial positions. Positions requiring no experience are available in housekeeping, laundry, maintenance, and front desk.

Hershey Entertainment & Resort Co.

300 Park Blvd.
PO Box 860
Hershey, PA 17033
Phone: (717)534-3156

Average Entry-Level Hiring: Three thousand seasonal rehires each year; 100 other full-time hires.

Opportunities: Due to the diversity of the company, a wide variety of positions exist. Most non-skilled positions are part-time or seasonal. Full-time positions are often filled internally.

Human Resources: Kendra J. Ruhl, Personnel Dir.; Heather Stuckey, Personnel Asst.

Application Procedures: Applications can be filled out on site Monday through Friday between 8:00 A.M. and 5:00 P.M.

▶ **Internships**

Type: Offers an internship program. Contact the company for more information.

Hertz Corp.

225 Brae Blvd.
Park Ridge, NJ 07656
Phone: (201)307-2000

Business Description: Operator of a passenger car rental service for short-term rentals.

Officers: Brian J. Kennedy, Exec. VP of Mktg.; Frank A. Olson, CEO & Chairman of the Board; William Sider, Exec. VP of Finance.

Employees: 18,000.

Average Entry-Level Hiring: Unknown.

Opportunities: Data base coordinator—technical background and computer experience required. Secretarial—one year experience or a graduate of a secretarial school. Accounting—college degree (accounting). Clerical—high school diploma and light typing required. At corporate office only. On-the-job training. Tuition reimbursement plan available.

Human Resources: Joanne Petraglia,

Personnel Mgr.; Gayle Schoch, Compensation Mgr.; Don Steel, Sr. VP of Employee Relations.

Application Procedures: Send resume and cover letter to the attention of Joanne Petraglia, Personnel Mgr.

Hilton Buffalo

120 Church St.
Buffalo, NY 14202
Phone: (716)845-5100

Employees: 350.

Average Entry-Level Hiring: Unknown.

Opportunities: No on-the-job training and no entry-level management positions. Most positions require hotel degree or work experience. Front desk, food and beverage—hotel experience helps but not required.

Human Resources: Debra, Personnel Dept.

Application Procedures: Applications can be filled out on site Wednesday and Thursday between 9:00 A.M. and 4:00 P.M. Department heads keep applications on file for six months.

▶ **Internships**

Type: The company may offer an internship program. Contact the company for more information.

Hilton Hawaiian Village

2005 Kalia Rd.
Honolulu, HI 96815
Phone: (808)949-4321

Business Description: Operator of hotels and/or motels.

Officers: Dieter Huckestein, Sr. VP; Phillip Valerio, Dir. of Sales; Andre Vonarb, Controller.

Employees: 2,100.

Human Resources: Cherlyn Logan, Human Resources Dir.

Hilton Hotels Corp.

9336 Civic Center Dr.
Beverly Hills, CA 90209
Phone: (213)278-4321

Business Description: The company owns, operates, and franchises 273 hotels, resorts, and hotel/casinos both in the United States and abroad. The company is also involved in planning and developing new hotels and resorts worldwide.

Officers: Barron Hilton, CEO, Pres. & Chairman of the Board; Maurice J. Scanlon, Sr. VP & Finance Officer.

Employees: 39,000.

Average Entry-Level Hiring: Unknown.

Opportunities: Hilton has a management trainee program, admission into which is predicated on experience. Inexperienced graduates should apply directly to independent hotels and work in an entry-level position to gain experience. 90 percent of entry-level recruits come from Hilton's once-a-year college visits; the others are recommended by employees.

Human Resources: Ana Bor, Human Resources Representative.

Application Procedures: Each hotel hires independently. In Beverly Hills, send resume and cover letter to the attention of Ana Bor, Human Resources Representative.

Hilton International Co.
605 3rd Ave.
New York, NY 10158
Phone: (212)973-2200

Business Description: Operates 150 international hotels.

Officers: Robert Bennett, Dir. of Systems; Andrew Bould, Sr. VP of Sales & Mktg.; Martin Gatto, CFO; Michael Hirst, Pres. & Chairman of the Board.

Employees: 40,000.

Average Entry-Level Hiring: Unknown.

Opportunities: Each hotel recruits and hires individuals for a management training program. Trainees either concentrate in food and beverage, room service, or choose a general management program.

Human Resources: Ron Hilvert, Human Resources President; David F. Hoffman, Sr. VP of Human Resources; Edwin Zephirin, Human Resources Representative.

Hilton Washington & Towers
1919 Connecticut Ave. NW
Washington, DC 20009
Phone: (202)483-3000

Employees: 1,000.

Average Entry-Level Hiring: 70-80.

Opportunities: All entry-level assistant managerial positions require a hotel management degree and prior experience. Inexperienced candidates start as front desk clerks or in rooms, food and beverage, etc.

Human Resources: Louis, Training Mgr.

Application Procedures: Applications can be filled out on site. Applications and/or resumes kept on file for 30 days. Applicant will be contacted by department head.

▶ **Internships**

Type: The company does not offer an internship program.

Holiday Inn Worldwide
3 Ravinia Dr., Ste. 2000
Atlanta, GA 30346-2149
Phone: (404)551-3500

Average Entry-Level Hiring: Unknown.

Human Resources: John Merkin, Sr. Recruiter.

Application Procedures: Send resume and cover letter to contact. Recruits at college campuses.

▶ **Internships**

Type: The company does not offer an internship program.

Holiday Inns Inc.
801 NW 57th Ave., Ste. 200
Miami, FL 33126
Phone: (305)266-0000

Business Description: The company has 19 properties, 13 domestic, 6 international.

Average Entry-Level Hiring: As needed.

Opportunities: During the fall and spring, Holiday Inns recruits at certain colleges for their management training program. Other entry-level positions are available in housekeeping, food & beverage and as a guest services representative.

Application Procedures: Send resume and cover letter.

▶ **Internships**

Type: The company does not offer an internship program.

Holiday Inns Inc.
Crowne Plaza Hotels
PO Box 888387
Atlanta, GA 30356
Phone: (904)804-8005

Business Description: Operates twenty hotels.

Average Entry-Level Hiring: Unknown.

Opportunities: Entry-level positions are available in food and beverage and front desk. Some regions have management training programs.

Application Procedures: Send resume and cover letter to the attention of Employment Center.

▶ **Internships**

Type: The company does not offer an internship program, however the company hopes to offer one in the future.

Holland America Line Westours Inc.
300 Elliot Ave. W.
Seattle, WA 98119
Phone: (206)281-3535

Business Description: Engaged in the transportation of passengers on the deep seas.

Officers: Larry Calkins, VP of Finance; A. Kirk Lanterman, President; Terry Underwood, VP of Mktg.

Employees: 2,600.

Human Resources: Wayne Byers, VP of Human Resources.

Hong Kong Tourist Association
333 N. Michigan Ave.
Chicago, IL 60601
Phone: (312)782-1960

Employees: 13.

Human Resources: Christina Puazon, Finance Officer.

Application Procedures: Send resume and cover letter.

Hotel Group of America
693 Sutter
San Francisco, CA 94102
Phone: (415)202-8700

Business Description: Operates the following major hotels: Diva Hotel, Hotel Union Square,

Hotel Kensington Park, UN Plaza, and Oxford-Cambridge Inn.

Average Entry-Level Hiring: Unknown.

Opportunities: Hotel Group hires front desk clerks, reservations agents, bellmen, night auditors, room cleaners, housemen, and parking lot attendants. Company employs 200 people and hires 70 entry-level people per year.

Application Procedures: Send resume and cover letter.

▶ **Internships**

Type: Summer and semester internships available for the following departments: front office, sales, and housekeeping.

Duties: Interns will receive an overall perspective of the hotel business by spending time with the management of each department and learning specific aspects of the business.

Application Procedure: Send resume and cover letter.

U.S. cities with the most expensive hotel room rates

1. New York, NY
2. Boston, MA
3. San Francisco, CA
4. Washington, DC
5. Honolulu, HI
6. New Orleans, LA
7. Chicago, IL
8. San Diego, CA
9. Miami-Hialeah, FL
10. Los Angeles-Long Beach, CA

Source: *Meeting News*

Hotel Operating Company of Hawaii Ltd.
2375 Kuhio Ave.
Honolulu, HI 96815
Phone: (808)921-6601

Business Description: Operator of hotels and/or motels.

Officers: Joe Durocher, VP of Info. Systems; Richard R. Kelley, CEO & Chairman of the Board; Jan Pang, VP of Sales; Bob Rostron, CFO.

Employees: 2,700.

Human Resources: William Brown, VP of Human Resources.

Hotel Pontchartrain
2 Washington Blvd.
Detroit, MI 48226
Phone: (313)965-0200

Employees: 290.

Average Entry-Level Hiring: Varies depending on business.

Opportunities: Sales—college degree in marketing. Accounting—college degree in accounting. Food and beverage—college degree and work experience. Entry-level management positions do not require a college degree but do require experience. Training includes both classroom and on-the-job instruction.

Human Resources: Debbie, Human Resources Asst.

Application Procedures: Apply Monday, Wednesday, and Thursday between 9:00 A.M. and 3:00 P.M. Manager reviews information and contacts applicant when positions are available. Applications and/or resumes kept on file for three months.

▶ **Internships**

Type: The company does not offer an internship program.

T he 400 employees at Hyatt Hotels company headquarters participate in In-Touch Day, an annual program designed to get Hyatt's top managers acquainted with the day-to-day routines of employees in the field and the problems they face. Participants work as bellmen, chambermaids, carpenters, and in other frontline jobs.

Source: *Working Woman*

J.B. Hunt Transport Services Inc.
Hwy. 71 N.
Lowell, AR 72745
Phone: (501)659-8800

Business Description: Provider of courier services for delivering letters and packages, using means other than air transportation and the U.S. Postal Service.

Officers: Paul R. Bergant, Exec. VP of Mktg.;

Bruce W. Jones, Exec. VP & CFO; Kirk Thompson, CEO & Pres.

Employees: 7,380.

Human Resources: Sherry Moneries, Personnel Dept.; Stephen L. Palmer, Exec. VP of Human Resources.

Application Procedures: Send resume and cover letter to the attention of Sherry Moneries, Personnel Dept, PO Box 130, Lowell, AR 72745.

Hyatt Cherry Hill
2349 W. Marlton Pike
Cherry Hill, NJ 08002
Phone: (609)662-1234

Employees: 330.

Average Entry-Level Hiring: 100.

Opportunities: Congenial personality a must for the following entry-level positions: front office cashier/receptionist—duties include checking guests in and out. System is computerized, but will train qualified individual. Food and beverage cashier—duties include working in room service, taking orders over the phone, and handling a cash bank; heavy customer contact. Concierge—part-time, servicing Regency Club level by setting up continental breakfast and evening hors d'oeuvres.

Human Resources: Joan Slater, Human Resources Representative.

Application Procedures: Applications taken daily between 9:00 A.M. and 5:00 P.M., and are subject to review. Applications are kept on file for six months. For more information, contact the human resources manager.

▶ **Internships**

Type: The company offers an internship program. Contact the company for more information.

Hyatt Corp.
200 W. Madison
Chicago, IL 60606
Phone: (312)750-1234

Business Description: Operates Hyatt hotels in the United States and abroad. The company also owns and operates retirement housing, specifically, the Classic Residence congregate-care facilities.

Officers: Jim Evans, Sr. VP of Sales; Gordon

Kerr, VP of Info. Systems; Ken Posner, Sr. VP & Finance Officer; Tom Pritzker, President.

Employees: 99,000.

Opportunities: Hyatt has management training programs in food and beverage, room operations, sales and marketing, accounting, human resources, and engineering. Graduates from hotel management schools are preferred but any college graduate is eligible to apply for admission. Candidates should be creative, flexible, energetic, able to communicate, and prepared to relocate. The training program is a nine-month rotation through the various departments of the hotel. Individuals get hands-on training in all areas of hotel management, participate in seminars, and sit in on executive meetings.

Human Resources: Dorothy Mrzlock, Corp. Personnel Dir.; Chuck Palid, Human Resources Representative.

Application Procedures: Send resume and cover letter to the attention of Dorothy Mrzlock, Corp. Personnel Dir.

▶ **Internships**

Type: Salaried (hourly pay for 40 hours/week), summer internships available for the Minority Internship Program. Meals are included. Hotels will help find housing if necessary.

Duties: Will gain hands-on experience through selected positions mainly in a hotel's operations division. Interns will be supervised and receive a formal evaluation twice during the program.

Qualifications: College students completing their sophomore or junior year with a working knowledge of the hospitality business, preferably pursuing a hotel/restaurant management, business administration, or liberal arts degree.

Application Procedure: See your campus placement office for details.

Hyatt Orlando

6375 W. Irlo Bronson Hwy.
Kissimmee, FL 32741
Phone: (407)396-1234

Employees: 675.

Average Entry-Level Hiring: 200.

Opportunities: Opportunities available for front desk clerks (promote from within), and entry-level management positions available in the housekeeping and food and beverage departments.

Human Resources: Wendy, Asst. Dir. of Human Resources.

Application Procedures: Applications can be filled out on site Monday through Wednesday between 9:00 A.M. and 12:00 noon, or by appointments. Applications kept on file for one year.

▶ **Internships**

Type: A culinary internship is available through a Johnson & Webb agreement.

Application Procedure: Contact the company for more information.

Hyatt Regency Atlanta

265 Peachtree St.
Atlanta, GA 30303
Phone: (404)577-1234
Fax: (404)588-4137

Average Entry-Level Hiring: Unknown.

Application Procedures: Available positions are sometimes posted with the Georgia Department of Labor. Applications kept on file for six months. For more information, contact the Hyatt receptionist.

▶ **Internships**

Type: Offers an internship program.

Hyatt Regency Columbus

350 N. High St.
Columbus, OH 43215
Phone: (614)463-1234

Employees: 500.

Average Entry-Level Hiring: Unknown.

Opportunities: Every department has entry-level opportunities, and the company is known for promoting from within. Entry-level management opportunities for employees or those with a college degree and hotel experience (preferred). Training includes both classroom and on-the-job instruction.

Human Resources: Christy, Asst. Dir. of Human Resources.

Application Procedures: Contact the company for more information.

▶ **Internships**

Type: The company may offer an internship program. Contact the company for more information.

Hyatt Regency Denver Downtown

1750 Welton St.
Denver, CO 80202
Phone: (303)295-1200

Employees: 350.

Average Entry-Level Hiring: Unknown.

Opportunities: Opportunities include front desk clerks and reservations. Training includes a management training program through the corporate headquarters.

Human Resources: Hope Stout, Employment Coordinator.

Application Procedures: Apply anytime on a walk-in basis Monday through Wednesday between 10:00 A.M. and 1:00 P.M. Applications are kept on file up to four months.

▶ **Internships**

Type: The company does not offer an internship program.

Hyatt Regency Minneapolis

1300 Nicollet Mall
Minneapolis, MN 55403
Phone: (612)370-1234

Employees: 400.

Average Entry-Level Hiring: Unknown.

Opportunities: Entry-level management opportunities in food and beverage, rooms, and accounting—hotel degree required; experience helps but not required. Training includes classroom and on-the-job instruction.

Human Resources: Stephanie, Employment Mgr.

Application Procedures: Applications can be filled out on site. Applications are kept on file for 90 days.

▶ **Internships**

Type: Internships available for the Hospitality Department.

Hyatt Regency Phoenix

122 N. 2nd St.
Phoenix, AZ 85004
Phone: (602)252-1234

Employees: 400.

Average Entry-Level Hiring: Unknown.

Opportunities: Assistant department heads in rooms and food and beverage—degree in hotel and hospitality not required, but experience is helpful. Business majors with good grades, extra-curricular activities, verbal and people skills, and ability to relocate.

Human Resources: Mike Dickey, Human Resources Dir.

Application Procedures: Applications accepted Tuesdays between 9:00 A.M. and 12:00 P.M., and Thursdays between 2:00 P.M. and 5:00 P.M. Applications are forwarded to specific departments and kept on file for six months.

▶ **Internships**

Type: The company does not offer an internship program.

Hyatt Regency Washington

400 New Jersey Ave. NW
Washington, DC 20001
Phone: (202)737-1234

Employees: 627.

Average Entry-Level Hiring: 25 (during peak season).

Opportunities: Entry-level management positions are available in Human Resources. Other entry-level positions are for housekeeping supervisors. All other positions require experience.

Human Resources: Paula, Benefits Mgr.

Application Procedures: Apply Monday through Wednesday between 9:00 A.M. and 12:00 noon. Applications are reviewed and kept on file three months.

▶ **Internships**

Type: The company does not offer an internship program.

Imperial Hotels Corp.

1000 Wilson Blvd.
Arlington, VA 22209
Phone: (703)524-4880

Business Description: Operator of hotels and/or motels.

Officers: Edward Blum, VP of Finance; Pat Buckley, Dir. of Data Processing; Douglas C. Collins, President; Linda Shiller, VP of Mktg. & Sales.

Employees: 749.

Human Resources: Lee A. April, VP of Human Resources.

Integra-A Hotel & Restaurant Co.

4441 W. Airport Fwy.
Irving, TX 75015
Phone: (903)258-8500

Business Description: Engaged in the operation of eating establishments. Operator of hotels and/or motels.

Officers: T.J. Corcoran, Jr., CEO & Pres.; Richard J. Cronin, Mktg. & Sales Mgr.; Ahmet Oner, VP of Info. Systems; Gil Turchin, Sr. VP & CFO.

Employees: 3,105.

Human Resources: Dorothy Wood, Sr. VP of Human Resources.

International Hospitality Consultants

1515 N. Federal Hwy., Ste. 110
Boca Raton, FL 33432
Phone: (407)394-3500

Employees: 7.

Average Entry-Level Hiring: The company has had the same employees for the past four years.

Opportunities: Corporate meeting planners—strong sales background, as well as a complete client base. College preferred, experience necessary.

Human Resources: Tony Tarrant, President.

Application Procedures: Send resume and cover letter.

International Travel Arrangers

2600 Eagan Woods Dr.
Eagan, MN 55121
Phone: (612)456-9280
Fax: (612)456-9340

Business Description: Engaged in the operation of travel agencies.

Officers: Mark Bassinger, Dir. of Systems; Don Poluha, VP of Finance; Stephen A. Russell, CEO & Pres.; Sid Walker, VP of Mktg.

Employees: 75.

Human Resources: Ron J. Novak, Dir. of Sales.

Interstate Hotels

Foster Plaza Bldg. 10
680 Anderson Dr.
Pittsburgh, PA 15220
Phone: (412)937-0600

Business Description: Operates 48 hotels.

Average Entry-Level Hiring: As needed per hotel.

Opportunities: Interstate has a Graduate in Development (GID) program open to graduates with majors in hotel management or accounting. Liberal arts majors are considered if they have experience in hotels. The program is 4-12 months in duration and is offered in the rooms and food and beverage departments.

Human Resources: Sharon Finn, Admin. Asst.

Application Procedures: Applicants should apply directly to the hotel of interest.

When you do your resume yourself, the process of sifting through your past helpfully forces you to zero in on the very things you will discuss at job interviews. Sam Marcus of Sibson & Company, a human-resources consulting firm in Princeton, NJ, suggests that you have a colleague or friend read your resume and ask them what message they get from it, to make sure you're highlighting your talents and the results of your labors. Use verbs like "improved," "planned," and "redesigned" followed by a briefly worded accomplishment.

Source: *U.S. News & World Report*

▶ **Internships**

Type: Summer and semester, salaried internships available for all departments.

Duties: Interns will work as entry-level employees with a chance to advance to supervisory positions.

Application Procedure: Send resume and cover letter to the hotel of interest.

Application Deadline: June.

Irish Tourist Board

757 3rd Ave., 19th Fl.
New York, NY 10017
Phone: (212)418-0800

Employees: 25.

Average Entry-Level Hiring: None.

Application Procedures: Send resume and cover letter.

Irvine Marriott Hotel
17900 Jamboree Blvd.
Irvine, CA 92714
Phone: (714)863-3111

Employees: 450.

Opportunities: Opportunities include front office clerk, restaurant cashier, and guest services.

Application Procedures: Contact the company for more information.

▶ Internships

Type: The company offers no formal internship program but will consider applications from interested students.

Application Procedure: Contact the company for more information.

Pay-for-performance plans start with reduced base wages and salaries but reward employees with sizeable bonuses for reaching production targets or meeting other goals. Workers under pay-for-performance plans typically earn from 10% less to 20% more than their jobs' average pay. About 4 million U.S. employees are currently paid under such plans.

Source: *Time*

Irving Convention & Visitors Bureau
3333 N. MacArthur, Ste. 200
Irving, TX 75062
Phone: (214)252-7476

Employees: 20.

Average Entry-Level Hiring: 1.

Opportunities: Clerical positions with room for growth. Sales positions require experience.

Application Procedures: Apply in person. For further information, contact the following office: PO Box 152288, Irvine, TX 75015. Phone: (214)721-2600.

Israel Ministry of Tourism
350 5th Ave.
New York, NY 10118
Phone: (212)560-0620

Employees: 10. (in New York).

Average Entry-Level Hiring: 1 to 5 per year.

Application Procedures: Applicants must be Israeli. Send resume and cover letter.

IVI Travel
400 Skokie Blvd.
Northbrook, IL 60062
Phone: (708)480-8400

Employees: 1,050.

Opportunities: A wide variety of entry-level opportunities, depending primarily on major. College degree or pertinent experience required. Training includes an in-house, 12-week program which teaches employees how to become travel agents.

Human Resources: Perry Sartori, Employment Specialist.

Application Procedures: Send resume and cover letter.

▶ Internships

Type: The company does not offer an internship program.

Jamaica Tourist Board
866 2nd Ave., 10th Fl.
New York, NY 10017
Phone: (212)688-7650

Employees: 20.

Average Entry-Level Hiring: Very few.

Human Resources: Bernie Rickman, Deputy Dir. of Tourism.

Application Procedures: Send resume and cover letter. 1320 S. Dixie Hwy., Ste. 1100, Coral Gables, FL 33146.

Japan Airlines
655 5th Ave.
New York, NY 10022
Phone: (212)838-4400
Fax: (212)310-1230

Average Entry-Level Hiring: The company has instituted a hiring freeze.

Application Procedures: Send resume and cover letter. Call (212)310-1451 for more information.

J.N.R. Inc.
4040 MacArthur Blvd.
Newport Beach, CA 92660
Phone: (714)476-2531
Fax: (714)955-3825

Average Entry-Level Hiring: 1.

Human Resources: Jenie Coch, Employment Contact.

Application Procedures: Send resume and cover letter.

▶ **Internships**

Type: The company does not offer an internship program.

JP Hotels
400 Mandalay
Clearwater, FL 34630
Phone: (813)878-0525

Human Resources: Karen Penna, Human Resources Dir.

Application Procedures: Send resume and cover letter.

KD German Rhine Line
170 Hamilton Ave.
White Plains, NY 10601
Phone: (914)948-3600

Human Resources: Marty, Reservationist.

Application Procedures: All resumes are sent to Germany.

▶ **Internships**

Type: The company does not offer an internship program.

Kempinski International Hotels
750 Lexington Ave., 24th Fl.
New York, NY 10022
Phone: (212)745-0890

Business Description: Operates nine hotels.

Average Entry-Level Hiring: Unknown.

Opportunities: Company is based in Germany and most hiring and management training is done through the German office.

Application Procedures: Send resume and cover letter to the corporate office in Germany.

Kimco Hotels
Galleria Parks Hotels
191 Sutter St.
San Francisco, CA 94104
Phone: (415)673-4064

Business Description: Operates eight hotels in San Francisco.

Average Entry-Level Hiring: 100.

Human Resources: Steve Pinetti, Vice Pres.

Application Procedures: Send resume and cover letter.

▶ **Internships**

Contact: Steve Pinetti, Vice Pres.

Type: Nonpaid internships available for the following departments: management, sales, and public relations. **Number Available Annually:** As needed.

Duties: Perform the actual work done by permanent staff.

Application Procedure: Contact the company for more information.

Application Deadline: None. The company hires year-round.

Kirby Tours
1 Kennedy Sq., Ste. 101
Detroit, MI 48226
Phone: (313)963-8585

Employees: 18.

Average Entry-Level Hiring: 20 (for tours).

Opportunities: Drivers and tour guides—license for commercial vehicle required and communication and people skills required. Travel agents—travel school diploma (preferred), knowledge of computers, personal travel and geographical experience. Training consists of taking the tours and watching the experienced employees.

Human Resources: Filip Kahn, Vice Pres.

Application Procedures: Send resume and cover letter.

Knott's Berry Farm

8039 Beach Blvd.
Buena Park, CA 90620
Phone: (714)220-5170
Fax: (714)220-5150

Employees: Positions are seasonal.

Average Entry-Level Hiring: 2,000.

Opportunities: Operations staff are trained to run park rides and other park activities.

Human Resources: Kathi Guiney, Employment Mgr.

Application Procedures: Apply in person Monday through Friday between 9:00 A.M. and 12:00 P.M., and between 1:00 P.M. and 4:30 P.M., or send resume and cover letter indicating position sought (i.e. administration or park operations).

▶ **Internships**

Type: Offers an internship program. Contact the company for more information.

Joan Sills is one of the few women to head a hotel company with international operations. At Colony Hotels & Resorts she is concentrating on the Pacific Rim, the continental U.S., and Hawaii, where Colony leads the time-share sector. New ventures include properties in Thailand and Israel.

Source: *Working Woman*

Korean Air

6101 W. Imperial Hwy.
Los Angeles, CA 90045
Phone: (213)417-5200

Employees: 570. (The number listed above is for United States employment only.).

Average Entry-Level Hiring: Unknown.

Opportunities: Opportunities include reservation agents, flight attendants, traffic agents, and clerical personnel. College education, experience, and bilingual preferred. Korean background helpful.

Application Procedures: Send resume (one-page if possible) directed to the Personnel Department.

Krisch Hotels, Inc.

PO Box 14100
Roanoke, VA 24022
Phone: (703)342-4531

Business Description: Operates 46 hotels.

Average Entry-Level Hiring: Unknown.

Opportunities: New employees participate in an 18-week training program.

Human Resources: Liz Carol, Manager.

Application Procedures: Recruits hospitality school graduates.

▶ **Internships**

Type: The company does not offer an internship program.

La Quinta Motor Inns Inc.

PO Box 790064
San Antonio, TX 78279-0064
Phone: (512)366-6000

Business Description: Operates 201 motels.

Officers: Sam Barshop, Pres. & Chairman of the Board; Walter J. Biegler, Sr. VP & Finance Officer.

Employees: 6,300.

Opportunities: LaQuinta rarely hires inexperienced people for managerial positions. Individuals who have experience dealing with the public can start as front desk clerks. Opportunities for advancement are good—promotions from within (up or to other motels in system).

Application Procedures: Contact the personnel director at each motel.

Larken Inc.

PO Box 1808
Cedar Rapids, IA 52406
Phone: (319)366-8201

Business Description: Operator of hotels and/or motels.

Officers: Larry Cahill, President; Bill Krueger, Controller; Derick Rackham, Director.

Employees: 6,000.

Application Procedures: Contact the company for more information.

Leisure Hotel Corp.
Stratford House Inns
PO Box 178
Hutchinson, KS 67504-0178
Phone: (316)663-1211

Business Description: Operates seven properties in Kansas, Missouri, and Oklahoma.

Average Entry-Level Hiring: Up to four.

Opportunities: "Leisure Hotel Corp. looks for hardworking, energetic people for our management in training (M.I.T.) program. A college degree helps but is not a prerequisite for admission. Other entry-level positions available: auditors, guest specialists, and salespersons. Opportunities exist in both our franchised and independent properites."

Application Procedures: Apply in person or send resume and cover letter. Contact Human Resources for more information.

▶ Internships

Type: The company does not offer an internship program.

Lexington Hotel Suites
3501 N. MacArthur Blvd., Ste. 403
Irving, TX 75062
Phone: (214)659-0220

Business Description: Operates 21 hotels in the Southwest.

Average Entry-Level Hiring: Unknown.

Human Resources: Karen Hensley, Personnel Dir.

Application Procedures: Send resume and cover letter.

Liberty Travel
69 Spring St.
Ramsey, NJ 07446
Phone: (201)934-3500
Fax: (201)934-3888

Opportunities: Provides training for new hires.

Application Procedures: Places newspaper advertisements for certain openings. Accepts unsolicited resumes and phone calls.

▶ Internships

Type: The company does not offer an internship program.

Lifeco Travel Management
(Express)
2901 Wilcrest Dr., Ste. 600
Houston, TX 77042
Phone: (713)789-3424

Average Entry-Level Hiring: Very few.

Human Resources: Dan Ehle, Human Resources.

Application Procedures: Send resume and cover letter.

Loew's Glenpointe Hotel
100 Frank W. Burr Blvd.
Teaneck, NJ 07666
Phone: (201)836-0600

Employees: 350.

Average Entry-Level Hiring: 200.

Opportunities: Opportunities include front desk attendants, reservation agents, concierge attendants, cooks, and switchboard operators. Training is as follows: front desk operations—three weeks; reservations—two weeks; and switchboard operators—one week.

Human Resources: Dorothy Bonatz, Asst. Personnel Mgr.

Application Procedures: Applications can be filled out on site Monday through Friday between 9:00 A.M. and 5:00 P.M. Applications and/or resumes kept on file for one year.

▶ Internships

Type: Occasionally, internships are available. Contact the Personnel Department for more information.

Loew's Hotels Inc.
667 Madison Ave.
New York, NY 10021
Phone: (212)545-2000

Business Description: Operates 14 hotels.

Officers: Richard Johnson, VP of Finance; C. Rockett, VP of Mktg.; Johnathan M. Tisch, CEO & Pres.

Employees: 4,500.

Human Resources: Allen Moneyer, Human Resources Dir.

Application Procedures: Send resume and cover letter to 1 Park Ave., New York, NY, 10016. Contact the Personnel department for more information.

Loew's Summit Hotel
569 Lexington Ave.
New York, NY 10003
Phone: (212)752-7000

Employees: 400.

Average Entry-Level Hiring: Unknown.

Opportunities: Opportunities include front desk clerks, reservation clerks, bellmen, busboys, and housemen.

Human Resources: Jerrylin, Personnel Sec.

Application Procedures: Applications can be filled out on site and accepts unsolicited resumes. Applicant is contacted when needed. Resumes kept on file six months.

▶ **Internships**

Type: The company does not offer an internship program.

Where jobs are rebounding, according to DRI/McGrawHill: the Pacific states, due to high-tech industries and trade with Asia; the southwest, due to free trade with Mexico and business diversification after the oil bust; the south Atlantic states, due to new investment lured by low labor and living costs.

Source: *Newsweek*

Long Beach Area Convention & Visitors Council, Inc.
1 World Trade Center, Ste. 300
Long Beach, CA 90831-0300
Phone: (213)436-3645

Employees: 22.

Opportunities: Opportunities include sales assistants, tourism assistants, public relations assistants, and membership assistants—college degree required for growth track but not for clerical positions. Training includes on-the-job and classroom instruction.

Human Resources: Judi Russi, Admin. Asst.

Application Procedures: Send resume and cover letter.

▶ **Internships**

Contact: Lorraine June, VP of Mktg.

Type: Nonpaid, college credit internships available. **Number Available Annually:** 2.

Duties: Internship duties include researching

media requests and assisting with the development of press researcher.

Application Procedure: Send resume and cover letter to the attention of Ms. Lorraine June.

Application Deadline: None.

Long Island Tourism & Convention Commission
Nassau Coliseum
Uniondale, NY 11553
Phone: (516)794-4222
Fax: (516)794-4639

Average Entry-Level Hiring: 3-5.

Human Resources: Michael Davidson, President.

Application Procedures: Send resume and cover letter or apply in person.

▶ **Internships**

Contact: Michael Davidson, President.

Type: Offers nonpaid internships for college credit. **Number Available Annually:** 3-5 per year.

Duties: Diverse duties may include the coordination of special events or conducting marketing research.

Application Procedure: Send resume and cover letter to contact.

Application Deadline: Applications are accepted year-round.

Maritz Travel
5245 Pacific Concord Dr., Ste. 200
Los Angeles, CA 90045
Phone: (310)536-7200

Average Entry-Level Hiring: Unknown.

Human Resources: Cindy Wudyka, Branch Mgr.

Application Procedures: Send resume and cover letter.

Maritz Travel Co.
1395 N. Highway Dr.
Fenton, MO 63099
Phone: (314)827-4000

Employees: 1,930. This number reflects employment at all branches.

Average Entry-Level Hiring: Unknown.

Human Resources: Stephanie Lappin, Employment.

Application Procedures: Send resume and cover letter.

Mark Allan Travel Inc.
9220 Sunset Blvd., No. 300
Los Angeles, CA 90069
Phone: (213)273-9330

Employees: 51.

Human Resources: Lara Bentley, Employment Contact.

Application Procedures: Send resume and cover letter.

Marriott Corp.
1 Marriott Dr.
Washington, DC 20058
Phone: (301)380-9000

Business Description: Provides lodging services, including full-service hotels and resorts, contract services, food service, and facilities management. Businesses include: Marriott Hotels, Resorts and Suites totalling 233 hotels in 41 states and 18 countries; Courtyard by Marriott comprising 196 moderately-priced hotels in 35 states; Residence Inn by Marriott offering 176 extended stay hotels in 42 states; Fairfield Inn totalling 93 economy hotels; 17 Marriott Golf facilities; Marriott Ownership Resorts made up of 18 timeshare resorts; Marriott Management Services supplying food service management to nearly 2,400 clients in business, healthcare, and education and facilities management to 500 clients; Host offering food, beverage, and merchandising services at stadiums, arenas, and other attractions as well as 51 airports; Travel Plazas operating nearly 100 restaurants, gift shops, and related facilities on 14 major tollroads in the United States; Marriott Senior Living Services comprising 13 retirement communities in nine states.

Officers: Stephen F. Bollenbach, Exec. VP & CFO; A. Bradford Bryan, Exec. VP; Sterling D. Colton, Sr. VP; J.W. Marriott, Pres. & Chairman of the Board; Richard E. Marriott, Vice Chairman of the Board; R. A. Rankin, Sr. VP; William J. Shaw, Exec. VP; William R. Tiefel, Exec. VP.

Employees: 230,000.

Average Entry-Level Hiring: Unknown.

Benefits: Benefits include medical insurance (including a health maintenance organization and a preferred provider organization), dental insurance, vacation days, overtime pay, a 401(K) plan, profit sharing, maternity leave, personal/sick days, and child-care programs.

Human Resources: Clifford J. Ehrlich, Sr. VP of Human Resources.

Application Procedures: The company has eighteen different human resource departments. For assistance, please call (302)380-1089.

▶ Internships

Type: Salaried, summer internship(s) available in food/beverage, front desk, housekeeping, and catering. Six resorts employ co-ops, including Voil, Marco Island, and Tan-Tara.

Duties: Perform duties as an entry-level employee, participating in training, tasks, and a smaller part of management.

Qualifications: College students between sophomore and junior year enrolled in a hotel/hospitality school.

Application Procedure: Send resume and cover letter.

Application Deadline: March-April. **Decision Date:** Within a few weeks of interview.

Marriott Downtown Chicago
504 N. Michigan Ave.
Chicago, IL 60611
Phone: (312)836-0100

Employees: 1,200.

Average Entry-Level Hiring: None in 1992.

Opportunities: Opportunities include front desk, gift shop, housekeeping, reservations, and food and beverage. Entry-level management positions for hotel school graduates only.

Human Resources: Byron Rodhs, Human Resources.

Application Procedures: Send resume and cover letter, or apply in person.

▶ Internships

Contact: Byron Rodhs, Human Resources.

Type: Nonpaid internships available. **Number Available Annually:** Unknown.

Duties: Decisions regarding interns are based on individual skills and the needs of the different areas of the organization. Training includes both classroom and on-the-job instruction.

Application Procedure: Send resume and cover letter.

Application Deadline: None.

One in ten Americans will change careers during a typical year, claims David Birch, head of Cognetics, a Cambridge, MA, consulting firm.

Source: *Better Homes and Gardens*

Massachusetts Office of Travel & Tourism

100 Cambridge St., 13th Fl.
Boston, MA 02202
Phone: (617)727-8886

Employees: 21.

Average Entry-Level Hiring: Low.

Opportunities: Opportunities exist in any of several departments, including Public Relations, International Marketing, Domestic Marketing, Group Tour Marketing, Marketing/Automation, and Research and Regional Marketing. "The description and duration of training is tailored to fit the candidate's skill levels in his or her respective areas."

Human Resources: Peter B. Lee, Intl. Mktg.

Application Procedures: Send resume and cover letter.

▶ **Internships**

Contact: Peter B. Lee.

Type: Paid, nonpaid, and college credit. **Number Available Annually:** 2-4.

Duties: Duties vary according to department.

Application Procedure: Send resume and cover letter to the attention of Mr. Lee.

Application Deadline: Applications are accepted year-round.

McCormick Center Hotel

23rd St. & Lakeshore Dr.
Chicago, IL 60616
Phone: (312)791-1900

Employees: 450.

Average Entry-Level Hiring: Unknown.

Opportunities: Front desk, concierge, and reservations—no specific requirements. Cooks—cooking school graduates. Training consists of a management training program—background in field or degree from hotel program required.

Human Resources: Leticia, Human Resources.

Application Procedures: Applications given out Monday and Tuesday between 9:00 A.M. and 2:00 P.M. Accepts unsolicited resumes. Applications and/or resumes kept on file for five months.

▶ **Internships**

Type: The company does not offer an internship program.

McLean Hilton

7920 Jones Branch Dr.
McLean, VA 22102
Phone: (703)847-5000

Employees: 358.

Average Entry-Level Hiring: Unknown.

Opportunities: Opportunities available for servers (restaurant, cocktail, and banquet), bartenders, front desk clerks, cooks, housekeepers, clerical personnel, secretaries, Business Department personnel, bell staff, van drivers, and cleaners. Training includes mostly on-the-job, but guest satisfaction and supervisory training available. Duration is from one to several weeks depending on position.

Medieval Times California/Florida/Spain

7662 Beach Blvd.
PO Box 5670
Buena Park, CA 90622
Phone: (714)525-1100

Employees: 300.

Average Entry-Level Hiring: Unknown.

Opportunities: Candidates without a college degree may qualify to work in the park or a show ("You don't need a degree to become a knight!"). Opportunities available for candidates with a college degree include: entry-level positions in marketing, accounting, cash handling, sales, and food service management. Training currently consists of only on-the-job instruction.

Medieval Times Dinner & Tournament
PO Box 2385
Kissimmee, FL 32742
Phone: (407)396-2900

Employees: 210.

Average Entry-Level Hiring: Unknown.

Opportunities: A college graduate serious about a career and with outstanding potential would start as an assistant manager in one of the following areas: Restaurant Management, Accounting, Finance, Food and Beverage, General Operations, or Show Management.

Human Resources: Kelly Yacono, Sales Coordinator.

Application Procedures: Apply at the employee entrance Monday-Friday, 10 A.M. to 1:00 P.M.

Meriden Hotels
888 7th Ave., 27th Fl.
New York, NY 10106
Phone: (212)956-3501

Business Description: Operates over 50 hotels worldwide.

Average Entry-Level Hiring: Varies.

Opportunities: Each hotel has a management training program.

Human Resources: Craig Keller, VP of Human Resources.

Application Procedures: Send resume and cover letter to the attention of Craig Keller.

▶ Internships

Type: The company may offer an internship program. Contact the company for more information.

Mexican Government Tourism Office
405 Park Ave., Ste. 1002
New York, NY 10022
Phone: (212)755-8233
Toll-free: 800-262-8900

Employees: 13.

Average Entry-Level Hiring: All hiring is done in Mexico City.

Human Resources: Francisco Gurria, Human Resources Representative.

MHM, Inc.
14651 Dallas Pkwy., Ste. 400
Dallas, TX 75240
Phone: (214)960-8990

Business Description: Operates 82 hotels.

Application Procedures: Send resume and cover letter to the Personnel Director at the hotel of choice.

Mon Valley Travel Inc.
100 Smithfield St.
Pittsburgh, PA 15222
Phone: (412)255-8747

Employees: 115.

Human Resources: Mark Zelenski.

Application Procedures: Send resume and cover letter.

Monaco Government Tourist Office
845 3rd Ave.
New York, NY 10022
Phone: (212)759-5227

Employees: 4.

Average Entry-Level Hiring: 1 or less per year.

Human Resources: Kathleen Herrera.

Application Procedures: Bi-lingual application is required. Apply in person, or send resume and cover letter.

Monteleone Hotel
214 Royal St.
New Orleans, LA 70140
Phone: (504)523-3341
Fax: (504)528-1019

Average Entry-Level Hiring: 20.

Human Resources: James Parro, Personnel Dir.

Application Procedures: Send resume and cover letter or apply in person.

Morris Travel-Ask Mr. Foster
240 E. Morris Ave.
Salt Lake City, UT 84115
Phone: (801)487-9731

Employees: 400.

Average Entry-Level Hiring: 10-25.

Opportunities: Accounting, administrative, and clerical—college degree (all majors considered).

Travel agents—should have graduated from a two-year travel school or have a college degree in a travel-related curriculum. Potential agents are started in phone message centers, where they answer phones, redirect calls, and handle preliminary client contact. They are also placed in the company's hotel chain to learn how to deal with clients.

Application Procedures: Send resume and cover letter.

Between 1926 and 1931 six small airlines merged as United Air Lines, eight as TWA and fourteen as American Airlines. After World War II nonscheduled airlines were organized by veterans with more zeal than business acumen. The resulting bankruptcies, buy-outs, and mergers echoed the frenzy of the 1920s and have a familiar ring today, when the industry is once more emerging from turmoil.

Source: *Flying*

Motel 6 L.P.
14651 Dallas Pkwy.
Dallas, TX 75240
Phone: (214)386-6161

Business Description: Operates a chain of 508 motels.

Officers: Robert L. Long, Dir. of Info. Systems; Joseph W. McCarthy, CEO & Pres.; Gary L. Mead, Exec. VP of Finance; Hugh Thrasher, Exec. VP of Mktg.

Employees: 5,000.

Opportunities: Motel 6 offers a management training program for two-person teams with no live-in dependents. Candidates should be able to deal with the public and be willing to relocate throughout the United States.

Human Resources: Thomas W. Higgins, VP of Human Resources.

Application Procedures: Contact the Personnel department for more information.

National Car Rental Systems Inc.
7700 France Ave., S.
Minneapolis, MN 55435
Phone: (612)830-2121

Business Description: Engaged in the automobile rental business. Operates the National auto rental franchise.

Officers: Chuck Lynch, CFO; Terrence Redmond, Exec. VP of Mktg.; Vincent A. Wasik, CEO.

Employees: 7,000.

Average Entry-Level Hiring: 200 (including 50 summer temps).

Opportunities: Reservations sales agents—high school diploma and strong customer service or telemarketing/sales background and orientation. Experience in the travel industry and/or travel school training is helpful but not required. Individuals in the Reservations department at the Minneapolis headquarters handle customer calls from around the country regarding rates and rental programs 24 hours a day, 365 days a year. Scheduling is assigned on a seniority basis with schedule changes every four months. Rental agent positions are available at many of the rental locations around the country (in 85 major cities) for individuals with strong customer service skills and experience to directly assist customers with their car rental needs. Both positions offer competitive salaries and an excellent benefit package. A 14-day, full-time paid training program is required. It involves hands-on training with the computer in conjunction with formal classroom teaching and simulated calls. Limited to 12 trainees per class.

Human Resources: Carrie Bertlsen, Sr. Personnel Admin.; Jeff Dowler, Human Resources Representative; Sandra Morrison, Human Resources Dir.

Application Procedures: Send resume and cover letter to the attention of Ms. Carrie Bertlsen, Sr. Personnel Admin.

National Hospitality Corp.
229 Main St.
Huntington, NY 11743
Phone: (516)351-7100

Business Description: The company has nine properties worldwide.

Average Entry-Level Hiring: The main office has two employees and rarely hires anyone.

Application Procedures: Send resume and cover letter.

New Orleans Paddlewheel Inc.

Cruise Terminal
Poydras St. Wharf
New Orleans, LA 70130
Phone: (504)529-4567

Business Description: This company is doing business as Creole/Cajun Queen Riverboats International.

Employees: 100.

Opportunities: College graduates may begin in computer input and operation, accounting, or general office. Some experience is required to begin in sales.

Application Procedures: Applications can be filled out on site. Applications and/or resumes kept on file indefinitely in the director's office. Applicant is contacted when needed.

▶ Internships

Type: The company does not offer an internship program.

New York Convention & Visitors Bureau

2 Columbus Circle
New York, NY 10019
Phone: (212)397-8215

Employees: 65. The company does not offer an internship program.

Average Entry-Level Hiring: 5-10.

Opportunities: Clerical, shipping—college preferred but not required. Management, sales—experience in tourism necessary. Convention sales—marketing background and contacts required.

Human Resources: Ken Durga, Office Mgr.

Application Procedures: Send resume and cover letter.

▶ Internships

Type: The company may offer an internship program.

New York Helmsey Hotel

212 E. 42nd St.
New York, NY 10017
Phone: (217)490-8900

Average Entry-Level Hiring: Unknown.

Opportunities: Management, payroll, restaurant, bar, accounting—specific experience

required. No experience required for telephone operators, front desk clerk or bellpersons.

Human Resources: Carol Sullivan, Accountant.

Application Procedures: Send resume and cover letter.

▶ Internships

Type: The company does not offer an internship program.

In recent years foreign tourism (foreign tourists visiting the U.S.) has generated more foreign earnings for the U.S. than such big-ticket exports as agricultural products and cars. In 1990 foreigners spent $3.1 billion more in the U.S. than Americans did overseas. Whenever the exchange rates on the dollar are favorable, affluent visitors from abroad are likely to spend. To encourage foreign travelers, U.S. resorts are more aggressively marketing to overseas tour operators, who book huge blocks of hotel reservations, airline tickets, and tours.

Source: *Business Week*

New York Hilton

1333 Avenue of the Americas
New York, NY 10019
Phone: (212)586-7000

Employees: 1,500.

Average Entry-Level Hiring: 150-180.

Opportunities: A degree in hotel management is helpful for all entry-level people. Experience is strongly preferred. All hiring and management training is done through the corporate office.

Human Resources: Stephen Koch, Human Resources.

Application Procedures: Send resume and cover letter, or apply in person.

New York Intercontinental Hotel

111 E. 48th St.
New York, NY 10017
Phone: (212)755-5900

Employees: 500.

Average Entry-Level Hiring: Unknown.

Opportunities: Entry-level positions are available in food and beverage and front office departments. Offers a management training and executive development program.

Human Resources: Michael Hollingsworth, Human Resources.

Application Procedures: Send resume and cover letter.

▶ **Internships**

Type: The company may offer an internship program.

New Zealand Tourist & Publicity Office

501 Santa Monica Blvd., Ste. 300
Santa Monica, CA 90401
Phone: (310)395-7480
Toll-free: 800-388-5494

Employees: 3.

Average Entry-Level Hiring: "Only if someone leaves.".

Human Resources: Christine Barber, Office Mgr.

Application Procedures: Send resume and cover letter. New Zealand citizenship preferred.

▶ **Internships**

Type: The company does not offer an internship program.

Newark Airport Marriott Hotel

Newark International Airport
Newark, NJ 017114
Phone: (201)623-0006

Employees: 450.

Average Entry-Level Hiring: Unknown.

Opportunities: Opportunities include front desk clerks, concierges, reservations personnel, drivers, bellhops, restaurant and banquet servers, aisle attendants, hosts/hostesses, bartenders, housekeepers, and lobby attendants.

Human Resources: Joseph Dembeck, Human Resources Dir.

Application Procedures: Send resume and cover letter.

▶ **Internships**

Contact: Joseph Dembeck, Human Resources Dir.

Type: The company offers the following paid internships: Banquets ($8.05/hr.) and Front Desk ($6.80/hr). **Number Available Annually:** Non-fixed.

Application Procedure: Apply in May for summer internships. Contact employer to arrange appointment for filling out application.

Nirro Hotels

160 Central Park S.
New York, NY 10019
Phone: (212)765-4894

Business Description: Operates twenty-three hotels worldwide.

Average Entry-Level Hiring: Unknown.

Opportunities: Opportunities include management training programs through individual hotels.

Application Procedures: Send resume and cover letter to the attention of Essex House/Human Resources. Resumes need to specify job interest.

Northwest Airlines Inc.

Minneapolis-St. Paul Intl. Airport
St. Paul, MN 55111
Phone: (612)726-2111

Business Description: Provider of regularly-scheduled air transportation.

Officers: A.B. Magary, Exec. VP of Mktg.; Fred Malek, President; William L. Trubeck, Exec. VP & CFO; Edwin S. Wright, VP of Info. Systems.

Employees: 40,000.

Average Entry-Level Hiring: 1,500-2,000.

Opportunities: Opportunities include reservation agents, flight attendants, mechanics, computer programmers, and engineers. College graduates preferred for all positions, especially when pursuing management. Recruiting also done at schools in Michigan, Chicago, Georgia, Indiana, and Iowa. Most programs have classroom training.

Human Resources: Jim Dixie, Human Resources Representative; Robert A. Reed, Human Resources Representative.

Application Procedures: Job hot-line (612)726-2215. Staffing Representative Dept. A1470, 5105 NW Dr., St. Paul, MN 55111-3034. Phone: (612)726-2215.

▶ **Internships**

Contact: Jim Dixie, Human Resources Representative.

Type: Salaried ($8.50/hour) and non-salaried, co-op positions available throughout the year for two-year durations. Internships available during the summer. Positions available in maintenance, engineering, finance, and marketing and sales.

Duties: Duties and responsibilities vary according to department.

Qualifications: Candidates should be enthusiastic. No specific GPA required.

Application Procedure: Recruits at participating schools.

Application Deadline: January-February. **Decision Date:** April.

Northwestern Business Travel

7250 Metro Blvd.
Minneapolis, MN 55439
Phone: (612)921-3700

Employees: 260.

Average Entry-Level Hiring: 20.

Opportunities: Entry-level people start in delivery, computer room, or ticketing (coding and splitting). Travel school or travel-related degree required. It takes nine months to be eligible for travel agent positions, if job is available. Accounting clerk—two years accounting experience. The company has two full-time in-house trainers who teach new hires the reservation system and guide them through their early months with the company.

Application Procedures: Send resume and cover letter.

▶ **Internships**

Type: The company may offer an internship program.

Norwegian Cruise Lines

1177 South America Way
Miami, FL 33132
Phone: (305)447-9660

Average Entry-Level Hiring: Unknown.

Application Procedures: Maintains a job hotline with directions on applying for employment

and sending resumes. Accepts unsolicited resumes.

▶ **Internships**

Type: The company does not offer an internship program.

Oakland Convention & Visitors Bureau

1000 Braodway, Ste. 200
Oakland, CA 94607
Phone: (510)839-9000

Employees: 15.

Average Entry-Level Hiring: 1-2. Work-study programs through the University of California.

Opportunities: Growth-oriented receptionist and support positions—college (preferred); experience required.

Human Resources: Veronica Carr, Dir. of Finance.

Application Procedures: Accepts walk-in applicants. Send resume and cover letter preferred.

▶ **Internships**

Contact: Veronica Carr.

Type: Nonpaid interships available for college credit in marketing, sales, and services. **Number Available Annually:** 4.

Duties: Comply as a standard employee performing specific duties and goals to meet department requirements as well as criteria needed by the student for their degree.

Application Procedure: Send resume and cover letter to the attention of Veronica Carr.

Application Deadline: Accepts applications all year long.

Omega World Travel

2 Skyline Pl.
5203 Leesburg Pike
Falls Church, VA 22041
Phone: (703)998-7171
Fax: (703)820-0983

Employees: 500.

Average Entry-Level Hiring: 25-50.

Opportunities: Travel school degree "pretty much" required. Travel agent trainee—handles accounts, but at a slower pace and lower quantity than experienced agents. Qualified trainees eventually move up to full agents and handle larger accounts from beginning to end. Accounting department—college degree required for some positions. The company has no formal training program, but classes and seminars are offered at all levels.

Application Procedures: May send resume and cover letter by mail or fax to personnel.

▶ Internships

Type: The company may offer an internship program.

---

n 1990 women's earnings as a percent of men's earnings for year-round, full-time workers in all occupations was 71%, up from 68% in 1989 and from 60% in 1980. Nonetheless, large pay differentials continue within job categories as well as across them. On average, women who are service workers or managers earn full-time pay closer to 60% of what men earn in the same occupations.

Source: *Business Week*

Omni Hotels Corp.
500 Lafayette Rd.
Hampton, NH 03842
Phone: (603)926-8911

Business Description: A chain of luxury hotels with more than 40 East Coast locations. Some of the hotels are franchised and some are wholly-owned.

Officers: Stephan H. Lewy, Sr. VP & Treasurer; Paul J. Sacco, Sr. VP of Sales & Mktg.; William J. Sheehan, CEO & Pres.

Employees: 10,000.

Opportunities: Omni recruits from campuses around the country for their management training program. The program is tailored to the needs of the individual. It provides an initial overview of the hotel and then allows trainees to specialize in the department of their choice. Graduates from hotel management schools are preferred.

Human Resources: Robert Young, Dir. of Training.

Application Procedures: If applying for a position at Omni's corporate headquarters in Hampton, New Jersey, send a resume and cover letter to the attention of Personnel Manager. If applying for a field position at one of Omni's hotel locations, make a phone inquiry to their headquarters for the name of the director of Human Resources at that particular hotel.

Omni Shoreham Hotel
2500 Calvert St. NW
Washington, DC 20008
Phone: (202)234-0700

Employees: 550.

Average Entry-Level Hiring: 10-12.

Opportunities: Desk clerks, housekeeping, floor supervisors, and reservations.

Human Resources: Sandra Simon, Employment Mgr.

Application Procedures: Send resume and cover letter or apply in person.

▶ Internships

Type: The company does not offer an internship program.

Opryland/Opryland USA, Inc.
2802 Opryland Dr.
Nashville, TN 37214
Phone: (615)889-6600
Fax: (615)871-8787

Average Entry-Level Hiring: Unknown.

Human Resources: Renae Udaco, Personnel Sec.

Application Procedures: Apply in person; applicants are interviewed the same day. Office hours are Monday through Friday between 9:00 A.M. and 4:00 P.M., and Saturday between 9:00 A.M. and 2:00 P.M.

Palmer House & Hilton
17 E. Monroe St.
Chicago, IL 60603
Phone: (312)726-7500

Employees: 1,300.

Average Entry-Level Hiring: Unknown.

Opportunities: Entry-level positions require college degrees. Opportunities exist in the front office, reservations, secretarial, restaurant (assistant manager or waiter), food and beverage, personnel, accounting, and sales. Most managers are transfers from other hotels or management trainees from corporate headquarters. Training includes both on-the-job and class-room programs.

Human Resources: Jeff Evans, Employment Mgr.

Application Procedures: Send resume and cover letter, or apply in person.

▶ Internships

Contact: Jeff Evans, Employment Mgr.

Type: Nonpaid internships available. **Number Available Annually:** Varies.

Application Procedure: Send resume and cover letter. Applicants must interview.

Application Deadline: None.

Pan Pacific Hotels
1717 West St.
Anaheim, CA 92802
Phone: (714)999-0990

Business Description: The company has 15 properties worldwide.

Average Entry-Level Hiring: 0 last year, 0-3 in past years.

Human Resources: Frank Morizaw, Human Resources Mgr.

Application Procedures: Applications can be filled out on site. Resume is helpful but not required.

▶ Internships

Type: The company does not offer an internship program.

Paragon Hotel Corp.
PO Box 7098
Phoenix, AZ 85011
Phone: (602)248-0811

Business Description: Operates 15 hotels.

Officers: Chet Corey, Dir. of Mktg.; James Rhead, President; Richard Scow, Exec. VP.

Employees: 850.

Human Resources: Andy Gullo, Asst. VP.

Passport Travel Inc.
6340 Glenwood, Bldg. No. 7
Overland Park, KS 66202
Phone: (913)677-7777

Employees: 120.

Average Entry-Level Hiring: 5.

Opportunities: Receptionist—previous experience preferred. Accounting clerks—experience in accounting. Support agents (reservations)—experience preferred. Training includes an on-site travel school for entry-level hirees. Contact Mileigh Hall for further information.

Human Resources: Susan Rice, VP of Admin.

Application Procedures: Advertises in local newspapers. Send resume and cover letter.

The Peabody Hotel
149 Union Ave.
Memphis, TN 38103
Phone: (901)529-4000

Employees: 700.

Average Entry-Level Hiring: Unknown.

Opportunities: No entry-level management positions, but the company promotes from within. Hourly positions available as a secretary, reservation clerk, in catering, or at the front desk.

Human Resources: Dave Maner, Human Resources Dir.; Sue Trobaugh, Human Resources Representative.

▶ Internships

Type: Paid/hourly (18 weeks). Culinary internships available only. **Number Available Annually:** 4 per year.

Application Procedure: Apply on campus.

Application Deadline: None.

The Peabody Orlando
9801 International Dr.
Orlando, FL 32819
Phone: (407)352-4000

Employees: 850.

Average Entry-Level Hiring: 20-25 per week.

Opportunities: Opportunities include front desk (Rooms Division), stewards, housekeeping, restaurant, and waiters. The company promotes from within. Everyone starts in an entry-level position; there is no separate route for managers.

Human Resources: Rosa Pettus, Asst. Dir. of Human Resources.

Application Procedures: Recruits from the Culinary Institute of America in New York twice yearly. Send resume and cover letter or apply in person.

▶ **Internships**

Contact: Rosa Pettus, Asst. Dir. of Human Resources.

Type: Paid, hourly 18-week internships available. **Number Available Annually:** 2, twice a year.

Duties: Culinary, cost-control, and practical experience.

Application Procedure: Apply at C.I.A. internship program office.

Application Deadline: None.

L ooking for a career counselor? Personal recommendation is the best route, but local psychologists and psychiatrists, outplacement firms, and college career-development offices often maintain lists of good counselors. A local chapter of the American Society for Training and Development will also give referrals.

Source: *Working Woman*

Philadelphia Convention & Visitors Bureau

1515 Market St., Ste. 2020
Philadelphia, PA 19102
Phone: (215)636-3300

Average Entry-Level Hiring: Unknown.

Opportunities: Opportunities include secretarial, administrative, and telemarketing—college not required, but it is the only path for promotion. Limited on-the-job training.

Human Resources: Wanda Daniels, VP of Finance & Admin.

Application Procedures: Apply in person, or send resume and cover letter. Applications and/or resumes kept on file for one year.

▶ **Internships**

Application Procedure: Apply in person, or send resume and cover letter.

Application Deadline: None.

Pickett Suite Hotels, Resorts & Inns Co.

655 Metro Place S.
Dublin, OH 43017
Phone: (614)889-6500

Business Description: The company has 12 properties.

Average Entry-Level Hiring: 0 in last few years, very irregular.

Human Resources: Marina Epple, Accountant.

Application Procedures: Send resume and cover letter.

▶ **Internships**

Type: The company does not offer an internship program.

The Pittsburgh Hilton & Towers

Gateway Ctr.
Pittsburgh, PA 15222
Phone: (412)391-4000

Employees: 530.

Average Entry-Level Hiring: 100.

Opportunities: Opportunities include concierges, hostesses, front desk personnel, and reservations personnel. Training includes a management development program through the corporate headquarters.

Human Resources: Kim Guarino, Personnel Representative.

Application Procedures: Send resume and cover letter, or apply in person.

▶ **Internships**

Contact: Carol Christian.

Type: Nonpaid and Paid internships available.

Duties: Duties vary according to department.

Application Procedure: Please send letter of application to Human Resources. The letter will be directed to the appropriate department, and the departmental manager will make a decision based on the department's needs.

Application Deadline: None.

Pointe At South Mountain

7227 N. 16th St., Ste. 100
Phoenix, AZ 85020
Phone: (602)997-7890

Employees: 3,200. (The number listed above reflects employment at three locations.).

Average Entry-Level Hiring: 1400.

Opportunities: Most entry-level people hired are not college educated; they start in the restaurant or housekeeping departments or as front desk clerks.

Human Resources: Chris Branham, Employment Mgr.

Application Procedures: Send resume and cover letter.

Portland Marriott Hotel

1401 SW Front Ave.
Portland, OR 97201
Phone: (503)226-7600

Employees: 450.

Average Entry-Level Hiring: 200-250.

Human Resources: Tracy Linne, Human Resources.

Application Procedures: Send resume and cover letter to contact.

▶ Internships

Contact: Tracy Linne, Human Resources.

Type: Offers nonpaid internship(s). College credit earned, depends on the academic institution. **Number Available Annually:** 10-12.

Duties: Interns choose area of interest from following: Sales and Marketing, Human Resources, Food and Beverage, and Housekeeping. Interns are also exposed to other areas.

Application Procedure: Apply in person or by mail before May 1. Interview is required. Potential interns may instead apply to the Marriott corporate offices at the beginning of the semester previous to desired starting semester. Send resume and cover letter to the attention of Chip Stuckmeyer, Human Resources for Hotel, Resorts, and Suites, Department No. 921.13, 1 Marriott Dr., Washington, DC 20058. Phone: 800-638-8108.

Application Deadline: May 1.

Pratt Hotel Corp.

2 Galleria Tower
Dallas, TX 75240
Phone: (214)386-9777

Business Description: Engaged in the operation of eating establishments. Operator of hotels and/or motels. Operator of miscellaneous sports, amusement or recreation establishments.

Officers: Albert J. Cohen, Exec. VP & CFO; Jack E. Pratt Sr., CEO & Chairman of the Board.

Employees: 6,550.

Application Procedures: Contact the company for more information.

Preferred Hotels Worldwide

1901 S. Meyers Rd., Ste. 220
Oakbrook Terrace, IL 60148
Phone: (708)953-0404

Business Description: The company has 91 properties worldwide.

Average Entry-Level Hiring: 1.

Human Resources: Dawn Hinds, Admin. Asst.

Application Procedures: Send resume and cover letter.

▶ Internships

Type: The company does not offer an internship program.

Prime Motor Inns Inc.

700 Rte. 46 E.
Fairfield, NJ 07006
Phone: (201)882-1010

Business Description: Owns and operates 132 motor inns, restaurants, and cocktail lounges worldwide. Also involved in the real estate and construction businesses.

Officers: P.E. Simon, CEO & Chairman of the Board.

Employees: 8,500.

Opportunities: Management trainees are hired for front desk positions. There are also entry-level positions available at individual hotels in food service. Individuals with hotel experience are preferred.

Human Resources: Harvey Bardell, VP & Dir. of Human Resources.

Application Procedures: Send resume and cover letter to the attention of Harvey Bardell, VP & Dir. of Human Resources.

Prince of Fundy Cruises

PO Box 4216, Ste. A
Portland, ME 04101
Phone: (207)772-7457
Fax: (207)773-3957

Employees: Positions are seasonal. Employees usually return every season.

Human Resources: Eric Hultkrantz, Supervisor.

Application Procedures: Send resume and cover letter to the attention of Floating Fleet at the above address.

▶ Internships

Type: The company does not offer an internship program.

Princess Cruises

2029 Century Park E.
Los Angeles, CA 90067

Application Procedures: All hiring is done by the head office in London. Ship employees must have British citizenship.

The concierge is the hallmark of the world's grand hotels. So important has the concierge become to modern hotellerie that he or she is now commonly removed from the service staff roster and listed among executive management. The chief concierge and staff have to play private secretary to a hotel full of guests. Much of their work consists of comforting a host of travelers who find themselves in a foreign city unable to speak the language, find the shops, recognize the monuments, or order in the restaurants. One concierge puts it this way: "The client's problems are my problems."

Source: *Smithsonian*

Princess Hotels International

805 3rd Ave.
New York, NY 10022
Phone: (212)715-7000

Business Description: The company has 7 properties.

Average Entry-Level Hiring: 0 in the last year. They rarely hire people for entry-level positions.

Human Resources: William Mullens, Personnel Asst.

Application Procedures: Send resume and cover letter if positions become available. Contact the company for more information (212)715-7049.

▶ Internships

Type: The company does not offer an internship program.

Quality Inn

8727 Colesville Rd.
Silver Springs, MD 20910
Phone: (301)589-5200

Average Entry-Level Hiring: Unknown.

Application Procedures: Apply in person.

Quality Inns International

10750 Columbia Pike
Silver Spring, MD 20901
Phone: (301)236-5025

Business Description: The company has 1,200 properties worldwide.

Average Entry-Level Hiring: 2.

Opportunities: While no formal internship program exists, interested students are encouraged to contact the department in which they're interested in working.

Human Resources: Susan Conlon, Human Resources Mgr.

Application Procedures: Send resume and cover letter. Contact the company for more information (301)236-4903.

Radisson Hotel Denver

1550 Court Pl.
Denver, CO 80202
Phone: (303)893-3333

Employees: 350.

Average Entry-Level Hiring: 400-500.

Opportunities: Opportunities include front desk.

Human Resources: Kel Heeth, Human Resources.

Application Procedures: The company does not accept unsolicited resumes. Applicants must call the Job Line (303)893-0642, and apply for a specific available position. Send resume and cover letter or apply in person.

▶ Internships

Type: The company does not offer an internship program.

Radisson Hotel South

7800 Normandale Blvd.
Bloomington, MN 55439
Phone: (612)835-7800

Employees: 450.

Average Entry-Level Hiring: Varies.

Opportunities: The company places a high emphasis on experience. No entry-level management positions. Entry-level opportunities available in the front office, reservations, and housekeeping.

Human Resources: Carole Anderson, Human Resources Dir.

Application Procedures: Send resume and cover letter, or apply in person.

▶ **Internships**

Contact: Carole Anderson, Human Resources Dir.

Type: Nonpaid and college credit internships available. **Number Available Annually:** 4-5.

Duties: Internship duties are very similar to the duties of the regular, full-time employees.

Application Procedure: Send resume and cover letter, or apply in person.

Application Deadline: April 1.

Radisson Hotels International Inc.
PO Box 59159
Minneapolis, MN 55459
Phone: (612)540-5526

Business Description: Operator of hotels and/or motels.

Officers: Tom Nalley, Dir. of Systems; John Norlander, President; Harriet Peterson, VP of Mktg.; Robert Zambrano, VP of Finance.

Employees: 30,000.

Human Resources: Sue Gordon, VP of Human Resources.

Radisson Seattle
17001 Pacific Hwy. S.
Seattle, WA 98188
Phone: (206)244-6000

Employees: 240.

Average Entry-Level Hiring: 30-40. Five college graduates, the rest lower-level employment.

Opportunities: Secretarial, catering secretary, front desk, food & beverage. Even persons with experience are considered entry-level. No entry-level management positions, but company is strongly committed to promotion from within. Classroom and on-the-job training provided.

Human Resources: Tessie Wilkerson, Personnel Recruiter.

Application Procedures: Send resume and cover letter or apply in person.

▶ **Internships**

Type: The company does not offer an internship program.

Ramada Inn Hotels
401 7th Ave. & Belmont St.
New York, NY 10001
Phone: (212)736-5000

Business Description: The company has 13 properties worldwide.

Average Entry-Level Hiring: 1-2 depending on needs.

Human Resources: Michael Weinstein, Asst. Personnel Dir.

Application Procedures: Send resume and cover letter.

▶ **Internships**

Type: The company does not offer an internship program.

Ramada International
2655 SW 42nd Ave., Ste. 800
Coral Gables, FL 33134

Business Description: Owns and operates 598 hotels and motels worldwide.

Officers: Wilfred Grau, President.

Employees: 3,400.

Average Entry-Level Hiring: Unknown.

Opportunities: Each hotel has a management training program.

Human Resources: Edwin Zephirim, Human Resources Dir.

Application Procedures: Places newspaper advertisements for certain openings. Accepts unsolicited resumes. Send resume and cover letter to the attention of Edwin Zephirim, Director, Human Resources, or contact the personnel director at each hotel. Reservations and computer jobs can be applied for at Phoenix location.

Ramada Pennsylvania
401 7th Ave. at 33rd St.
New York, NY 10001
Phone: (212)736-5000

Employees: 900.

Average Entry-Level Hiring: Unknown.

Opportunities: There are no entry-level management positions. Opportunities exist in front desk, guest services, customer complaints, and sales, all of which offer a good way to learn about the business from the bottom up. Company promotes from within.

Application Procedures: Apply in person.

▶ **Internships**

Type: The company does not offer an internship program.

Squeezed by foreign competition and a slowing economy, employers are increasingly shunning fixed raises in favor of pay plans where employees can enrich themselves only by enriching the company. From hourly workers to managers in pin stripes, those who boost earnings, productivity, or other results prosper. Those who turn in a lackluster performance take home less.

Source: *U.S. News & World Report*

Rank Hotels North America

15303 Dallas Pkwy., Ste. 610
Dallas, TX 75248
Phone: (214)458-7265

Business Description: The company has four properties, two in California, one each in South Carolina, and Colorado.

Average Entry-Level Hiring: 0-2 per year.

Opportunities: Rank hires entry-level managers in accounting, front office, restaurant, housekeeping and human resources. Trainees must have a bachelor's degree. Graduates of hospitality schools are preferred for the front office management positions. Interested students should send their resumes to Pam Tolley.

Human Resources: Pam Tolley, Human Resources Dir.

Application Procedures: Send resume and cover letter.

▶ **Internships**

Type: The company does not offer an internship program.

Red Lion Hotels & Inns

4001 Main St.
Vancouver, WA 98663
Phone: (206)696-0001

Business Description: Operates 54 hotels.

Officers: Cliff Barry, Dir. of Data Processing; Jerry Best, CEO & Pres.; Raymond Bingham, CFO; Steve Giblin, Exec. VP of Mktg.

Employees: 11,000.

Opportunities: Red Lion has a management training program for which they recruit graduates of hotel management schools. The program lasts 90 days. Trainees are rotated through the different departments during the first six weeks and choose an area of concentration during the second six-week period.

Human Resources: Steve Hubbard, VP of Human Resources; Susan Rivenbark, Human Resources Representative.

Red Roof Inns Inc.

4355 Davidson Rd.
Hilliard, OH 43026-2491
Phone: (614)876-3200
Fax: (614)771-7838

Business Description: Operates a chain of 200 motor inns.

Officers: Richard Bibart, President; Gary Qualmann, CFO; David Wible, Dir. of Mktg.; Jeff Winslow, Dir. of Systems.

Employees: 5,000.

Average Entry-Level Hiring: Unknown.

Opportunities: Red Roof offers a nine-week management training program for which they recruit students from more than 25 universities. While candidates with a bachelor's degree in hotel management, business administration, or communication are preferred, any individual with an interest in hospitality will be considered. The program is divided into three distinct phases. Phase I is a hands-on, task-oriented session at a training center. Phase II is a four-week class given at the corporate offices in Columbus, Ohio. The final phase is an integration period in which trainees are asked to demonstrate what they have learned at their inn of assignment. Trainees must be able to relocate.

Human Resources: Doug Bruce, Human Resources Representative.

▶ Internships

Contact: Doug Bruce, Human Resources Representative.

Type: Internships are offered sporadically.

Application Procedure: Contact Doug Bruce for more information.

The Registry Hotel Corp.

16250 Dallas Pkwy., Ste. 105
Dallas, TX 75248
Phone: (214)248-4300

Business Description: The company has 15 properties.

Average Entry-Level Hiring: 1.

Opportunities: Each hotel offers a Management Training Program.

Human Resources: Rockie Garza, Office Admin.

Application Procedures: Send resume and cover letter.

▶ Internships

Type: The company does not offer an internship program.

The Residence Inn Co.

1 Marriott Dr.
Washington, DC 20058
Phone: (301)380-9000
Toll-free: 800-228-9290

Average Entry-Level Hiring: Unknown.

Application Procedures: Send resume and cover letter, or applications will be mailed upon request. Contact the company for more information at the Corporate Headquarters.

▶ Internships

Type: The company offers an internship program. **Number Available Annually:** 2.

Duties: Interns will spend a week in every department and two to three weeks in sales.

Application Procedure: Send resume and cover letter.

Application Deadline: A semester in advance.

Revere Travel Inc.

1891 N. Olden Ave.
Trenton, NJ 08638
Phone: (609)882-0052

Application Procedures: Revere Travel has been acquired by American Express Corp. For employment information at Revere Travel, contact World Finance Center, 200 Vesey St., New York, NY 10285.

Richfield Hotel Management

4600 S. Ulster St., Ste. 1200
Denver, CO 80237
Phone: (303)220-2000
Fax: (303)799-6367

Business Description: Engaged in the operation of eating establishments. Operator of hotels and/or motels.

Officers: John A. Eriksson, Exec. VP & CFO; Robert M. James, CEO, Pres. & Chairman of the Board.

Employees: 360.

> **B**y the year 2000, 41% of new jobs created will require average or above-average skills, compared with fewer than 24% in 1992.
>
> Source: *The Futurist*

Riser Foods, Inc.

5300 Richmond Rd.
Bedford Heights, OH 44146
Phone: (216)292-7000

Average Entry-Level Hiring: Varies.

Human Resources: Lorraine Hulsman, Human Resources.

Application Procedures: Send resume and cover letter.

▶ Internships

Type: The company does not offer an internship program.

The Ritz-Carlton Hotel

160 E. Pearson St.
Chicago, IL 60611
Phone: (312)266-1000

Employees: 650.

Average Entry-Level Hiring: 50-80.

Opportunities: Supervisors in front office, restaurant (background in food and beverage preferred), and housekeeping—experience working with public; college degree (liberal arts major acceptable). Provides both classroom and on-the-job training.

Human Resources: Darren Oliver, Human Resources Dir.

Application Procedures: Send resume and cover letter. Applications and/or resumes kept on file for 6 months.

▶ Internships

Type: The company may offer an internship program.

---

al Rosenbluth is president and CEO of Philadelphia based Rosenbluth Travel, Inc., one of the country's most distinguished travel agencies. When he "wanted feedback from clients and associates, he took the advice on the back of a 64-pack of Crayola crayons: crayons help people express thoughts they can't always put into words. He sent 100 of his clients and associates construction paper and a box of crayons and asked them to illustrate what Rosenbluth Travel meant to them. A tradition was created; never has a mailing failed to produce valuable insights into the business."

Source: *Working Woman*

Ritz Carlton Hotel Co.
3414 Peachtree Rd., NE, Ste. 300
Atlanta, GA 30326
Phone: (404)237-5500
Fax: (404)261-0119

Business Description: Operates 12 hotels.

Officers: Leo Hart, Dir. of Mktg. & Sales; William B. Johnson, CEO; Richard Stephens, CFO.

Employees: 10,000.

Human Resources: Libby Dawson; Owen Dorsey, VP of Human Resources.

Rivership Romance
433 N. Palmetto Ave.
Sanford, FL 32771
Phone: (407)321-5091

Human Resources: Judy, Reservationist.

Application Procedures: Applications can be filled out on site Monday through Friday between 8.30 A.M. and 5:00 P.M. Applications and/or resumes kept on file for six months to one year.

▶ Internships

Type: The company does not offer an internship program.

Robustelli World Travel
30 Spring St.
Stamford, CT 06901
Phone: (203)965-0200

Employees: 150.

Average Entry-Level Hiring: 10.

Opportunities: Travel agents and ticketing and packaging personnel—travel school certification preferred. Accounting—high school diploma required; accounting courses or experience preferred.

Human Resources: Lisa Smith, Human Resources.

Application Procedures: Send resume and cover letter.

Rosenbluth Travel Agency Inc.
1650 Market St.
Philadelphia, PA 19103
Phone: (215)981-1710
Fax: (215)981-0140

Business Description: A travel management firm. Rosenbluth Travel was named Service Company of the Year in 1989 by Tom Peters, an "internationally acclaimed expert on excellence." ("Transcending the Travel Industry: Hal Rosenbluth Rose Up Through a Family Business." *Focus.* 25 Oct. 1989.)

Officers: David Fisher, CFO; David Miller, Dir. of Data Processing; Hal F. Rosenbluth, President.

Employees: 2,300.

Opportunities: Support agents—if interested in the travel industry, this position is a good place to start. Airline reporting commission—previous office experience of any kind (not necessarily travel). Job entails producing ARC reports and issuing tickets. Travel agents—no experience needed; hirees will participate in the company's training program. When hired, new employees are placed with senior agents who will act as supervisors. New employees are considered trainees for six to eight weeks. Technology, customer service, client services, accounting, operations, and administration—all require the desire to be involved in the travel industry; previous office experience is helpful. You have to be in a position for a year before moving up. There is a two-day orientation to the company.

Human Resources: Cecily Carel, Human Resources Dir.; Meg Wolf, Human Resources Representative.

Application Procedures: For reservations positions, send resume and cover letter to the attention of Carolyn Wible at W. Valley Business Center, 900 W. Valley Rd., No. 2200, Wayne, PA 19087. For other positions, send resume and cover letter to the attention of Corporate Staffing, Human Resources Department, Rosenbluth Travel Agency Inc., 1911 Arch St., Philadelphia, PA 19103. Phone: 215/557-8700.

▶ **Internships**

Type: Salaried and/or college credit. Summer or semester. Internships available for support, airline reporting commission, travel agency, technology, customer service, accounting, operations, and administration. **Number Available Annually:** 15.

Duties: Duties/responsibilities are same as an entry-level employee. Sometimes the company will create a job description based on needs.

Qualifications: Qualifications include an interest in travel (or specific area such as accounting, etc.).

Application Procedure: Call the Human Resources Department for further information.

Application Deadline: Ongoing. **Decision Date:** Soon after receiving resume.

Royal Caribbean Cruise Line

1050 Caribbean Way
Miami, FL 33132
Phone: (305)634-7748

Business Description: Considered to be the "country club of the sea" and specializes in providing luxury cruises with fine foods and excellent service.

Average Entry-Level Hiring: Unknown.

Opportunities: The crew is international. Positions are available through Royal Caribbean in the following areas: shipboard contact, shore side contact, restaurant and bar staff, and hotel stewards. In addition, related positions are avail-able through companies that provide services to Royal Caribbean. These include scuba instructor, child care, entertainers, cosmetologist, massage therapist, gift shop attendant, casino staff, photographer, food and beverage, medical doctor and nurse, ship officer, and engineering staff. Contact the Cruise Line for details on how to apply for these positions.

Application Procedures: Send resume and cover letter to Human Resources.

Sabena Belgian World Airlines

1155 Northern Blvd.
Manhasset, NY 11030
Phone: (516)562-9200
Toll-free: 800-955-2000

Employees: 320.

Average Entry-Level Hiring: Unknown.

Opportunities: Opportunities include clerical positions. Candidates must have experience. A college degree is helpful but not necessary. Instruction includes classroom and on-the-job instruction.

Human Resources: Maria, Secretary.

Application Procedures: Applications and/or resumes kept on file for one year.

▶ **Internships**

Type: The company does not offer an internship program.

St. Louis Convention & Visitors Commission

10 S. Broadway, Ste. 1000
St. Louis, MO 63102
Phone: (314)421-1023

Employees: 40.

Average Entry-Level Hiring: 1.

Opportunities: Clerical, administrative—no educational or skill requirements specified by company. Sales—experience required.

Human Resources: David Austin, Senior VP-Finance & Administration.

Application Procedures: Send resume and cover letter.

▶ **Internships**

Type: The company does not offer an internship program.

San Antonio Convention and Visitor's Bureau

PO Box 2277
San Antonio, TX 78298
Phone: (512)270-8700

Employees: 54.

Average Entry-Level Hiring: 1-2.

Opportunities: Opportunities may be found in the convention sales, convention services, film, administration, public relations, and visitor divisions.

Application Procedures: Contact City Personnel at 299-7283. Maintains a job hotline at 299-7280.

▶ Internships

Application Procedure: Contact company, or city personnel at 299-7283.

San Diego Zoo/San Diego Wild Animal Park

PO Box 551
San Diego, CA 92112
Phone: (619)231-1515

Employees: 1,400.

Average Entry-Level Hiring: 500.

Opportunities: Very low turnover in professional positions. Minimal employment opportunities for college graduates without experience. On-the-job training for all positions except managers, for whom there is a full-time trainer on staff.

Human Resources: Gabriela Valverde, Human Resources Mgr.

Application Procedures: Applications can be filled out on site Monday through Friday 1:00 to 4:00 P.M. Applications and/or resumes kept on file and active for six months.

▶ Internships

Type: The company does not offer an internship program.

San Francisco Convention & Visitors Bureau

PO Box 426676
San Francisco, CA 94101
Phone: (415)974-6900

Employees: 65.

Average Entry-Level Hiring: 4.

Opportunities: All positions are clerical.

Human Resources: Joy Creese, Admin. Services Mgr.

Application Procedures: Send resume and cover letter.

▶ Internships

Contact: Sharon Rooney, Public Relations Dir.

Type: College credit and honorarium. **Number Available Annually:** 3.

Duties: Duties include writing press releases, assisting with mailings, and assisting with journalists inquiries.

Application Procedure: Contact the company for more information.

San Jose Convention & Visitors Bureau

333 W. San Carlos, Ste. 1000
San Jose, CA 95110
Phone: (408)295-9600

Employees: 26.

Average Entry-Level Hiring: 3-5.

Opportunities: Project coordinator—experience in marketing, public relations or business. Sales—one or two years experience required (hotel sales preferred).

Human Resources: Chris Jasper, Admin. Asst.

Application Procedures: Send resume and cover letter.

▶ Internships

Type: The company does not offer an internship program.

Sands Hotel & Casino Inc.

3355 Las Vegas Blvd. S.
Las Vegas, NV 89109
Phone: (702)733-5495

Business Description: Operator of hotels and/or motels.

Officers: Ty Chamberlain, Dir. of Data Processing; Henri Lewin, President; Colleen Myler, VP of Mktg.; Tom Steinbauer, VP of Finance.

Employees: 800.

Human Resources: Jeannette Armstrong, Human Resources Dir.

Scandinavian Tourist Board
655 3rd Ave., 18th Fl.
New York, NY 10017
Phone: (212)949-2333

Employees: 5.

Average Entry-Level Hiring: Personnel only hired through the headquarters in Sweden.

▶ **Internships**

Type: The company does not offer an internship program.

Sea Escape
1080 Port Blvd.
Miami, FL 33132
Phone: (305)476-4300

Employees: 1,000.

Opportunities: Deck, engine, hotel departments, entertainment—pertinent experience necessary. Pursers—college graduate (public relations or banking majors).

Human Resources: Sam Wiggins, Controller.

Application Procedures: Applications can be filled out on site. Applications and/or resumes kept on file for six months.

▶ **Internships**

Type: The company does not offer an internship program.

Sea World
70077 Sea Harbor Dr.
Orlando, FL 32821
Phone: (407)351-3600

Opportunities: There are excellent opportunities for college graduates with or without experience. These opportunities include accounting, finance, sales, marketing, management, and many other areas. Animal handling—scuba, CPR, and communication skills plus a B.A. in a marine biology-related major required.

Human Resources: Christina, Sr. Employment Representative.

Application Procedures: Applications can be filled out on site. Applications are routed to representatives and are kept on file for six months, for both professional and nonprofessional positions.

▶ **Internships**

Type: Internships are available through the Marketing Department.

Sea World of San Diego
1720 S. Shores Rd.
San Diego, CA 92109
Phone: (619)226-3901
Fax: (619)226-3996

Average Entry-Level Hiring: Heavy seasonal turnover rate each year.

> **M**ore casino operators are getting into family resorts, theme-park-like amenities and casinos for low- and middle-income gamblers, a market first identified by Circus Circus Enterprises. With more revenue-hungry states looking at legalizing gambling, this could be a timely move for the Nevada casino operators.
>
> Source: *Forbes*

Seattle/King County Convention & Visitors Bureau
520 Pike St., Ste. 1300
Seattle, WA 98101
Phone: (206)461-5800

Human Resources: Claudia Mitchell, Mgr. of Admin. Services.

Application Procedures: Advertises in Seattle papers. Contact the company for more information.

▶ **Internships**

Contact: Anais Winant, Vice Pres.

Type: Nonpaid with college credit. Paid minority positions available through the Minority Affairs Office. **Number Available Annually:** 1.

Duties: Substantive internship. The intern will work on projects as a member of the staff.

Application Procedure: Recruits at college campuses.

Application Deadline: Varies.

Servico Inc.
1601 Belvedere Rd.
West Palm Beach, FL 33406
Phone: (407)689-9970

Business Description: Operates fifty hotels.

Officers: A.I. Meyer, CEO & Chairman of the Board.

Employees: 9,150.

Application Procedures: Contact the personnel director at each hotel for more information.

Sheraton Brickell Point Miami

495 Brickell Ave.
Miami, FL 33131
Phone: (305)373-6000

Business Description: Hotel.

Employees: 300.

Average Entry-Level Hiring: Depends on qualifications.

Opportunities: Front desk clerk or Supervisor.

Human Resources: Sophie Blanc, Human Resources Mgr.

Application Procedures: Send resume and cover letter or applications can be filled out on site.

▶ **Internships**

Contact: Maria Elena Rodriguez.

Type: Paid internships available for a period of 18 weeks. Contact the company for more information (305)373-6000. **Number Available Annually:** 4. **Applications Received:** 18.

Duties: Culinary internships only.

Application Procedure: Apply on campus or contact the company for more information at (305)373-6000.

Application Deadline: None.

Sheraton Cleveland City Centre Hotel

777 St. Clair Ave.
Cleveland, OH 44114
Phone: (216)771-7600

Employees: 295.

Average Entry-Level Hiring: Unknown.

Opportunities: Servers, bussers, cashiers, bartenders, cooks, sous chef, dishwashers, desk clerks, desk supervisors, concierge. On-the-job training conducted by management or supervisor.

Human Resources: Annette Dix, Personnel Dir.

Application Procedures: Send resume and cover letter; applications and/or resumes kept on file for one year.

▶ **Internships**

Type: Interns serve as front desk agents. This program is currently informal; a formal internship program is being developed.

Sheraton Corp.

60 State St.
Boston, MA 02109
Phone: (617)367-3600-

Business Description: Operates 465 hotels in 65 countries.

Officers: William Buxton, Sr. VP & Controller; Robert Collier, Sr. VP of Mktg.; Mark Hurwitz, Dir. of Data Processing; John Kapioltas, CEO, Pres. & Chairman of the Board.

Employees: 3,000.

Average Entry-Level Hiring: Unknown.

Opportunities: Sheraton has a management training program for which they will consider individuals with a bachelor's degree, preferably in hotel management or business administration. 1-2 years working experience is also preferred, though not a prerequisite for admission into the program. Trainees can choose a specific department, such as food & beverage, systems, human resources, or comptroller, or enter a more general management program. Inexperienced people who are not yet eligible for the management training program are encouraged to join the line staff and work as a front desk clerk, hostess, or bellman to gain the necessary experience. "There is an excellent opportunity for people who come in at rock bottom level to be promoted within a year's time, sometimes less."

Human Resources: Brett Hutchens, Human Resources Representative.

▶ **Internships**

Contact: Brett Hutchens, Human Resources Representative.

Type: Salaried, summer internships available in human resources, accounting, and marketing. **Number Available Annually:** 3-4.

Duties: Vary according to the needs of the department.

Qualifications: Graduate students only—working toward masters in hospitality.

Application Procedure: Send resume/cover letter to contact.

Application Deadline: Early spring. **Decision Date:** May-June.

Sheraton New Orleans Hotel

500 Canal St.
New Orleans, LA 70130
Phone: (504)525-2500

Employees: 824.

Average Entry-Level Hiring: 840.

Opportunities: Entry-level positions include front desk staff, PBX telephone operators, and Food & Beverage positions. Offers a management training program for college graduates, preferably those with hotel experience. Program duration is one year. Trainees can specialize in Food & Beverage or follow the general management path. The company promotes from within.

Human Resources: Sharon Price, Employment Mgr.

Application Procedures: Send resume and cover letter, or apply in person.

▶ **Internships**

Type: The company may offer an internship program.

Sheraton Phoenix

111 N. Central
Phoenix, AZ 85004
Phone: (602)257-1525

Employees: 375. Peak season employment.

Average Entry-Level Hiring: Unknown, 200 percent turnover.

Opportunities: Rarely hires anyone without experience. Non-experienced start in kitchen; experienced at front desk.

Human Resources: Kelly Stoner, Human Resources.

Application Procedures: Send resume and cover letter or apply in person.

▶ **Internships**

Type: The company does not offer an internship program.

Sheraton Tara Hotel

Tara Blvd.
Nashua, NH 03062
Phone: (603)888-9970

Employees: 320.

Average Entry-Level Hiring: 40-50.

Opportunities: Assistant management and management positions in all departments—hotel degree; experience not required but helpful.

Human Resources: Michelle Faust, Personnel Dir.

Application Procedures: Send resume and cover letter or apply in person.

▶ **Internships**

Contact: Michelle Faust, Personnel Dir.

Type: Nonpaid internships available. College credit offered. **Number Available Annually:** 2 or 3.

Duties: Applicants are accepted in all phases of hotel work.

Application Procedure: Send resume and cover letter or apply in person.

Application Deadline: Ongoing.

> Many spas now offer weekend retreat specials for busy executive women. These include Canyon Ranch in the Berkshires and Rowes Wharf Health Club & Spa, both in Massachusetts; the Peninsula Spa in New York; the Aveda Spa Osceola in Wisconsin; Le Meridien Spa in California, and the Doral Saturnia in Florida.
>
> Source: *Working Woman*

Sheraton Tara Hotels

50 Braintree Hill Office Pk.
Braintree, MA 02184
Phone: (617)848-2000

Business Description: The company has 11 properties in the Northeast.

Average Entry-Level Hiring: 2-3 per year.

Human Resources: Kristen Seaman, Personnel Asst.

Application Procedures: Send resume and cover letter.

Sheraton Tucson El Conquistador

10000 N. Oracle Rd.
Tucson, AZ 85737
Phone: (602)742-7000

Employees: 630.

Average Entry-Level Hiring: 200-300.

Opportunities: Front desk, concierge, restaurant servers, and cashiers.

Human Resources: Matt Van Der Peet, Personnel Dir.

Application Procedures: Send resume and cover letter or apply in person.

▶ **Internships**

Type: The company may offer an internship program.

Sheraton Universal

333 University Terrace Pkwy.
Universal City, CA 91608
Phone: (818)980-1212

Employees: 450.

Average Entry-Level Hiring: 12.

Opportunities: Hotel has low turnover. Opportunities for assistant restaurant manager, housekeeping, front desk supervisor. Latter requires supervisory experience and computer skills.

Human Resources: Virginia Page, Human Resources Dir.

Application Procedures: Apply in person on Monday, Tuesday between 9:00 A.M. and 12 noon or Wednesday, Thursday betwen 3:00 P.M. and 5:00 P.M.

▶ **Internships**

Type: The company does not offer an internship program in 1992.

Sheraton Washington

2660 Woodley Rd.
Washington, DC 20008
Phone: (202)328-2000

Employees: 950.

Average Entry-Level Hiring: 450.

Opportunities: Guest service agents, front office, and reservations—opportunity for promotion to manager after about a year. Restaurant—the company will hire supervisors straight out of college if they have some experience.

Human Resources: Catherine Dimare, Human Resources Mgr.

Application Procedures: Apply in person.

Sheraton World Resort

10100 International Dr.
Orlando, FL 32821
Phone: (407)352-1100

Employees: 330.

Average Entry-Level Hiring: 175.

Opportunities: Guest service agent (front desk), hospitality host/hostess (guest services desk)—requires excellent communication and interpersonal skills and some cash handling experience. Reservations agent—requires excellent communication and telephone skills and typing skills (35 wpm). Accounting clerks—requires good mathematical skills and some basic accounting background. Deli attendant, restaurant hostperson/cashier (food service)—requires good guest relations skills and some cash-handling experience. Food and beverage servers—excellent interpersonal skills and some previous food and beverage experience required. Guest room attendant (housekeeping)—requires the ability to stand and bend for long periods of time. The Sheraton has five training programs: Systems, Personnel, Controllership, Food and Beverage, and General Management. Four-year college degree required. For more information, contact: Brett Hutchens, The Sheraton Corporation, 60 State St., Boston, MA 02109.

Human Resources: Yolanda Gonzalez, Personnel Mgr.

Application Procedures: Apply in person and arrange an interview. Applications will be mailed upon request.

▶ **Internships**

Type: The company offers an internship program through its corporate office in Boston.

Shilo Inns

11600 SW Barnes Rd.
Portland, OR 97225
Phone: (503)641-6565

Business Description: Operator of hotels and/or motels.

Officers: Linda S. Burt, Dir. of Mktg.; Mark S. Hemstreet, CEO; Cathy Marconi, Dir. of Data Processing; Marge Taylor, Controller.

Employees: 2,500.

Human Resources: Darlene Wruble, Human Resources Dir.

Showboat Inc.

2800 Fremont St.
Las Vegas, NV 89104
Phone: (702)385-9123

Business Description: Operator of hotels

and/or motels. Engaged in the operation of bowling centers.

Officers: Frank Modica, CEO & Pres.; Leann Schneider, VP & CFO; Dominic Virga, Dir. of Info. Systems; Steve Waldman, Dir. of Mktg.

Employees: 4,750.

Human Resources: Walter Reid, Human Resources.

Application Procedures: Contact the company for more information.

Signature Inns Inc.

8335 Allison Point, No. 300
Indianapolis, IN 46250
Phone: (317)577-1111

Business Description: Operator of hotels and/or motels.

Officers: J.D. Bontreger, President; Robert Goodwell, CFO; David Miller, Dir. of Mktg. & Sales.

Employees: 900.

Average Entry-Level Hiring: 50.

Opportunities: Signature Inns Inc. offers many openings at all different levels. Individuals with a bachelor's degree in any area are eligible for an assistant manager's position. Duties include making sales calls to the community, generating business for the motel, and assisting in management responsibilities. Future promotion to manager is possible. Other entry-level possibilities offer advancement potential and do not require a college degree. Administrative coordinator—excellent communication and interpersonal skills; bookkeeping, secretarial, and clerical skills; computer interest helpful. Duties include conducting motel tours and publishing a monthly newsletter. Front desk personnel—excellent communication skills; must enjoy working with people and computers. Night auditor—bookkeeping/accounting and excellent communication skills; must enjoy working with people and computers. Assistant managers go through three to four weeks of training; administrative coordinators, eight weeks; front desk and night auditors, two weeks.

Human Resources: David Proctor, Human Resources Dir.

Small Luxury Hotels

339 S. Robertson Blvd., Ste. 103
Beverly Hills, CA 90211
Phone: (213)659-5050

Business Description: The company has 30 properties worldwide.

Employees: 4.

Average Entry-Level Hiring: A very small company, no entry level positions.

Human Resources: Jan Bell, Admin. Asst.

Application Procedures: Send resume and cover letter.

▶ **Internships**

Type: The company does not offer an internship program.

According to the Bureau of Labor Statistics, the rapid growth of women entering the workforce—about 2.3% per year from 1975 to 1990—is expected to slow, growing at a rate of 1.6% per year in the next fifteen years. By 2005, minorities are expected to account for more than 25% of all working people in the U.S., with the fastest growth occurring among Hispanics, who will make up over 11% of the workforce by 2005.

Source: *Forbes*

Sonesta International Hotels Corp.

200 Clarendon St.
Boston, MA 02116
Phone: (617)421-5400

Business Description: Operates six hotels located in Maine, Massachusetts, Florida, and Los Angeles, California.

Officers: Brian Owen, Treasurer; Jules Sieburgh, VP of Info. Systems; R.P. Sonnabend, CEO & Chairman of the Board; Stephanie Sonnabend, VP of Mktg.

Employees: 1,680.

Opportunities: Sonesta offers entry-level positions both in its individual hotels and in the corporate office. Opportunities in the corporate office include positions as sales assistants, reservations agents, advertising assistants, design/purchasing assistants, and marketing/sales/public relations assistants. Opportunities in the hotels include positions as front desk clerks, restaurant supervisors, hosts/hostesses, chefs, housekeeping supervisors, guest service representatives, and administrative office staff. There are also opportunities for sales assistants in the following regional sales offices: Washington, DC, New York, and Chicago. The company offers intensive in-house training for all managers and an employee educational assistance program.

Human Resources: Grace Andrew, Personnel Coordinator; Jackie Sonnabend, VP of Human Resources.

▶ Internships

Contact: Kathleen Powers, Personnel Coordinator.

Type: Salaried ($7.00/hour). Internships begin January 1 and July 1 and last six months. Internships are available for central reservations.

Duties: Airline reservationists—will confirm reservations from airline computer to travel agents, act as liaison between hotel and travel agents, and compile daily and weekly transactional reports. Hours are Monday through Thursday between 12:00 noon and 8:30 P.M., and Saturday between 9:00 A.M. and 5:00 P.M. Reservation agents—must have excellent telephone skills. This internship is ideal for someone who would like an overview of the travel industry. Interns will be trained in all aspects of hotel telemarketing sales and learn the operations of a central reservations office. This internship must be taken for course credit.

Qualifications: Airline reservationists must be familiar with airline reservation systems such as Sabre, PARS, Apollo, or System One. Courses in the travel industry are helpful.

Southwest Airlines Co.
Love Field
PO Box 36611
Dallas, TX 75235-1611
Phone: (214)904-4000

Business Description: Offers primarily short haul service to thirty-one airports in 29 cities in the midwestern, southwestern, and western regions of the United States. The average flight time is usually one hour or less.

Officers: Colleen C. Barrett, VP of Admin. & Sec.; Gary A. Barron, Exec. VP; Herbert D. Kelleher, CEO, Pres. & Chairman of the Board; Gary C. Kelly, VP of Finance & CFO; James F.

Parker, VP & General Counsel; Donald G. Valentine, VP of Mktg.

Employees: 7,760.

Average Entry-Level Hiring: 500-600.

Opportunities: Opportunities include ticket agents, ramp agents, flight attendants, reservations, clerical, accounting, secretarial, and provisioning. College degree or two years of working experience required. The company promotes from within. Training includes classroom or on-the-job instruction.

Benefits: Benefits include a profit sharing plan.

Human Resources: Ann Rhodds, VP of Human Resources.

Application Procedures: Send resume and cover letter to the attention of Human Resources.

Stevens Travel Management
432 Park Ave., S.
New York, NY 10016
Phone: (212)696-4300

Employees: 51.

Average Entry-Level Hiring: 10.

Opportunities: Expediting—must be ambitious and trustworthy. Job entails getting ticket books organized. Accounting—no experience necessary. Will be working on sales reports. Clerical—basic clerical experience. Administrative—secretarial background required.

Human Resources: Dwayne Jacobsen, Dir. of Finance & Info. Systems.

Application Procedures: Send resume and cover letter.

▶ Internships

Type: The company does not offer an internship program.

Stouffer Concourse Hotel
5400 W. Century Blvd.
Los Angeles, CA 90045
Phone: (213)216-5858

Employees: 750.

Average Entry-Level Hiring: 2-4.

Opportunities: Front desk, concierge, secretarial, and clerks.

Human Resources: John Atchison, Personnel Dir.

Application Procedures: Apply in person on Tuesday and Thursday between 9:00 A.M. and 12 noon, or Wednesday between 9:00 A.M. and 4:00 P.M. They will accept mailed resumes. Internships available through corporate office. Contact the company for more information (216)248-3600.

▶ Internships

Duties: Manager Trainee Program—college degree (any major) and interest mandatory; experience helpful but not required.

Stouffer Hotels & Resorts
29800 Bainbridge Rd.
Solon, OH 44139
Phone: (216)248-3600

Business Description: The company has 34 properties.

Average Entry-Level Hiring: 0-5.

Opportunities: Stouffer recruits and interviews students at schools that offer a four-year degree in hospitality. Graduates with different degrees are considered if they have experience in the hotel field. Training program is 10-12 months and concentrates on all areas of hotel operation.

Human Resources: Laura Kenney, Employment Mgr.

Application Procedures: Send resume and cover letter.

▶ Internships

Type: The company does not offer an internship program.

Sun Line Cruises
1 Rockefeller Plaza
New York, NY 10020
Phone: (212)397-6400
Toll-free: 800-445-6400

Employees: 370 employees per ship.

Opportunities: Hostess—must be bilingual, including English and Spanish, Italian, or French.

Application Procedures: Usually hires personnel overseas; must be bilingual.

Sunbelt Travel
909 E. Las Colinas Blvd., Ste. 200
Irving, TX 75039
Phone: (214)401-0210

Employees: 250.

Average Entry-Level Hiring: None.

Opportunities: Travel agents must have two years experience as travel agents in order to be hired.

Application Procedures: Send resume and cover letter to the attention of Human Resources.

Taj International Hotels
230 Park Ave., Ste. 466
New York, NY 10169
Phone: (212)949-2798

Business Description: The company has 42 properties worldwide.

Average Entry-Level Hiring: 0-2 per year.

Human Resources: Celine Cannon, Employment Mgr.

Application Procedures: Send resume and cover letter.

▶ Internships

Type: The company does not offer an internship program.

Thumb Fun Amusement Park
Hwy 42, PO Box 128
Fish Creek, WI 54212
Phone: (414)868-3418

Employees: 4 full time, 75 seasonal.

Human Resources: Lois, Office Mgr.

Application Procedures: Applications can be filled out on site anytime. Mainly hires seasonal employees.

▶ Internships

Type: The company does not offer an internship program.

Total Travel Management Inc.
1441 E. Maple Rd.
Troy, MI 48083
Phone: (313)528-8000

Business Description: Handles travel arrangements for corporate clients.

Employees: 250.

Average Entry-Level Hiring: 10.

Opportunities: Ticket department—opportunity to learn the business from the bottom up. Duties include running tickets, breaking them down, and preparing them for delivery. Hotel department—responsibilities include working with blocked hotel space and "sell out" situations that arise throughout the system. Frequent travelers department—keeps track of miles and awards earned by the clients. The company has four full-time trainers. There is generally a two-week, hands-on training period for all departments.

Human Resources: Paul Pinto, Human Resources Representative.

▶ **Internships**

Contact: Paul Pinto, Human Resources Representative.

Type: Offers nonpaid internships.

Application Procedure: Send resume and cover letter.

Application Deadline: None.

What to do when you're thinking about changing careers: 1) evaluate what you really want to do; 2) keep your resume and portfolio constantly updated; 3) check out organizations in your new field; 4) collect background information on your new field; 5) learn all sides of the job you want, the negatives and the positives; 6) make sure your financial and status expectations are realistic.

Source: *Better Homes and Gardens*

Trans-Mark Travel
1100 Main St., No. 1510
Kansas City, MO 64105
Phone: (816)842-1002

Employees: 120. (In 13 branches).

Average Entry-Level Hiring: 11.

Opportunities: Travel agent—must train for one year. Accounting—degree not necessary but experience is required. One-year training period for travel agents is conducted under direction of an experienced employee.

Human Resources: Debbie Williams, Human Resources Representative.

Application Procedures: Send resume and cover letter.

Trans World Airlines Inc.
100 S. Bedford Rd.
Mount Kisco, NY 10549
Phone: (914)242-3000

Business Description: Provides regularly-scheduled air transportation services.

Officers: R.B. Cozzi, VP of Mktg.; Carl C. Icahn, CEO & Chairman of the Board; Mark S. Mulvany, Sr. VP & CFO.

Employees: 32,000.

Application Procedures: Accepts unsolicited resumes. Send resume and cover letter to the attention of Personnel. Hangar 12, 217 Box 3-Z, JFK Airport, Jamaica, NY 11430.

Travaco Management Systems
2550 Som Center Rd.
Willoughby Hills, OH 44094
Phone: 800-435-1495

Average Entry-Level Hiring: Unknown.

Opportunities: Applicants must have two to three years of experience and formal training and must be familiar with the SABRE system.

Human Resources: Carol Sweda, Manager.

Application Procedures: Apply in person, or send resume and cover letter.

Travel & Transport
9777 M St.
Omaha, NE 68127
Phone: (402)592-4100

Employees: 450.

Average Entry-Level Hiring: Unknown.

Opportunities: Travel school or previous experience a must for any position. Travel consultants (agents)—making reservations for commercial or leisure accounts. Accounting—degree required for accountants, not for support staff. Secretarial. Training includes Travel Careers Institute, run by the company, trains travel agents and issues certification. The company's training staff teaches computers and automated functions.

Human Resources: Evelyn Sobzzyk, Acctg. Supervisor.

Application Procedures: Schooling or experience in travel business is required. Apply at location of interest; applications are forwarded.

Tropicana Resort & Casino

3801 Las Vegas Blvd. S.
Las Vegas, NV 89109
Phone: (702)739-2222

Business Description: Operator of hotels and/or motels.

Officers: John Chiero, President; Bill Dayton, VP of Mktg.; Al DelSarto, Dir. of Info. Systems; Mike Shaunnessy, VP of Finance.

Employees: 2,700.

Human Resources: M. Seay, Vice Pres.

United Airlines Inc.

PO Box 66100
Chicago, IL 60666
Phone: (708)952-4000
Fax: (708)952-7345

Business Description: Provider of regularly-scheduled air transportation.

Officers: J. Donald Karmazin, VP of Info. Systems; John C. Pope, CFO; John C. Pope, Exec. VP of Mktg.; Stephen M. Wolf, CEO, Pres. & Chairman of the Board.

Employees: 71,000.

Average Entry-Level Hiring: 30 management; 800 non-management.

Opportunities: Programmer trainees—college degree in computer science with knowledge of COBAL. Jobs available in Chicago and Denver. Service representatives and Reservation sales representatives—familiarity with computers. Personnel clerks—typing skills. Food service management trainees—college degree in hotel and restaurant management or nutrition. Jobs in Chicago, Denver, and San Francisco. Management trainees—college degree. Training includes classroom and on-the-job instruction.

Human Resources: Paul G. George, Sr. VP of Human Resources.

Application Procedures: Job hot-line (708)952-4090.

▶ **Internships**

Contact: Mr. Gene Krop, Employment Mgr.

Type: Salaried, summer internships are avail-

able in management information systems. **Number Available Annually:** 2.

Qualifications: College junior or senior preferred with a GPA above 3.0. Must be at least 18 years old.

Application Procedure: Send resume and cover letter.

United Inns Inc.

5100 Poplar Ave.
Suite 2300
Memphis, TN 38137
Phone: (901)767-2880

Business Description: Manufacturer of upholstered household furniture on wood frames. Engaged in the operation of eating establishments. Operator of hotels and/or motels.

Officers: J. Richard Barton, Dir. of Mktg.; Don Wm. Cockroft, President; John Magee, Dir. of Info. Systems; J. Donald Miller, VP of Finance.

Employees: 3,335.

Human Resources: George Hill, Human Resources Dir.

U.S. Air

PO Box 2720
Winston Salem, NC 27156
Phone: (919)767-5727

Average Entry-Level Hiring: None recently due to hiring freeze.

Opportunities: Opportunities include flight attendants, customer service, clerical, mechanics, and pilots—high school graduate (college preferred); public-oriented background. Most promotions from within. Flight attendants use both on-the-job and classroom instruction, while other positions use mainly on-the-job training.

Application Procedures: Send resume and cover letter.

U.S. Travel

55 Farmington
Hartford, CT 06105
Phone: (203)278-4000

Human Resources: Lilly Simons, Human Resources Representative.

▶ **Internships**

Contact: Lilly Simons, Human Resources Representative.

Type: The company may offer an internship program. Contact the company for more information.

Application Procedure: Contact the company for more information.

U.S. Virgin Islands Division of Tourism

PO Box 6400
St. Thomas, VI 00804
Phone: (809)774-8784

Employees: 20.

Average Entry-Level Hiring: Unknown.

Human Resources: Eric Dawson, Comm. of Econ. Development & Agriculture.

Application Procedures: Send resume. It will be directed to specific department. Departments include Public Relations, Tourism, Commissioners Office. Personnel department works out of Virgin Islands.

▶ Internships

Type: The company does not offer an internship program.

In 1992 Chicago-based UAL, the parent of United Airlines, instituted a 4-year, $15.8 billion spending program for 223 fuel-efficient Boeing planes. This is part of a plan to make United a global leader. The goal is to have one seamless airline that can feed in customers from small-town airports and take them across the country or around the globe.

Source: *Forbes*

US Travel System, Inc.

1776 Yorktown
Houston, TX 77056
Phone: (713)968-5900

Employees: 140.

Average Entry-Level Hiring: 5 or less.

Opportunities: Travel school is required for all entry-level positions. Entry-level person runs errands, does mailings, and posts and tears tickets.

Human Resources: Bruce Arnold, Employment Admin.; Maren Dreyling.

Application Procedures: Currently a hiring freeze is in effect.

Vagabond Hotels Inc.

6170 E. Cornerstone
San Diego, CA 92121-3710
Phone: (619)535-0390

Business Description: Operates 40 hotels in California, Nevada, and Arizona.

Officers: Les Biggins, VP of Finance; Tom Evans, President; Jane Innes, VP of Mktg.

Employees: 150.

Human Resources: Marianne Dowdy, Human Resources Dir.

Application Procedures: Contact the personnel director at each hotel.

Van Alphen Travel Service, Inc.

15 Fishers Rd., Ste. 200
Pittsford, NY 14534

Employees: 70.

Average Entry-Level Hiring: 2.

Opportunities: Opportunities for college or travel school graduates include starting as messengers or ticket processors. Depending on the individual's capacity, company demand, and openings available, it could take from one to three years to move up to travel agent. The company has an in-house training staff. The length of training depends on the individual. Training teaches computerized and automated aspects of the agent's function.

▶ Internships

Contact: Norman C. Barlow.

Type: Internships available for college credits. **Number Available Annually:** As needed.

Duties: The company hires students who need hours to complete school training. The student's primary objective should be to become familiar with operations on various levels.

Application Procedure: Send resume and cover letter.

Virgin Atlantic

96 Morton St.
New York, NY 10014
Phone: (212)206-6612

Employees: 200-300 (United States).

Average Entry-Level Hiring: Unknown.

Opportunities: Opportunities include reservations and secretarial positions—college is preferred but not mandatory. Positions are mainly located in New Jersey, New York, and Miami. The company promotes from within. Training includes classroom instruction.

Application Procedures: Send resume and cover letter. Applications and/or resumes kept on file for three to six months.

Wagons-Lits Travel
30 Commerce Rd.
Stamford, CT 06904-2180
Phone: (203)967-3200
Toll-free: 800-888-7397

Employees: 525.

Average Entry-Level Hiring: As needed.

Opportunities: Applicants should have some backgroung in the travel industry. Training includes hands-on experience as a ticket agent.

Human Resources: Marilyn Adelbung, Human Resources Representative.

Application Procedures: Places newspaper advertisements for certain openings. Send resume and cover letter.

Waldorf Astoria
301 Park Ave.
New York, NY 10022
Phone: (212)355-3000

Employees: 2,000.

Average Entry-Level Hiring: Unknown.

Opportunities: Management training is available through Hilton Corp.

Application Procedures: Apply in person, or send resume and cover letter to the attention of Employment Manager.

▶ **Internships**

Type: The company does not offer an internship program.

Walt Disney World Resort
PO Box 10090
Lake Buena Vista, FL 32830
Phone: (407)828-2850

Average Entry-Level Hiring: The company reports that all entry-level positions are filled by in-house applicants.

Opportunities: Provides a 13-week training period for animators and artists. Provides a six-month hospitality training period.

Human Resources: Diane Bradley, Manager.

Application Procedures: Send resume and cover letter; state position sought. Resumes are kept on file for one year.

Washington, D.C. Convention & Visitors Association
1212 New York Ave., NW
Washington, DC 20005
Phone: (202)789-7013

Employees: 38.

Average Entry-Level Hiring: 3.

Opportunities: Marketing, communications, public relations, journalism—college degree required. "We don't mind hiring people right out of college."

Human Resources: Jill Ransom, Human Resources Mgr.

Application Procedures: Send resume and cover letter.

▶ **Internships**

Type: The company may offer an internship program.

Westin Hotel Co.
Westin Bldg.
Seattle, WA 98121
Phone: (206)443-5248

Business Description: Operates 65 hotels worldwide.

Officers: Michael Corr, Sr. VP; Larry Magnan, CEO & Pres.; Ray Whitty, CFO.

Employees: 28,000.

Average Entry-Level Hiring: Unknown.

Opportunities: Westin offers a "learner-controlled" management training program that is tailored to the needs of the individual. It is a skills-specific program in which trainees choose an area of concentration, such as food and beverage, front office, human resources, cost control, accounting, housekeeping, or sales and marketing. A hotel degree is preferred, but not required. Practical experience is as important as education.

Human Resources: Jim Purvis, Human Resources Dir.

Application Procedures: Contact the college relations manager.

Westin Hotel, Copley Place
10 Huntington Ave.
Boston, MA 02116
Phone: (617)262-9600

Employees: 800.

Average Entry-Level Hiring: 100-200.

Opportunities: Entry-level positions are primarily in Rooms Division and Food and Beverage. All require guest contact. Front office agent—college degree, typing skills required. Concierge—must be bilingual, have a college degree, and be familiar with Boston. Luggage attendant. Garage attendant—must have knowledge of standard shift autos and a Massachusetts drivers license. Linen room attendant—previous housekeeping experience required. Greeter—knowledge of food and beverages. Server—previous serving exprience. Refreshment center attendant. Cashier—cash handling experience. The company provides complete training, depending on department, lasting two weeks or more. Has a six-week course for new managers. Other training includes a one-day session on guest relations and one-day supervisory workshops.

Human Resources: Janet Breen, Employment Contact.

Environment fervor has given rise to a fast-growing low-environmental-impact travel business, sometimes called ecotourism. The idea is to gain an appreciation of undeveloped areas, which are disappearing fast, without harming them. The ecotourism business isn't only about conservation. Kurt Kutay, a co-founder of Wildland Journeys, says most of his customers are mainly after adventure.

Source: *Fortune*

Application Procedures: Applications are accepted Tuesdays and Thursdays between 9:00 A.M. and 1:00 P.M.

▶ Internships

Type: The company does not offer an internship program.

Westin Hotel Seattle
1900 5th Ave.
Seattle, WA 98101
Phone: (206)728-1000

Employees: 700. The company holds a job fair once a year. Apply in person, or send resume and cover letter.

Average Entry-Level Hiring: 100.

Opportunities: College graduates with a degree in hotel management or business administration preferred. Employees may apply for the management training program. Two phases include a general overview of all departments, and specific work in one department. Program lasts one year.

Human Resources: Lynn Elle-Caudill, Human Resources Representative.

▶ Internships

Type: Summer and semester, Salaried internships available for the following departments: public relations, marketing, or you may create your own program.

Application Procedure: Contact the company for more information.

Westin St. Francis
335 Powell St.
San Francisco, CA 94102
Phone: (415)397-7000

Employees: 1,000.

Average Entry-Level Hiring: 30-50.

Opportunities: Food and beverage, rooms, housekeeping—prefer hotel school graduate, but not required. Company promotes from within. Numerous other entry-level positions exist, from dishwasher to sales coordinator. Offers a one-year management training program through corporate office.

Human Resources: Sarah Williams, Human Resources.

Application Procedures: They accept applications on Monday, Tuesday, and Thursday between 9:00 A.M. and 12 noon. You may also send in a resume, but they prefer applications.

▶ Internships

Contact: Jerry Evans, Human Resources.

Type: Non-salaried, (but occassionally paid) Summer semester internships available in human resources and in other departments on an as need basis. **Number Available Annually:** Varies.

Duties: First-hand experience in different departments of the hotel—could be anything from clerical to special project assignments.

Application Procedure: Send resume and cover letter.

Application Deadline: Two to three months before starting date. **Decision Date:** Within one week.

The Westin William Penn Hotel

530 William Penn Pl.
Pittsburgh, PA 15219
Phone: (412)281-7100

Employees: 435.

Average Entry-Level Hiring: 50-100.

Opportunities: Maids, dishwashers, and room servers (latter may be promoted to front office). Front desk clerk—must have degree from travel school or experience. Management trainee positions available in all departments.

Application Procedures: Applications accepted on Monday-Wednesday between 9:00 A.M. and 11:30 P.M. Places newspaper advertisements for certain openings in Pittsburgh newspapers.

▶ Internships

Type: The company does not offer an internship program.

World Travel and Incentives, Inc.

701 4th Ave. S., No. 1500
Minneapolis, MN 55415
Phone: (612)333-0920
Fax: (612)333-9627

Average Entry-Level Hiring: Varies.

Opportunities: Entry-level people go through a three-step ladder: 1. distribution department—match airline tickets with invoices and handle mail; 2. support desk—book hotels for agents; 3. travel agents—handle accounts from beginning to end. Some new hires are very quickly promoted, which increases the need to fill entry-level positions. Normally, the company prefers employees to remain in their new position for

six months, although employees will be promoted sooner if merited.

Human Resources: Colleen Good, Training Specialist.

Application Procedures: Accepts unsolicited resumes. Recruits at college campuses.

Wyndham Franklin Plaza Hotel

2 Franklin Plaza
Philadelphia, PA 19103
Phone: (215)448-2000

Employees: 450.

Average Entry-Level Hiring: Unknown.

Opportunities: Candidates without experience: line-level front desk, and reservations. Experienced candidates: Management Development Program, leading to direct placement as an assistant manager. Those with a college degree get promoted faster once hired.

Human Resources: Anne Lutz, Employment Mgr.

Application Procedures: Interviews conducted on Tuesday from 10:00 A.M. and 12 noon, and Wednesday between 1:00 P.M. and 4:00 P.M. The company requests that applicants apply in person.

▶ Internships

Contact: Anne Lutz, Employment Mgr.

Type: There isn't a standard internship program in place at this time; however, internships are granted on an individual basis.

Application Procedure: Send resume and cover letter.

Application Deadline: Hires throughout the year.

Wyndham Hotels & Resorts

3200 Trammell Crow Center
2001 Ross Ave.
Dallas, TX 75201-2997
Phone: (214)978-4578

Opportunities: Entry-level positions are available in sales, rooms, food and beverages, engineering, catering, accounting, and human resources. The company employs 5,000 people nationwide and has two entry-level positions available per Garden Hotel each year and several more at their full-service hotels each year.

Training is handled by department managers, general managers, and by the corporate human resources department. Cross training will be provided in all departments for employees. Time spent in each department will vary depending on previous background and interests. The company is committed to promoting from within.

▶ Internships

Contact: Elizabeth Brannon, Mgr. of Staffing & Development.

Type: Offers paid internships in sales, rooms, food and beverage, housekeeping, engineering, human resources, and front desk. Internships are available year-round and last one semester or quarter. **Number Available Annually:** 6.

Duties: Will function as a regular employee and be supervised by a department manager or the General Manager. There is a chance for cross-training in other departments of the hotel.

Application Procedure: Send resume and cover letter to contact.

Application Deadline: Applications are accepted on an ongoing basis.

Wynfrey Hotel at Riverchase Galleria

1000 Riverchase Galleria
Birmingham, AL 35244
Phone: (205)987-1600
Fax: (205)988-4597

Average Entry-Level Hiring: Unknown.

Application Procedures: Send resume and cover letter or apply in person. If applying in person, be prepared for same-day interview.

▶ Internships

Contact: Laura Fleming, Human Resources Mgr.

Type: No formal internship program is available. However, interns are hired on an as-needed basis.

Zenith Travel, Inc.

16 E. 34th St.
New York, NY 10016
Phone: (212)889-6969
Fax: (212)251-1492

Average Entry-Level Hiring: Does not hire entry-level staff.

Application Procedures: Send resume and cover letter. For more information, contact Marsha at (212)545-5680.

Additional Companies

Arvida Co.
PO Box 100
Boca Raton, FL 33429
Phone: (407)479-1100

Bally's Grand Hotel and Casino
PO Box 1737
Atlantic City, NJ 08404
Phone: (609)347-7111

Bally's Las Vegas
3645 Las Vegas Blvd., S.
Las Vegas, NV 89109
Phone: (702)739-4848

Bally's Park Place, Inc.
Park Pl. and Boardwalk
Atlantic City, NJ 08401
Phone: (609)340-2000

Beehive Tours and Travel
1325 S. Main St.
Salt Lake City, UT 84115
Phone: (801)487-1731

Bermuda Star Line Inc.
1066 Teaneck Rd.
Teaneck, NJ 07666
Phone: (201)837-0400

California Hotel and Casino
12 Ogden St.
Las Vegas, NV 89109
Phone: (702)732-6111

Dayton's Travel Service
700 Nicolet Mall
Minneapolis, MN 55402
Phone: (612)375-3452

Del Webb Corp.
2231 E. Camelback Rd.
Phoenix, AZ 85016
Phone: (602)488-6800

Desert Inn Hotel/Casino
3145 Las Vegas Blvd.
Las Vegas, NV 89109
Phone: (703)733-4444

Discover the World
14455 N. Hayden
Scottsdale, AZ 85260
Phone: (602)998-5566

Dunes Hotels and Casinos
4045 Spencer
Las Vegas, NV 89119
Phone: (702)732-7474

El Rancho Hotel
2755 Las Vegas Blvd.
Las Vegas, NV 89109
Phone: (702)796-2222

Elsinore Corp.
202 E. Fremont St.
Las Vegas, NV 89101
Phone: (702)385-4011

First Family of Travel
2809 Butterfield
Oak Brook, IL 60521
Phone: (312)571-5500

Getz Travel Inc.
4720 Kingsway
Indianapolis, IN 46205
Phone: (317)251-9555

Harley Hotels, Inc.
2100 Terminal Tower
Cleveland, OH 44113
Phone: (216)623-3900

Hawes International Travel Service
20 E. 46th St.
New York, NY 10017
Phone: (212)682-4088

Kyo-Ya Co. Ltd
255 Kalakaua Ave.
Honolulu, HI 96815
Phone: (808)922-4422

Maupintour Inc.
PO Box 807
Lawrence, KS 66044
Phone: (913)843-1211

McGiffin and Co., Inc.
PO Box 3
Jacksonville, FL 32201
Phone: (904)353-1741

MGM Grand, Inc.
9755 Wilshire Blvd.
Beverly Hills, CA 90212
Phone: (213)271-3793

Miller Travel Ltd.
901 French St.
Erie, PA 16501
Phone: (814)456-2024

Pacifico Creative Service
770 Wilshire Blvd.
Los Angeles, CA 90017
Phone: (213)239-2400

Riviera Hotel and Casino
2901 Las Vegas Blvd.
Las Vegas, NV 89109
Phone: (702)734-5110

Safaris Inc.
5350 Riley St.
San Diego, CA 92110
Phone: (619)293-7870

Sahara Resorts
2535 Las Vegas Blvd.
Las Vegas, NV 89109
Phone: (702)737-2111

Showboat-Atlantic City
801 Boardwalk
Atlantic City, NJ 08401
Phone: (609)343-4000

Somes World of Travel
62 Rte. 10
East Hanover, NJ 07936
Phone: (201)884-9000

Stardust Hotel and Casino
3000 Las Vegas Blvd., S.
Las Vegas, NV 89109
Phone: (702)732-6111

Texas Air
333 Clay St.
Houston, TX 77002
Phone: (713)658-9588

Trade Wind Tours Ltd.
PO Box 2198
Honolulu, HI 96805
Phone: (808)923-2071

Travelcenter Inc.
2000 W. International Airport
Anchorage, AK 99502
Phone: (907)266-6622

Union Plaza Hotel/Casino
PO Box 760
Las Vegas, NV 89125
Phone: (702)386-2110

Vacations to Go, Inc.
2411 Fountain
Houston, TX 77057
Phone: (713)974-2121

Woodside Management System
131 Tremont St.
Boston, MA 02111
Phone: (617)426-7661

World Travel Bureau Inc.
PO Box 1228
Santa Ana, CA 92702
Phone: (714)835-8111

Xenia International Travel
1026 W. Washington
San Diego, CA 92103
Phone: (619)291-2815

CAREER
RESOURCES

Career Resources

The Career Resources chapter covers additional sources of job-related information that will aid you in your job search. It includes full, descriptive listings for sources of help wanted ads, professional associations, employment agencies and search firms, career guides, professional and trade periodicals, and basic reference guides and handbooks. Each of these sections is arranged alphabetically by organization, publication, or service name. For complete details on the information provided in this chapter, consult the introductory material at the front of this directory.

Sources of Help Wanted Ads

A/C Flyer
McGraw-Hill Inc.
7205 Corporate Center Dr., Ste. 301
Miami, FL 33126
Phone: (305)591-0656
Toll-free: 800-327-2052
Fax: (305)592-0294

Monthly. Publication covering the aviation industry. Features a broker/dealer directory, and news of the aircraft resale industry.

ADNET
National On-Line Classified, Inc.
1465 Andrews Ln.
East Meadow, NY 11554
Phone: (516)481-9222

Contains personnel and consulting firm listings and job seeker profiles. Enables the user to match employers seeking permanent and temporary personnel with entry-level and experienced job candidates, consultants, personnel recruiters, and technical consulting firms. Employer entries typically include company name, address, benefits, environment, and technical information. Job seeker listings generally contain candidate's name, skills, experience, and specific job criteria.

Advance Job Listings
PO Box 900
New York, NY 10020

Affirmative Action Register
Affirmative Action, Inc.
8356 Olive Blvd.
St. Louis, MO 63132
Phone: (314)991-1335
Toll-free: 800-537-0655
Fax: (314)997-1788

Monthly. Publication containing listings of

vacant administrative jobs in business, industry, government, and schools. Designed to aid advertising professionals in complying with equal employment guidelines.

Air Jobs Digest
World Air Data
PO Box 70127
Washington, DC 20088

Tim and Nina Zagat publish the Zagat restaurant guides, slim red volumes full of pithy comments that, over the past decade, have become to food lovers what AAA guides are to motorists. The guides started as a photocopied one-page set of comments on New York restaurants; now the line includes 26 cities and netted revenues of approximately $3 million in 1991.

Source: *Business Week*

Air Transport World
Penton Publishing
1100 Superior Ave.
Cleveland, OH 44114
Phone: (216)696-7000
Fax: (216)696-1267

Monthly. Magazine covering the international airline industry. Reports on such topics as legislative, financial, and technical developments, and industry trends.

Airline Executive
Communication Channels, Inc.
6255 Barfield Rd.
Atlanta, GA 30328
Phone: (404)256-9800
Fax: (404)256-3116

The AOPA Pilot
Aircraft Owners and Pilots Assn.
421 Aviation Way
Frederick, MD 21701
Phone: (301)695-2000
Fax: (301)695-2375

Monthly. $18.00/year; $2.00/issue. Magazine for general aviation pilots and aircraft owners who are members of the association.

Black Careers
Project Magazine, Inc.
PO Box 8214
Philadelphia, PA 19101
Phone: (215)387-1600

Bimonthly. Magazine focusing on black men and women looking for job opportunities in government, industry, and commerce. Designed to serve mainly high school and college counselors, college graduates currently working in industry, and college seniors in black colleges.

The Black Collegian
1240 S. Broad St.
New Orleans, LA 70125-2091
Phone: (504)821-5694
Fax: (504)821-5713

Quarterly. $10.00/year; $5.00/year for students; $2.50/issue. Career and job-oriented publication for black college students.

Black Employment & Education Magazine
Hamdani Communications, Inc.
13428 Maxella Ave., Ste. 283
Marina Del Ray, CA 90292
Toll-free: 800-726-3907

7x/year. Magazine covering career opportunities for black people in the United States and abroad.

The Bottomline
The International Assn. of Hospitality Accountants
PO Box 27649
Austin, TX 78755-2649
Phone: (512)346-5680
Fax: (512)346-5760

Bimonthly. Publication covering the hospitality industry. Features articles on such topics as accounting, economics, finance, management, and technology.

Business and Commercial Aviation
4 International Dr., Ste. 260
Rye Brook, NY 10573-1065
Phone: (914)939-1184

Monthly. $36.00/year. Magazine focusing on operation and maintenance of business and commercial aircraft.

Business Travel News

CMP Publications, Inc.
600 Community Dr.
Manhasset, NY 11030
Phone: (516)562-5772
Fax: (516)562-5465

27x/year. Publication serving the travel industry, including travel agents, and corporate executives who plan travel activities. Covers market trends, international business travel, and general news of airlines, hotels, car rentals, and more.

California Inntouch

Naylor Publications, Inc.
9812 Old Winery Pl., Ste. 1
Sacramento, CA 95827
Phone: (916)363-1913
Toll-free: 800-873-4800
Fax: (916)363-1934

Bimonthly. Publication featuring news and information for hospitality professionals. Covers such topics as legislation, real estate developments, and market trends.

Canadian Hotel & Restaurant

Maclean-Hunter Ltd.
Maclean-Hunter Bldg.
777 Bay St.
Toronto, ON, Canada M5W 1A7
Phone: (416)596-5782
Fax: (416)593-3189

Monthly (except July). Magazine covering the hotel and restaurant industry in Canada.

Canadian Travel Press Weekly

Baxter Publishing
310 Dupont St.
Toronto, ON, Canada M5R 1V9
Phone: (416)968-2377

46x/year. Publication covering the Canadian travel industry. Includes such features as marketing information, tour package reviews, profiles of travel professionals, and cruise and airline schedules.

Career Opportunity Update

Career Research Systems, Inc.
PO Box 28799
Santa Ana, CA 92799-8799
Phone: (714)556-1200
Fax: (714)556-6548

Monthly, except December. $72.00/year;

$24.00/three issues; $9.00/issue. Covers about 100 employers nationwide who anticipate having technical, professional or management employment opportunities in the coming six months. Consists of five regional editions for Pacific, Western, Midwestern, Southern, and Eastern states. Entries include: Company name, address, phone, name of contact, date established, number of employees, description of the company and its products, and general description of openings expected. Arranged alphabetically and geographically.

According to the Bureau of Labor Statistics, the total labor force in the U.S. is projected to grow by about 1.3% per year between 1992 and 2005, down from about 2% per annum in the past 15 years. At the projected rate, the number of people employed in 2005 will be a little over 142 million, up from 123 million in 1992.

Source: *Forbes*

Career Placement Registry (CPR)

Career Placement Registry, Inc.
302 Swann Ave.
Alexandria, VA 22301
Phone: (703)683-1085
Fax: (703)683-0246

Contains brief resumes of job candidates currently seeking employment. Comprises two files, covering college and university seniors and recent graduates, and alumni, executives, and others who have already acquired substantial work experience. Entries typically include applicant name, address, telephone number, degree level, function, language skills, name of school, major field of study, minor field of study, occupational preference, date available, city/area preference, special skills, citizenship status, employer name, employer address, description of duties, position/title, level of education, civil service register, security clearance type/availability, willingness to relocate, willingness to travel, salary expectation, and overall work experience. Available online through DIALOG Information Services, Inc.

Career Woman
Equal Opportunity Publications, Inc.
44 Broadway
Greenlawn, NY 11740
Phone: (516)261-8899
Fax: (516)261-8935

3x/year. Magazine addressing affirmative action issues for career-seeking college students. Covers such topics as career guidance, and opportunities in banking, communications, insurance, nursing, the government, and industry. Offers a free resume service.

Catering Today
ProTech Publishing and Communications, Inc.
PO Box 222
Santa Claus, IN 47579
Phone: (812)937-4464

Bimonthly. Magazine covering the catering industry in the United States. Features include computer information, new products and equipment, book reviews, recipes, and market trends.

CHRIE Communique
Council on Hotel, Restaurant and Institutional Education (CHRIE)
311 1st St., NW
Washington, DC 20001
Phone: (202)628-0038

Semimonthly. $50.00/year. Newsletter containing information and features on hospitality education, including employment opportunities for hospitality educators.

Club Industry
Sportscape, Inc.
492 Old Connecticut Path, 3rd Fl.
Framingham, MA 01701
Phone: (508)872-2021
Toll-free: 800-541-7706

Monthly. Magazine serving the interests of health club, golf, tennis, country club, hotel club, and recretional spa operators. Features include market trends, program design, finance, operation, and equipment reviews.

Club Management
Finan Publishing Co., Inc.
8730 Big Bend Blvd.
St. Louis, MO 63119
Phone: (314)961-6644

9x/year. Publication covering issues of interest to club operators. Includes such topics as food and beverage management and service, purchasing, inventory, cost control systems, and party ideas.

College Recruitment Database (CRD)
Executive Telecom System, Inc.
College Park N.
9585 Valparaiso Ct.
Indianapolis, IN 46268
Phone: (317)872-2045

Contains resume information for graduating undergraduate and graduate students in all disciplines at all colleges and universities for recruitment purposes. Enables the employer to create and maintain a private "skill" file meeting selection criteria. Typical entries include student identification number, home and campus addresses and telephone numbers, schools, degrees, dates of attendance, majors, grade point averages, date available, job objective, curricular statement, activities/honors, and employment history. Available online through the Human Resource Information Network.

Collegiate Career Woman
Equal Opportunity Publications, Inc.
44 Broadway
Greenlawn, NY 11740

Three times/year. $25.00/year. Recruitment magazine for women. Provides free resume service and assists women in identifying employers and applying for positions.

Community Jobs
Community Careers Resource Center
1601 Connecticut Ave., NW, 6th Fl.
Washington, DC 20009
Phone: (202)667-0661
Fax: (202)387-7915

Monthly. $30.00/year to institutions; $20.00/year to nonprofit organizations; $18.00/year to individuals; $3.50/issue. Covers: Jobs and internships available with nonprofit organizations active in issues such as the environment, foreign policy, consumer advocacy, housing, education, etc. Entries include: Position title, name, address, and phone of contact; description, responsibilities, requirements, salary. Arrangement: Geographical.

Commuter Air
6255 Barfield Rd.
Atlanta, GA 30328
Phone: (404)256-9800
Fax: (404)256-3116

Monthly. $27.00/year.

Commuter World
The Shephard Press Ltd.
14 S. Hill Rd.
Colonia, NJ 07067
Phone: (908)388-4245
Toll-free: 800-873-2147

6x/year. Publication covering the state of, the problems, and the trends of the commuter aircraft industry.

Convene
Professional Convention Management Assn.
100 Vestavia Office Park, Ste. 220
Birmingham, AL 35216
Phone: (205)823-7262

10x/year. Publication covering news and information of interest to convention and meeting planners of non-profit organizations and associations.

Corporate Travel
Miller Freeman Inc.
1515 Broadway
New York, NY 10036
Phone: (212)869-1300
Toll-free: 800-869-1300
Fax: (212)302-6273

Monthly. Magazine focusing on business travel news and information.

Equal Opportunity Magazine
44 Broadway
Greenlawn, NY 11740

Three times/year. $13.00/year. Minority recruitment magazine. Includes a resume service.

Exhibit Review
Phoenix Communications, Inc.
3800 SW Cedar Hills Blvd., Ste. 251
Beaverton, OR 97005
Phone: (503)643-2783
Fax: (503)644-7107

Quarterly. Publication listing consumer and trade shows from 45 different industries.

Flight Training
Flight Training, Ltd.
405 Main St.
Parkville, MO 64152
Phone: (816)741-1165
Fax: (816)741-6458

Monthly. Publication for and about pilots. Features articles on flight training, regulations, techniques, and avionics.

Florida Hotel & Motel Journal
Florida Hotel & Motel Assn., Inc.
Accomodations, Inc.
PO Box 1529
Tallahassee, FL 32302
Phone: (904)224-2888
Toll-free: 800-476-3462
Fax: (904)222-3462

Monthly. Magazine covering the Florida lodging industry. Includes marketing ideas, news of insurance and security, technological developments, travel trends, housekeeping, and more.

> **S**ome companies are using "behavioral interviewing" to gain greater insight into job candidates. By asking the interviewee to address hypothetical situations relating to the job, interviewers go behind the resume to assess likely performance. "What you get on a resume are education and experience," explains Jim Kennedy, president of Management Team. "You want to find out how a person is going to do a job, not only whether he has the credentials to do it."
>
> Source: *Business Week*

Flying
Hachette Publications, Inc.
500 W. Putnam Ave., 2nd Fl.
Greenwich, CT 06830
Phone: (203)622-2700
Fax: (203)622-2725

Monthly. $18.00/yr. General aviation magazine.

Food Production/Management
CTI Publications, Inc.
2619 Maryland Ave.
Baltimore, MD 21218
Phone: (410)467-3338
Fax: (410)467-7434

Monthly. $25.00/year; $40.00/year for foreign subscribers.

Hispanic Times Magazine
Hispanic Times Enterprises
PO Box 579
Winchester, CA 92396
Phone: (714)926-2119

Bimonthly. Magazine focusing on issues of interest to Hispanic and American Indian college students and professionals.

L'Hospitalite'
Communications Vero Inc.
1600 Henri Bourassa O., Ste. 420
Montreal, PQ, Canada H3M 3E2
Phone: (514)332-8376
Fax: (514)332-2666

6x/year. Publication covering the restaurant, hospitality, and food service industries.

> **T**he roots of takeover trends in the airline industry go back to the late 1970s, when deregulation began a decade of competitive warfare. A handful of megacarriers emerged from that long struggle with more than 90% of the U.S. market and considerable weaponry to maintain their sway, including huge fleets, elaborate maintenance centers and long-term airport leases, sophisticated computer reservations systems, frequent-flier programs, financial control of commuter airlines to feed traffic into central hubs, and marketing deals with foreign carriers.
>
> Source: *Fortune*

Hotel & Resort Industry
Coastal Communications Corp.
488 Madison Ave.
New York, NY 10022
Phone: (212)888-1500
Fax: (212)888-8008

Monthly. Publication covering issues of interest to managers and operators of hotels, motels, resorts, and conference centers.

Inn Touch
Wisconsin Innkeepers Assn.
509 W. Wisconsin Ave., Ste. 622
Milwaukee, WI 53203
Phone: (414)271-2851
Fax: (414)271-3050

Monthly. Magazine covering the Wisconsin hospitality industry.

The Job Finder: A Checklist of Openings for Administrative and Governmental Research Employment in the West
Western Governmental Research Assn.
California State University, Long Beach
c/o Graduate Center for Public Policy and Administration
1250 Bellflower Blvd.
Long Beach, CA 90840

Monthly. $20.00/year. Listing of openings in city, county, and state government in 13 western states.

Job Opportunities Bulletin
Airline Employee Association
5600 S. Central Ave.
Chicago, IL 60638
Phone: (312)767-3333

Monthly. Free to members. Contains information on opportunities in the airline industry. Provides information on job responsibilities, requirements, benefits, salary, and application process as available.

Job Ready
Quantum Publishing Inc.
1211 N. Westshore Blvd., Ste. 102
Tampa, FL 33607
Phone: (813)874-5550
Fax: (813)286-3649

Monthly. Magazine concerning disabled people in the workforce. Designed to help human resource professionals understand disabilities, and with interviewing techniques, and adaptive technology.

Jobs Available
PO Box 1222
Newton, IA 50208-1222
Phone: (515)791-9019

Biweekly. $18.00/year. Lists a wide range of employment opportunities in the public sector. Published in Midwest/Eastern and Western editions.

Journal of Career Planning and Employment

College Placement Council, Inc.
62 Highland Ave.
Bethlehem, PA 18017
Phone: (215)868-1421
Fax: (215)868-0208

Quarterly. $65.00/year. Can be used to provide assistance to students in planning and implementing a job search.

Liberal Arts Jobs

Peterson's
PO Box 2123
Princeton, NJ 08543-2123
Phone: (609)243-9111

Nadler, Burton Jay. 1989. $9.95. 110 pages. Presents a list of the top 20 fields for liberal arts majors, covering more than 300 job opportunities. Discusses strategies for going after those jobs, including guidance on the language of a successful job search, informational interviews, and making networking work.

Mature Group Traveler

Meetings Info-Resources Inc.
1 Atlantic St., No. 413
Stamford, CT 06901
Phone: (203)975-1416
Fax: (203)975-1418

Quarterly. Publication offering news and information for travel planners for senior or 50-plus groups.

The Meeting Manager

Meeting Planners International, INFOMART
1950 Stemmons Fwy., Ste. 5018
Dallas, TX 75207
Phone: (214)746-5222
Fax: (214)746-5248

Monthly. Publication designed to help meeting managers plan activities, conferences, seminars, and trade shows.

Meeting News

Miller Freeman, Inc.
Gralla Publications
1515 Broadway
New York, NY 10036
Phone: (212)869-1300
Fax: (212)302-6273

Monthly. Magazine designed to help meeting managers plan trade shows, conventions, and incentive travel programs.

Minority Employment Journal

C.L. Lovick & Associates
1341 Ocean Ave., Ste. 228
Santa Monica, CA 90401
Phone: (213)338-8444
Fax: (213)338-0901

Bimonthly. Publication covering career opportunities in the aerospace, computer, financial, manufacturing, and retail industries for executives, community leaders, and minority professionals.

> With big corporations no longer rewarding loyalty and performance with lifetime guarantees of employment, individuals are transforming themselves into itinerant professionals who sell their human capital on the open market. "Instead of climbing up the ladder, people now have to develop a portfolio of skills and products that they can sell directly to a series of customers," explains Charles Handy, visiting professor at the London Business School and author of *The Age of Unreason*, a book about the changing nature of work. "We are all becoming people with portfolio careers."
>
> Source: *Business Week*

The National Ad Search

National Ad Search, Inc.
PO Box 2983
Milwaukee, WI 53201

Fifty issues/year. $215.00/year; $135.00/six months; $75.00/three months. Contains listings of "over 2,000 current career opportunities from over 72 employment markets."

National Employment Listing Service Bulletin

Sam Houston State University
College of Criminal Justice
Huntsville, TX 77341

Monthly. $30.00/year for individuals; $65.00/year for institutions/agencies.

National Job Market

Careers Information, Inc.
PO Box 1411
Alexandria, VA 22313-2011
Phone: (703)548-8500

Biweekly. $150.00/year; $6.50/issue. Career advancement magazine for professionals, containing articles and job listings.

If you've been out of school a while, you can still obtain access to career counseling through your local university or community college at no or low cost. Some programs offer group sessions, most include standardized tests as well as seminars and workshops. Some university alumni clubs also deliver high-quality career-counselling services.

Source: *Working Woman*

Nation's Restaurant News

Lebhar-Friedman, Inc.
425 Park Ave.
New York, NY 10022
Phone: (212)756-5000

Weekly. Publication serving the commercial and institutional food service industry, including hotels and motels, restaurants, government institutions, schools and colleges, hospitals, and health and welfare facilities.

Networking News

Networking Unlimited, Inc.
c/o Alina Novak
337 44th St., No. 6
Brooklyn, NY 11220-1105

Quarterly. $10.00/year. Newsletter concerned with career management, change, skills, problems, and prospects. Carries features about networking as a career strategy and practical articles on leadership and communication in business and professional spheres. Recurring features include reports of conferences, panel discussions, and speakers.

New England Employment Week

PO Box 806
Rockport, ME 04856

New England Minority News

New England Minority News, Inc.
46 Battles St.
Hartford, CT 06120
Phone: (203)549-0809
Fax: (203)293-2402

Biweekly. Magazine aiming to help the minority community and business and government communicate. Highlights business and employment opportunities.

OAG Travel Planner Hotel & Motel Redbook (Pacific Asia Edition)

Official Airline Guides
2000 Clearwater Dr.
Oak Brook, IL 60521
Phone: (708)574-6000
Fax: (708)574-6373

Quarterly. Publication covering news and information of interest to travelers in the Pacific area. Lists hotels, car rental companies, and railroads; gives contact information of many cities in the Pacific area; provides maps and a calendar of events.

Occupational Outlook Quarterly

U.S. Government Printing Office
Superintendent of Documents
Washington, DC 20402-9322
Phone: (202)783-3238
Fax: (202)512-2250

Quarterly. Contains articles and information about career choices and job opportunities in a wide range of occupations.

Opportunity Report

Job Bank, Inc.
PO Box 6028
Lafayette, IN 47903
Phone: (317)447-0549

Biweekly. $252.00/year. Lists 3,000-4,000 positions across the United States, from entry-level to upper management, in a variety of occupational fields. Ads are derived from newspapers, primarily in growth markets. Ads contain position description, employment requirements, and contact information.

Plane and Pilot

Werner Publishing Corp.
12121 Wilshire Blvd., Ste. 1220
Los Angeles, CA 90025-1175
Phone: (310)820-1500
Fax: (310)826-5008

Monthly. $16.95/year.

The Private Pilot

PO Box 57900
Los Angeles, CA 90057-0900
Phone: (213)385-2222

Monthly. $17.97/year.

Resort and Hotel Management

2431 Morena Blvd.
San Diego, CA 92110

Restaurant News of the Rockies

D & H Communications
8962 E. Hampden Ave.
PO Box 156
Denver, CO 80231-4911
Phone: (303)751-5788

Monthly. Covers news and information of interest to the Rocky Mountain region food service industry, including C-stores, healthcare, in-plant, hotels, military, and restaurants.

Restaurants and Institutions

Cahners Publishing Co.
1350 E. Touhy Ave.
PO Box 5080
Des Plaines, IL 60017-5080
Phone: (708)635-8800
Fax: (708)635-6856

Biweekly. $99.95/year. Magazine focusing on food service and lodging.

Rotor Magazine

Helicopter Assn. International
1619 Duke St.
Alexandria, VA 22314
Phone: (703)683-4646
Fax: (703)683-4745

Quarterly. Publication covering the civilian helicopter industry. Includes articles on regulations, costs, safety, developments, and trends.

Rotor and Wing

Phillips Publishing, Inc.
7811 Montrose Rd.
Potomac, MD 20854
Phone: (301)340-2100
Fax: (301)340-0542

Monthly. $36.00/year; $44.00/year for foreign subscribers; $4.00/issue. Magazine focusing on helicopters.

Top city-center hotels

1. The Pierre Hotel, New York, NY
2. Royalton Hotel, New York, NY
3. Morgans Hotel, New York, NY
4. The Lowell Hotel, New York, NY
5. Boston Harbor Hotel, Boston, MA
6. Ritz-Carlton Hotel, Chicago, IL
7. The Mark, New York, NY
8. The Hay-Adams Hotel, Washington, DC
9. Fairmont Hotel, San Francisco, CA
10. The Willard Inter-Continental, Washington, DC

Source: *Lodging Hospitality*

Ski Area Management

Beardsley Publishing Corp.
45 Main St., N.
PO Box 644
Woodbury, CT 06798
Phone: (203)263-0888

Bimonthly. Publication covering the North American ski resort industry.

Southeast Food Service News

Southeast Publishing Co.
PO Box 47719
Atlanta, GA 30362
Phone: (404)452-1807
Fax: (404)457-3829

Monthly. Magazine focusing on the food service industry in Southeast United States, including hotels and motels, country clubs, restaurants, schools and colleges, food service distributors, and equipment manufacturers.

Special Events

Miramar Publishing Co.
6133 Bristol Pkwy.
PO Box 3640
Culver City, CA 90231-3640
Phone: (310)337-9717
Toll-free: 800-543-4116
Fax: (310)337-1041

12x/year. Magazine covering news and information of interest to professionals who specialize in special event planning and execution.

---

n a survey of companies that are experimenting with alternative approaches to pay, Marc J. Wallace Jr., of the University of Kentucky's business school, found two main directions: 1) skill-based pay—where the company grants raises as workers learn to perform new job-related tasks; and 2) gainsharing—where the team or unit gets incentive pay for meeting certain quality or productivity goals.

Source: *Newsweek*

Tradeshow Week

Reed Publishing, Inc.
Tradeshow Week, Inc.
R.R. Bowker
12233 W. Olympic Blvd., Ste. 236
Los Angeles, CA 90064-9956
Phone: (310)826-5696
Fax: (310)826-2039

Weekly. Publication covering the exposition industry in the United States, Canada, and abroad. Features such topics as budget planning, market trends, and labor and equipment rates.

Travel New England

Air Travel Publications
1 Harborside Dr.
East Boston, MA 02128
Phone: (617)561-4000

Monthly. Magazine covering the travel industry in New England and the United States.

Travel Weekly

Reed Travel Group
500 Plaza Dr.
Secaucus, NJ 07096
Phone: (201)902-1500
Fax: (201)319-1755

2x/week. Publication covering news and features of interest to travel professionals.

Travelage East

Official Airline Guides
Travel Magazines Div.
1775 Broadway
New York, NY 10019
Phone: (212)237-3050
Fax: (212)237-3007

Weekly. Magazine covering the eastern U.S. travel industry, including Delaware, Maryland, New England, New Jersey, New York, Pennsylvania, Washington D.C., and south to Florida.

Travelage Midamerica

Official Airline Guides
Travel Magazines Div.
320 N. Michigan, Ste. 601
Chicago, IL 60601
Phone: (312)346-4954
Fax: (312)346-5034

Weekly. Magazine covering the mid-American travel industry, including Arkansas, Illinois, Indiana, Iowa, Kansas, Michigan, Minnesota, Missouri, Nebraska, North Dakota, Ohio, Oklahoma, South Dakota, Texas, Wisconsin, and the Canadian provinces of Manitoba and Ontario.

Travelage West

Official Airline Guides Inc.
Travel Magazines Div.
49 Stevenson, No. 460
San Francisco, CA 94105-2909
Phone: (415)905-1160
Fax: (415)905-1145

Weekly. Magazine covering the Western U.S. travel industry, including Alaska and Hawaii, and the Canadian provinces of Alberta, British Columbia, and Saskatchewan.

Western Association News

Western Assn. News, Inc.
1516 S. Pontius Ave.
Los Angeles, CA 90025
Phone: (310)478-0215
Fax: (310)312-6684

Monthly. Magazine covering news and information for meeting managers, executives, and association officers.

Professional Associations

Air Line Pilots Association, International (ALPA)

1625 Massachusetts Ave., NW
Washington, DC 20036
Phone: (703)689-2270
Fax: (202)797-4052

Membership: Collective bargaining agent for air line pilots. **Publication(s):** *Air Line Pilot: The Magazine of Professional Flight Crews*, monthly. • *Newsletter*, periodic. • Also publishes memoranda.

Air Traffic Control Association (ATCA)

2020 N. 14th St., Ste. 410
Arlington, VA 22201
Phone: (703)522-5717
Fax: (703)527-7251

Membership: Air traffic controllers; private, commercial, and military pilots; private and business aircraft owners and operators; aircraft and electronics engineers; airlines, aircraft manufacturers, and electronic and human engineering firms interested in the establishment and maintenance of a safe and efficient air traffic control system. **Purpose:** Conducts special surveys and studies on air traffic control problems. Participates in aviation community conferences. Bestows awards and scholarships. **Publication(s):** *Bulletin*, monthly. • *Fall Conference Proceedings*, annual. • *Journal of Air Traffic Control*, quarterly.

Air Transport Association of America (ATA)

1709 New York Ave., NW
Washington, DC 20006
Phone: (202)626-4000
Membership: Airlines engaged in transporting persons, goods, and mail by aircraft between fixed terminals on regular schedules. **Purpose:** Maintains resource library of transportation texts and congressional, administrative, and legal histories of civil aviation. **Publication(s):** *Air Transport*, annual. • Also publishes fact sheets, press releases, studies, speeches, testimonies, and references.

American Car Rental Association (ACRA)

927 15th St. NW, Ste. 1000
Washington, DC 20005
Phone: (202)789-2240

American Helicopter Society

217 N. Washington St.
Alexandria, VA 22314
Phone: (703)684-6777
Fax: (703)739-9279

Purpose: Conducts research and educational and technical meetings concerning professional training and updated information. **Publication(s):** *Journal of the American Helicopter Society*, quaterly.

American Hotel & Motel Association (AH&MA)

1201 New York Ave. NW, Ste. 600
Washington, DC 20005
Phone: (202)289-3100
Fax: (202)289-3199

Membership: Federation of 50 state and regional hotel associations, representing over 1 million hotel and motel rooms. **Purpose:** Promotes business of hotels and motels through publicity and promotion programs. Works to improve operating methods through dissemination of information on industry methods. Conducts educational institute for training at all levels, through home study, adult education, and colleges. Provides guidance on member and labor relations. Reviews proposed legislation affecting hotels. Sponsors study group programs. Maintains speakers' bureau; conducts research; compiles statistics; sponsors competitions and presents awards. **Publication(s):** *AH&MA Leadership Directory*, annual. • *Construction and Modernization Report*, monthly. • *Lodging*, monthly. • *Directory of Hotel and Motel Systems*, annual. • Also publishes surveys, guidelines, manuals, brochures, prints of articles and makes available hotel information kits; produces videos and bilingual (English/Spanish) energy conservation reference cards.

American Society of Travel Agents (ASTA)

1101 King St.
Alexandria, VA 22314
Phone: (703)739-2782

Membership: Travel agents; allied members are representatives of carriers, hotels, resorts, sightseeing and car rental companies, official tourist organizations, and other travel interests. **Purpose:** Purposes are to: promote and encourage travel among people of all nations; to promote the image and encourage the use of professional travel agents worldwide; serve as an information resource for the travel industry worldwide; promote and represent the views and interests of travel agents to all levels of government and industry; promote professional and ethical conduct in the travel agency industry worldwide; facilitate consumer protection and safety for the traveling public. Maintains biographical archives and travel hall of fame. Sponsors competitions; bestows awards; conducts research and education programs. **Publication(s):** *ASTA Educational System Catalog*, annual. • *ASTA Stat*, monthly. • *ASTA Travel Agency Management Magazine*, monthly. • *AstaNotes*, weekly. • *ASTA Officials Directory*, annual. • *ASTA Stat*, monthly. • *Membership Directory*, annual. • *Travel Industry Honors*, periodic. • Also publishes pamphlets.

Association for Convention Operations Management (ACOM)

c/o William H. Just and Associates, Inc.
1819 Peachtree St., NE, Ste. 560
Atlanta, GA 30309
Phone: (404)355-2400
Fax: (404)351-3348

Membership: Convention service directors and managers of hotels, convention centers, and convention bureaus; suppliers of services and products to the convention and meetings industry are affiliate members. **Purpose:** Provides placement services. Works to increase the effectiveness, productivity, and quality of meetings, conventions, and exhibitions. Works to establish high ethical standards, improve professional management techniques, and increase awareness of client, employer, and supplier needs. Holds summer classes. Maintains speakers' bureau and resource center; bestows awards; compiles statistics. Conducts research programs.

Association of Flight Attendants (AFA)

1625 Massachusetts Ave. NW
Washington, DC 20036
Phone: (202)328-5400

Association for International Practical Training (AIPT)

Park View Bldg.
Ste. 320
10480 Little Patuxent Pkwy.
Columbia, MD 21044-3502
Phone: (301)997-2200

Purpose: U.S. affiliate of the International Association for the Exchange of Students for Technical Experience, which arranges reciprocal exchanges among 49 member countries for students of engineering, architecture, agriculture, mathematics, and the sciences to obtain on-the-job practical training with educational institutions, research organizations, and industry in another country. Training periods are from eight weeks to 12 months and include students from the sophomore through graduate level. Operates a Career Development and Hotel/Culinary Exchange providing reciprocal practical training exchanges for recent graduates from the U.S. and Australia, Austria, Federal Republic of Germany, Finland, France, Ireland, Japan, Malaysia, Netherlands, Switzerland, and the United Kingdom.

Club Managers Association of America (CMAA)

1733 King St.
Alexandria, VA 22314
Phone: (703)739-9500
Fax: (703)739-0124

Membership: Professional managers and assistant managers of private golf, yacht, athletic, city, country, luncheon, university, and military clubs. **Purpose:** Maintains placement service and operates Executive Career Service Committee. Encourages education and advancement of members and promotes efficient and successful club operations. Conducts seminars, workshops, and exhibitions; provides reprints of articles on club management Supports courses in club management and awards scholarships. Compiles statistics; operates library of 625 volumes on food preparation and service, beverages and wines, and maintenance and management.

Council on Hotel, Restaurant, and Institutional Education (CHRIE)

1200 17th St. NW
Washington, DC 20036-3097
Phone: (202)331-5990
Fax: (202)331-2429

Membership: Schools and colleges offering specialized education and training in cooking, baking, tourism and hotel, restaurant, and institutional administration; individuals, executives, and students. **Purpose:** Sponsors competitions; bestows awards. **Publication(s):** *CHRIE Communique*, semimonthly. • *Guide to Hospitality Education*, annual. • *Hospitality Education and Research Journal*, 3/year. • *Hospitality and Tourism Educator*, quarterly.

Future Aviation Professionals of America (FAPA)

4959 Massachusetts Blvd.
Atlanta, GA 30337
Phone: (404)997-8097
Fax: (404)997-8111

Membership: Commercial pilots, flight attendants, aviation maintenance personnel, and persons aspiring to careers in those areas. **Purpose:** Purpose is to channel career information to aviation personnel and those seeking careers in aviation. Conducts bimonthly seminar and job fair. **Publication(s):** *Career Pilot*, monthly. • Also publishes brochures and flyers.

Hotel-Motel Greeters International (HMGI)

PO Box 20017
El Cajon, CA 92021
Phone: (619)561-5869

Membership: Owners, managers, executives,

clerks, and other personnel in hotels, motor hotels, clubs, and apartment hotels. **Purpose:** Provides educational services to members. Offers guest referral service to member hotels and motels. Bestows awards.

computerized airline reservation systems also schedule such services as car rental, cruise ship packages, and hotel reservations. Some may also handle ticketing for sporting events, plays, and other entertainment. Every time a travel agent writes a ticket on a CRS terminal, the operator collects a fee.

Source: *Business Week*

Institute of Certified Travel Agents (ICTA)

148 Linden St.
PO Box 82-56
Wellesley, MA 02181
Phone: (617)237-0280
Fax: (617)237-3860

Membership: Individuals who have been accredited as Certified Travel Counselors (CTC) after meeting the institute's requirements (5 years' travel industry experience, 4 travel management courses, 4 examinations, and an original research project). **Purpose:** Seeks to increase the level of competence in the travel industry. Provides educational guidance, continuing education, and examination and certification program; conducts workshops and executive management seminars. Operates Travel Career Development Program to increase skills of pre-management personnel and Destination Specialist Program to enhance the geographical knowledge of sales agents. Organizes study groups of instruction with enrolled student bodies in most major cities. Maintains library on travel agency management and travel reference topics. **Publication(s):** *CTCs Newsletter*, monthly. • *ICTA News*, monthly. • *Institute of Certified Travel Agents—Directory*, annual. • *Travel Trainers Network*, semiannual. • Also publishes catalog and books.

International Agricultural Aviation Foundation (IAAF)

405 Main St.
Mt. Vernon, WA 98275
Phone: (206)336-9737
Fax: (206)336-2506

Membership: Crop duster pilots, aerial applicators, fire bomber pilots, and agricultural aviation operators licensed by the FAA. **Purpose:** Provides placement service. Presents scholarships to pilots; aids survivors of decedents of the industry. Maintains speakers' bureau and biographical archives. Conducts specialized education.

International Association of Hospitality Accountants (IAHA)

Box 27649
Austin, TX 78755
Phone: (512)346-5680

Membership: Professional society of hotel, motel, casino restaurant, and club controllers and financial officers. **Purpose:** Offers placement service. Develops uniform system of accounts. Conducts education, training, and certification programs, bestows scholarship awards.

International Association of Tour Managers - North American Region (IATM-NAR)

1646 Chapel St.
New Haven, CT 06511
Phone: (203)777-5994

Membership: Travel agents, travel wholesalers, airlines, hotel associations, shipping lines, tourist organizations, restaurants, shops, and entertainment organizations. **Purpose:** Offers placement service and computerized job bank matching tour managers with groups (offers members access). Works to: maintain the highest possible standards of tour management; guarantee excellence of performance; educate the travel world on the role of the tour manager (also referred to as tour director, tour escort, or tour leader) in the successful completion of the tour itinerary and in bringing business to related industries. Represents members in influencing legislation and advising on travel policy. Offers courses in tour management, travel marketing, and sales promotion through New York University in New York City and Metropolitan State College in Denver, Colorado. Trains tour managers to plan, research, and lead tours for domestic and foreign travelers; operates Advisory Board in Professional Tour Management; conducts Professional Tour Management, U.S.A. Certificate Program. Affiliated with: American Society of Travel Agents; Universal Federation of Travel Agents' Associations.

International Caterers Association (ICA)

220 S. State St., Ste. 1416
Chicago, IL 60604
Phone: (312)922-0966

Membership: Caterers; restaurants, hotels, hospitals, country clubs, and delicatessens with catering services. **Purpose:** Provides job placement service and nationwide referrals for potential customers. Seeks to provide assistance and information to caterers. Maintains consulting staff to help members with the catering business. Aids in advertising and marketing efforts. Sponsors the Certified Catering Professional Program for marketing, expansion, and specialization in the industry. Offers group insurance policies and discounts on supplies; conducts seminars, workshops, in-house training, and demonstrations. Maintains speakers' bureau; sponsors competitions; bestows awards; compiles statistics.

National Air Traffic Controllers Association (NATCA)

444 N. Capitol St. NW, Ste. 845
Washington, DC 20001
Phone: (202)347-4572

Purpose: Represents U.S. air traffic controllers within the aviation industry and before the government. Negotiates on members' behalf with the Federal Aviation Administration. Conducts educational programs; compiles statistics. Maintains speakers' bureau. **Publication(s):** *Newsletter*, monthly. • Also publishes brochures; plans to publish a quarterly journal. Compuserve.

National Association of Black Hospitality Professionals (NABHP)

PO Box 5443
Plainfield, NJ 07060
Phone: (201)354-5117

Membership: Individuals involved in the hospitality profession on a managerial or supervisory level, and those interested in careers in the field. **Purpose:** Operates placement service. Purposes of NABHP are: to provide a forum for the sharing of ideas, experiences, and job opportunity information; to improve the image of blacks in the hospitality industry; to provide support to educational institutions. Conducts educational and research programs. Compiles statistics on blacks in hospitality management.

National Association of Business Travel Agents (NABTA)

3255 Wilshire Blvd., Ste. 1514
Los Angeles, CA 90010
Phone: (213)382-3335
Fax: (213)480-7712

Membership: Travel agents who specialize in servicing corporate and business accounts and provde travel services for businesses and organizations holding out-of-town meetings and conventions. **Purpose:** To educate and inform members of practical methods of servicing and increasing their accounts. Prepares detailed descriptions of convention facilities, hotels, restaurants, tour operators, and tourist attractions for members.

National Association of Trade and Technical Schools (NATTS)

2251 Wisconsin Ave. NW
Washington, DC 20007
Phone: (202)333-1021

Membership: Private schools providing career education. **Purpose:** Provides general career information and publications containing listings of accredited private trade and technical schools offering programs in hotel-motel management. Also informs members of the accreditation process and regulations affecting vocational education. Has established Career Training Foundation to support research into private vocational education. **Publication(s):** *Career News Digest*, 3-4/year. • *Career Training*, quarterly. • *Classroom Companion*, quarterly. • *Handbook of Trade and Technical Careers and Training*, annual. • *NATTS News and Views*, bimonthly. • Also publishes *Career Guidance Handouts*.

National EMS Pilots Association (NEMSPA)

c/o Tom Einhorn
5810 Hornwood
Houston, TX 77081
Phone: (713)668-6144

Membership: Aeromedical helicopter pilots; organizations providing goods and services to the emergency medical service (EMS) industry; medical professionals; interested individuals and organizations. **Purpose:** Maintains placement service. Serves as a forum for the exchange of information concerning equipment, operations, and safety procedures. Compiles statistics on EMS aviation accidents and incidents. Has developed EMS guidelines to address pilot, aircraft, and operating standards for EMS helicopter operations. Plans to: develop a database; offer training and professionalism certification; sponsor a landing zone coordinator course; monitor legislative and administrative decisions that affect the industry; conduct research projects; bestow awards.

The best business-travel guides: *Economist Business Traveller's Guides*, scholarly essays combined with Michelin-like hotel and restaurant capsule recommendations; *Birnbaum's for Business Travelers* series, leisure-minded, with strength in the time-off part of the trip; Fodor's *The Wall Street Journal Guides to Business Travel* series, pocketbook-size manuals with maps, hotel and restaurant descriptions, and Fortune 500 CEO ratings.

Selected by Melinda Marshall

National Executive Housekeepers Association (N.E.H.A.)

1001 Eastwind Dr., Ste. 301
Westerville, OH 43081
Phone: (614)895-7166
Fax: (614)895-1248

Membership: Persons engaged in institutional housekeeping management in hospitals, hotels and motels, schools, and industrial establishments. **Purpose:** Has established educational standards. Sponsors certificate and collegiate degree programs. Holds annual National Housekeepers Week celebration during the second week in September. Created the N.E.H.A.

Educational Foundation to allocate financial awards to recognized schools to assist students in institutional housekeeping. Maintains referral service. **Publication(s):** *Executive Housekeeping Today*, monthly. • *Shop Talk*, quarterly.

entitling winners to advanced flight training or courses in specialized branches of aviation; awards Amelia Earhart Research Scholar Grant to a specialized, professional scholar. Maintains biographical archives; compiles statistics.

Negro Airmen International (NAI)

PO Box 1340
Tuskegee, AL 36008

Membership: Individuals holding at least a student pilot license who are active in some phase of aviation; members include both aviation professionals and others who are qualified pilots. **Purpose:** Provides placement service. Seeks greater participation by blacks in the field of aviation through the encouragement of broader job opportunities; promotes awareness by government and industry of the needs, attitudes, and interests of blacks concerning aviation. Encourages black youth to remain in school and to enter the field of aviation. Maintains Summer Flight Academy for teenagers each July at Tuskegee Institute in Alabama. Sponsors competitions; bestows awards. Operates speakers' bureau and library.

Ninety-Nines, International Women Pilots

Will Rogers Airport
PO Box 59965
Oklahoma City, OK 73159
Phone: (405)685-7969

Membership: International organization of women pilots. **Purpose:** Operates placement services and maintains computerized information on women interested in aviation careers. Sponsors seminars on safety education; works with schools and youth organizations to develop programs and courses designed for a better understanding of aviation. Encourages cross-country flying; endorses air races. Maintains resource center and 700 volume library and display area dedicated to the preservation of women's achievements in aviation. Participates in flying competitions. Members give indoctrination flights, act as consultants, teach ground school subjects, and lecture on personal aviation experience. Flies missions for charitable assistance programs; sponsors charitable events to benefit hospitals, schools, and children. Bestows Amelia Earhart Memorial Scholarship Award,

Organization of Black Airline Pilots (OBAP)

PO Box 86
La Guardia Airport
New York, NY 11371
Phone: (201)568-8145

Membership: Cockpit crew members of commercial air carriers, corporate pilots, and interested individuals. **Purpose:** Offers job placement service and has computerized job placement bank. OBAP seeks to enhance minority participation in the aerospace industry. Maintains liaison with airline presidents and minority and pilot associations. Conducts lobbying efforts, including congressional examinations into airline recruitment practices. Provides scholarships; cosponsors Summer Flight Academy for Youth at Tuskegee Institute in Alabama. Conducts charitable program; operates speakers' bureau; compiles statistics on airline hiring practices. Affiliated With: Negro Airmen International; Tuskegee Airmen.

Pilots International Association (PIA)

PO Box 907
Minneapolis, MN 55440
Phone: (612)588-5175

Membership: Private, commercial, airline, military, and student pilots; associate members are persons other than pilots who are interested in flying. **Purpose:** Maintains job placement service. Promotes the use of the airplane; works for aircraft safety; cooperates with government agencies and private and public flying organizations for the general safety of flying; encourages development and use of convenient landing and service facilities and use of aircraft fuel taxes for development of aviation; seeks international understanding through common aviation problem-solving techniques. Offers aircraft title search service, travel service, chart service, group life and health insurance, weather information service and free items to members. Maintains film-lending library and collection of general flying periodicals and statistical surveys. Bestows awards for meritorious service to the association and/or aviation.

Self-Help Clearinghouse

St. Clares-Riverside Medical Center
Pocono Rd.
Denville, NJ 07834
Phone: (201)625-9565

Edward Madara, Director. A central source of information on self-help groups across the U.S. and in Canada. Can direct interested persons to clearinghouses in their own states which in turn can provide help in finding local self-help groups for job hunters. (A variety of self-help groups exist for job hunters: 40-plus; disabled; those in certain professions such as social work; etc.)

Society of Incentive Travel Executives (SITE)

271 Madison Ave., Ste. 904
New York, NY 10016
Phone: (212)889-9340
Fax: (212)889-0646

Membership: Individuals responsible for the administration or sale of incentive travel including corporate users, incentive travel houses, cruise lines, hotel chains, resort operators, airlines, and tourist boards. **Purpose:** Provides placement service. Supports expansion of incentive travel through public relations, promotion, and speakers' bureau activities. Contributes to the continuing professional education of members through meetings, publications, and research services. Helps upgrade standards through educational services to nonmembers. Holds regional incentive travel seminars. Sponsors awards competition for outstanding incentive travel accomplishments. Bestows Certified Incentive Travel Executive title. Compiles statistics.

United States Pilots Association

483 S. Kirkwood Rd., Ste. 10
St. Louis, MO 63122
Phone: (314)843-2766

Purpose: Promotes aviation safety and education. **Publication(s):** *United States Pilots Association Newsletter,* quarterly.

Women Executives International Tourism Association (WEXITA)

c/o SATH
26 Court St.
Brooklyn, NY 11242

Membership: Female executives from the travel, transportation, tourism, recreation, and leisure industries, as well as travel-related and allied industries. **Purpose:** Offers placement service. Works for the establishment of networks and support systems among executives in the travel industry. Encourages the exchange of knowledge and experience within the industry. Focuses on the aims and issues of women executives in the travel industry, seeking new solutions to problems. Spotlights the achievements and talents of members. Bestows awards; conducts regional seminars; maintains speakers' bureau. Affiliated with: National Council of Women of the U.S. Presently inactive.

Employment Agencies and Search Firms

ABC Employment Service

25 S. Bemiston
St. Louis, MO 63105
Phone: (314)725-3140

Employment agency.

A.C. Personnel Consultants

262 Havana St., Ste. 1018
Aurora, CO 80010
Phone: (303)341-5477

Alpha Resource Group, Inc.

10300 N. Central Expy.
Bldg. V, Ste. 190
Dallas, TX 75231

Executive search firm.

Alpine Consultants

10300 SW Greenburg Rd., Ste. 290
Portland, OR 97223
Phone: (503)244-3393

Employment agency.

Amherst Personnel Group Inc.
550 Old Country Rd., Ste. 203
Hicksville, NY 11801
Phone: (516)433-7610

Employment agency. Executive search firm. Other offices in Milltown, NJ, and Rochelle Park, NJ.

Best Personnel Services
9229 Ward Pkwy., Ste. 335
Kansas City, MO 64114
Phone: (816)361-3100

Employment agency. Fills openings on a regular or temporary basis.

Jobs are increasingly determined by skills, and titles are meaningless. A resume that reads "Executive VicePresident for Marketing" won't guarantee employment. Companies want people who can solve problems and complete projects. Security derives from the salability of a "can-do" reputation in a job market that spans all industries.

Source: *Business Week*

Career Specialties
210 G St., NE, 1st Fl.
Washington, DC 20002

Executive search firm. Recruits for a variety of fields.

Dartmouth Consultants
275 Madison Ave.
New York, NY 10016
Phone: (212)889-9600

Employment agency. Handles placements in variety of fields.

Domenico/Brown Group
2151 Michelson Dr., Ste. 217
Irvine, CA 92715

Executive search firm. Concentrates on placement to the food and lodging industry.

Dunhill of Falls Church
PO Box 4935
Falls Church, VA 22044
Phone: (703)241-8788

Employment agency. Member of Dunhill Personnel Systems. This office specializes in the hospitality industry.

Dunhill Personnel Systems, Inc.
1 Old Country Rd.
Carle Place, NY 11514

Executive search firm. Over 300 affiliated locations coast-to-coast.

Dussick Management Associates
149 Durham Rd.
Madison, CT 06443

Executive search firm.

Employment Advisor, Inc. of Minneapolis
526 Nicollet Mall
Minneapolis, MN 55402
Phone: (612)339-0521

Employment agency. Also located in Bloomington, Minnesota. Places candidates in variety of fields.

Esquire Personnel Services, Inc.
222 S. Riverside Plaza, Ste. 320
Chicago, IL 60606
Phone: (312)648-4600

Employment agency. Places individuals in variety of fields. Handles temporary assignments as well.

Ferree and Associates, Inc.
PO Box 3997
Federal Way, WA 98063-3997
Phone: (206)941-4950

Employment agency. Executive search firm.

Fox-Morris
1617 JFK Blvd., Ste. 210
Philadelphia, PA 19103

Executive search firm. Branch locations in many states throughout the U.S.

Harry E. Fear and Associates
Deer Creek Country Club
Box 8645
Deerfield Beach, FL 33441

Employment agency. Executive search firm.

J.D. Hersey and Associates
6099 Riverside Dr., Ste. 104
Dublin, OH 43017

Executive search firm.

Hospitality International
Davis Rd.
Box 906
Valley Forge, PA 19481

Executive search firm. Branch office in Lombard, IL.

Hospitality Recruiters of America, Inc.
Atlanta, GA 30305
Phone: (404)233-3530

Employment agency. Executive search firm.

Hotel and Restaurant Personnel of America, Inc.
561 Boylston St.
Boston, MA 02116

Executive search firm.

Hotelmen's Executive Recruitment
305 W. End Ave., Ste. 5B
New York, NY 10023

Employment agency. Executive search firm.

HRI Services, Inc.
150 Wood Rd., Ste. 205
Braintree, MA 02184
Phone: (617)848-9110

Employment agency.

Mell D. Leonard and Associates Inc.
Florida Federal Bldg., Ste. 260
919 West Hwy., No. 436
Altamonte Springs, FL 32714
Phone: (407)869-6355

Employment agency. Executive search firm. Places individuals in variety of fields.

MBC Systems Ltd.
7444 Dulaney Valley Ct., Ste. 11
Towson, MD 21204
Phone: (301)583-8600

Employment agency.

Miriam Factors Employment Agency
9763 W. Pico Blvd., Ste. 203
Los Angeles, CA 90035
Phone: (213)553-8677

Employment agency. Serves the hotel and food service industries.

B ill Costa, director of placement for Jet Professionals, a corporate pilot placement service based in Fairfield, CT, claims that some companies are "flying like crazy," but warns that the jobs are going to the best qualified pilots. Corporate pilot candidates are more likely to be hired if they possess the specific type rating and time in type for the aircraft they'd like to be hired to fly. Aspiring professional pilots should concentrate on one thing: getting qualified for the jobs they want.

Source: *Flying*

National Hospitality Associates, Inc.
PO Box 27965
Tempe, AZ 85282

Executive search firm. Specializes in placements to hospitality industry.

The Pathfinder Group
295 Danbury Rd.
Wilton, CT 06897
Phone: (203)762-9418

Employment agency. Executive search firm. Recruits staff in a variety of fields.

Peter, Mann and Associates
250 S. Stommons, Ste. 300
PO Box 1552
Lewisville, TX 75067
Phone: (214)221-7516

Employment agency.

Remer-Ribolow and Associates
275 Madison Ave., Ste. 1605
New York, NY 10016
Phone: (212)808-0580

Employment agency.

Ritt-Ritt and Associates
1400 E. Touhy Ave.
Des Plaines, IL 60018
Phone: (708)298-2510

Employment agency.

Some typical questions for the job candidate: "Give me an example of a problem in which you and your manager disagreed over how to accomplish a goal." "Do your talents lean more toward strategy or tactics, being creative or analytical?" "How would you compare, say, the marketing of consumer goods vs. financial services?" "A year from now, what might your boss say about your work for the company during a performance review?"

Source: *Business Week*

Sanford Rose Associates
265 S. Main St.
Akron, OH 44308
Phone: (216)762-6211

Executive search firm. Over 80 office locations nationwide.

RitaSue Siegel Agency, Inc.
60 W. 55th St.
New York, NY 10019

Executive search firm. Affiliate office located in London.

Snelling and Snelling
4000 S. Tamiami Tr.
Sarasota, FL 33581
Phone: (813)922-9616

Employment agency. Over 50 offices across the country.

The Stanford Gilbert Agency
1377 Westwood Blvd.
Los Angeles, CA 90024
Phone: (213)473-3097

Employment agency. Also located in Hollywood, CA.

Career Guides

After College: The Business of Getting Jobs
The Career Press
62 Beverly Rd.
PO Box 34
Hawthorne, NJ 07507
Phone: 800-227-3371

Falvey, Jack. $9.95. 192 pages. Provides students with the perspective and tools to meet career and job-hunting challenges.

Air Traffic Control: How to Become an FAA Air Traffic Controller
Random House
201 E. 50th St.
New York, NY 10022
Phone: (212)751-2600
Toll-free: 800-726-0600

Walter S. Luffsey. 1990.

Air Traffic Control Specialist
Chronicle Guidance Publications, Inc.
Aurora St. Extension
PO Box 1190
Moravia, NY 13118-1190
Phone: (315)497-0330
Toll-free: 800-622-7284

1989. Career brief describing the nature of the job, working conditions, hours and earnings, education and training, licensure, certification, unions, personal qualifications, social and psychological factors, location, employment outlook, entry methods, advancement, and related occupations.

Air Traffic Controller
Careers, Inc.
PO Box 135
Largo, FL 34649-0135
Phone: (813)584-7333
Toll-free: 800-726-0441

1992. Eight-page brief offering the definition, history, duties, working conditions, personal qualifications, educational requirements, earnings, hours, employment outlook, advancement, and careers related to this position.

Air Traffic Controller

Vocational Biographies, Inc.
PO Box 31
Sauk Centre, MN 56378-0031
Phone: (612)352-6516

1986. Four-page pamphlet containing a personal narrative about a worker's job, work likes and dislikes, career path from high school to the present, education and training, the rewards and frustrations, and the effects of the job on the rest of the worker's life. The data file portion of this pamphlet gives a concise occupational summary, including work description, working conditions, places of employment, personal characteristics, education and training, job outlook, and salary range.

Airline Attendants

Chronicle Guidance Publications, Inc.
PO Box 1190
Moravia, NY 13118-1190
Phone: (315)497-0330
Toll-free: 800-622-7284

1990. This career brief describes the nature of the work, working conditions, hours and earnings, education and training, licensure, certification, unions, personal qualifications, social and psychological factors, employment outlook, entry methods, advancement, and related occupations.

Airline Pilot

Arco Publishing Co.
15 Columbus Circle
New York, NY 10023
Phone: (212)373-8931
Toll-free: 800-223-2336

Edited by the Future Aviation Professionals of America (FAPA). 1990. Professional guide for aspiring pilots. Covers job qualifications, requirements, application procedures, and training programs.

Airline Pilot

Prentice Hall
Rte. 9W
Englewood Cliffs, NJ 07632
Phone: (201)592-2000

Edited by Future Aviation Professionals of America Staff. 1990. Includes illustrations.

Airline Pilots, Commercial

Chronicle Guidance Publications, Inc.
PO Box 1190
Moravia, NY 13118-1190
Phone: (315)497-0330

1987. This career brief describes the nature of the job, working conditions, hours and earnings, education and training, licensure, certification, unions, personal qualifications, social and psychological factors, location, employment outlook, entry methods, advancement, and related occupations.

---

n 1970 nearly half of all airline passengers traveled on routes dominated by one airline. Now only about 20% face that situation. As competition grew, fares dropped. The Brookings Institution calculates that between 1978 and 1988, as a result of deregulation, air travelers saved about $100 billion. For that same ten-year period airlines reported a net profit margin averaging 1.6%, compared with 4.6% for U.S. manufacturers. And from 1978 to 1987 fatal airline accidents per million miles traveled declined by 57%.

Source: *Fortune*

Airline Reservations Sales Agent

Vocational Biographies, Inc.
PO Box 31, Dept. VF10
Sauk Centre, MN 56378
Phone: (612)352-6516
Toll-free: 800-255-0752

1990. This pamphlet profiles a person working in the job. Includes information about job duties, working conditions, places of employment, educational preparation, labor market outlook, and salaries.

Airline Ticket Agent

Careers, Inc.
PO Box 135
Largo, FL 34649-0135
Phone: (813)584-7333

1988. Two-page occupational summary card describing duties, working conditions, personal qualifications, training, earnings and hours, employment outlook, places of employment, related careers and where to write for more information.

The Art and Science of Hospitality Management

American Hotel & Motel Assn.
1201 New York Ave., NW. Ste. 600
Washington, DC 20005
Phone: (202)289-3100

James R. Abby and Jerome J. Vallen; edited by Jim Purvis. 1987. Offers a clear understanding of the skills specific to managing a hotel, motel, or restaurant, including management responsibilities, operational responsibilities, and the personal and professional demands of managing and maintaining the management image.

A s corporate America struggles through its own identity crisis during the next decade, the burden will be on employees to be both adaptable and opportunistic. From learning to cope with paychecks that are increasingly tied to a company's or department's overall performance to designing flexible work schedules that make raising a family and pursuing a career compatible goals, being successful in the 1990s will more than ever be synonymous with achieving personal satisfaction.

Source: U.S. News & World Report

Becoming an Airline Pilot

TAB Books
PO Box 40
Blue Ridge Summit, PA 17294-0850
Phone: (717)794-2191
Toll-free: 800-822-8138

Jeff Griffin. 1990.

The Berkeley Guide to Employment for New College Graduates

Ten Speed Press
PO Box 7123
Berkeley, CA 94707
Phone: (415)845-8414

Briggs, James I. $7.95. 256 pages. Basic job-hunting advice for the college student.

The Big Book of Free Career Services and Programs

Ready Reference Press
PO Box 5249
Santa Monica, CA 90405
Phone: (213)474-5175

$95.00. Two-volume set. Presents thousands of free or low-cost career and job-hunting resources. Includes such things as job referral services, vocational testing programs, and job training. Entries include organization name, type of service offered, background, description, audience served, hours, address, and telephone number. Subject and geographic indexes.

Breaking into the Travel Business

Jeffrey Norton Publishers, Inc.
96 Broad St.
Guilford, CT 06437

Berman, Richard. $10.95. Audiocassette.

California Connections

CALCON
PO Box 90396
Long Beach, CA 90809-0396
Phone: (213)434-7843
Fax: (213)434-4202

Includes job opportunities in California listed by city, county, federal, school district, community college, and university personnel offices. Typical entries contain employer name, address, telephone number, job title, salary, benefits offered, and job description. Available online through CompuServe.

Career in Air Transport Flight Services

Morris Video
2730 Monterey St., No. 105
Monterey Business Park
Torrance, CA 90503
Phone: (213)533-4800

Videocassette. 15 mins. Learn what types of jobs are available in flight service from flight attendants to commercial jet pilots. Discover what the educational requirements are and what background skills are needed.

Career in Air Transport Ground Services

Morris Video
2730 Monterey St., No. 105
Monterey Business Park
Torrance, CA 90503
Phone: (213)533-4800

Videocassette. 15 mins. Discover the different jobs available in ground services from air traffic controller to ramp attendant.

The Career Fitness Program: Exercising Your Options

Gorsuch Scarisbrick Publishers
8233 Via Paseo del Norte, Ste. F-400
Scottsdale, AZ 85258

Sukiennik et al. 1989. $15.00. 227 pages. Textbook, with second half devoted to the job search process.

Career Information System (CIS)

National Career Information System
1787 Agate St.
Eugene, OR 97403
Phone: (503)686-3872

Includes information on job search techniques and self-employment options. Also provides extensive career planning information.

Career Opportunities News

Garrett Park Press
PO Box 190 C
Garrett Park, MD 20986-0190
Phone: (301)946-2553

Calvert, Robert, Jr., and French, Mary Blake, editors. Bimonthly. $30.00/year; $4.00 sample issue. Each issue covers such things as resources to job seekers, special opportunities for minorities, women's career notes, and the current outlook in various occupations. Cites free and inexpensive job-hunting materials and new reports and books.

Careering and Re-Careering for the 1990's

Consultants Bookstore
Templeton Rd.
Fitzwilliam, NH 03447
Phone: (603)585-6544
Fax: (603)585-9221

Krannich, Ronald. 1989. $13.95. 314 pages. Details trends in the marketplace, how to identify opportunities, how to retrain for them, and how to land jobs. Includes a chapter on starting a business. Contains index, bibliography, and illustrations.

Careers and the College Grad

Bob Adams, Inc.
260 Center St.
Holbrook, MA 02343
Phone: (617)767-8100
Fax: (617)767-0994

Ranno, Gigi. 1990. $12.95. Approximately 150 pages. An annual resource guide addressing the career and job-hunting interests of undergraduates. Provides company profiles and leads.

Careers as a Flight Attendant: Flight to the Future

Rosen Publishing Group, Inc.
29 E. 21st St.
New York, NY 10010
Phone: (212)777-3017

Catherine Okray Lobus. 1991. Discusses the work, personal characteristics of successful flight attendants, physical and educational qualifications, the application process, and airline training programs. Lists major airlines and outlines their application processes, policies and benefits, and training programs.

"Most job seekers are not successful because they don't have support during the search," reveals Debbie Featherston of JIST Works, Inc., a career-planning and job-search company in Indianapolis. Featherston says the group approach to realizing career goals really works, and "success teams" inspired by the 1980 book *Wishcraft* are springing up all over the country. Team members encourage each other to act: to develop career plans, find jobs, or build independent businesses. To find a success team near you, send a self-addressed, stamped envelope to: Wishcraft and Success Teams, Box 20052 Park West Station, New York, NY 10025.

Source: *Working Woman*

Careers in Travel

Solitaire Publishing
216 S. Bungalow Park Ave.
Tampa, FL 33609
Phone: (813)876-0286
Toll-free: 800-226-0286

Claudine Dervaes. 1988.

Chronicle Career Index

Chronicle Guidance Publications
PO Box 1190
Moravia, NY 13118-1190
Phone: (315)497-0330

Annual. $14.25. Provides bibliographic listings of career and vocational guidance publications and other resources. Arrangement: Alphabetical by source. Indexes: Occupation; vocational and professional information.

Coming Alive from Nine to Five
Mayfield Publishing
1240 Villa St.
Mountain View, CA 94041

Micheolzzi, Betty N. 1988. $12.95. In addition to general job-hunting advice, provides special information for women, young adults, minorities, older workers, and persons with handicaps.

When times get tough in the travel business, hotel managers have to react. "We've got a commodity—a room—that's only got a one-day shelf life, so we have to move it," remarks Bill Evans, general manager of Bahia Resort Hotel on San Diego's Mission Bay. The quick fix: price cuts. Other techniques used in the industry to stimulate business include free breakfasts, hotel-paid recreational fees (such as for golf or skiing), two-for-one deals, giveaways, air-and-lodging packages, and increased marketing blitzes at home and abroad.

Source: Business Week

Communication Skills
Travel Text Associates
12605 State Fair
Detroit, MI 48205
Phone: (313)527-6971

Chris Hoosen. 1989. Part of Travel Agent Training Series.

The Complete Job Search Book
John Wiley and Sons
General Books Div.
605 3rd Ave.
New York, NY 10158
Phone: (212)850-6000
Fax: (212)850-6088

Beatty, Richard H. 1988. $12.95. 256 pages.

The Complete Job-Search Handbook
Consultants Bookstore
Templeton Rd.
Fitzwilliam, NH 03447
Phone: (603)585-6544
Fax: (603)585-9221

Figler, Howard. 1988. $11.95. 366 pages. Contains information on how to look for career opportunities every day. Focuses on twenty life skills in self-assessment, detective work, communication skills, and selling oneself. Includes skill-building exercises.

Exploring Careers in the Travel Industry
Rosen Publishing Group, Inc.
29 E. 21st St.
New York, NY 10010
Phone: (212)777-3017

Edgar Grant. 1989. Provides an overview of the travel and tourism industries. Describes the work of the travel agent, skills, training, pay, and employment outlook. Offers job hunting advice.

Federal Career Opportunities
Federal Research Service, Inc.
370 W. Maple Ave.
Vienna, VA 22180
Phone: (703)281-0200

Biweekly. $147.00/year; $71.00/six months; $37.00/three months; $7.50/copy. Provides information on more than 4,200 current federal job vacancies in the United States and overseas; includes permanent, part-time, and temporary positions. Entries include: Position title, location, series and grade, job requirements, special forms, announcement number, closing date, application address. Arrangement: Classified by federal agency and occupation.

Federal Jobs Digest
Federal Jobs Digest
325 Pennsylvania Ave., SE
Washington, DC 20003
Phone: (914)762-5111

Biweekly. $110.00/year; $29.00/three months; $4.50/issue. Covers over 20,000 specific job openings in the federal government in each issue. Entries include: Position name, title, General Schedule grade and Wage Grade, closing date for applications, announcement number, application address, phone, and name of contact. Arrangement: By federal department or agency, then geographical.

Flight Attendant

Careers, Inc.
PO Box 135
Largo, FL 34649-0135
Phone: (813)584-7333

1989. Eight-page brief offering the definition, history, duties, working conditions, personal qualifications, educational requirements, earnings, hours, employment outlook, advancement possibilities, and related occupations.

Flight Attendant

Arco/Prentice Hall Press
1 Gulf & Western Plaza
New York, NY 10023
Phone: (212)373-8500

Future Aviation Professionals of America; David Massey. 1990. Career planning guide covering the work, pay, benefits, places of employment, training, and employment outlook. Lists major airlines and national airline flight attendant bases. Offers tips about filling out applications, writing resumes, and interviewing.

Flight Attendant Interview Handbook

State of the Art, Ltd.
1625 S. Broadway
Denver, CO 80210
Phone: (303)722-7177
Fax: (303)744-9825

Ken Rebalais. 1987.

Flight Instructors

Chronicle Guidance Publications, Inc.
PO Box 1190
Moravia, NY 13118-1190
Phone: (315)497-0330

1990. This career brief describes the nature of the job, working conditions, hours and earnings, education and training, licensure, certification, unions, personal qualifications, social and psychological factors, location, employment outlook, entry methods, advancement, and related occupations.

Flying High in Travel: A Complete Guide to Careers in the Travel Industry

John Wiley and Sons, Inc.
605 3rd Ave.
New York, NY 10158
Phone: (212)850-6000
Fax: (212)850-6088

Karen Rubin. 1986.

Sibson & Company, a human-resource firm based in Princeton, NJ, reports that 53% of the 630 companies it surveyed in 1990 provided variable incentives to workers below the executive level, up from 46% in 1989.

Source: *U.S. News & World Report*

Free-lance Travel Writer

Vocational Biographies, Inc.
PO Box 31
Sauk Centre, MN 56378-0031
Phone: (612)352-6516

1986. Four-page pamphlet containing a personal narrative about a worker's job, work likes and dislikes, career path from high school to the present, education and training, the rewards and frustrations, and the effects of the job on the rest of the worker's life. The data file portion of this pamphlet gives a concise occupational summary, including work description, working conditions, places of employment, personal characteristics, education and training, job outlook, and salary range.

Front Desk Courtesy

National Educational Media, Inc.
21601 Devonshire St.
Chatsworth, CA 91311-9962
Phone: (818)709-6009

Videocassette. 1981. 11 mins. A demonstration of the importance of proper guest relations at the hotel front desk in a variety of challenging situations.

Future Aviation Professionals of America

Arco Publishing Co.
15 Columbus Circle
New York, NY 10023
Phone: (212)373-8931
Toll-free: 800-223-2336

1990. This career and educational planning and

job hunting guide for pilots includes information on pay and advancement possibilities. Lists Federal Aviation Administration approved pilot training schools and collegiate aviation programs. Lists new pilot qualifications for major airlines.

A narrow focus on a single specialty doesn't do much for your employability quotient. The more tasks you've performed and the more problems you've solved, the greater your chances of getting another job. A diverse resume should also help you ride out the twists of the economy and the whims of financial fashion. Since no one knows exactly which skills will be in demand in the future, you'd better have several to offer.

Source: *Business Week*

Get a Better Job!

Peterson's
PO Box 2123
Princeton, NJ 08543-2123
Phone: (609)243-9111

Ed Rushlow. 1990. $11.95. 225 pages. Counsels the reader on job search techniques. Discusses how to win the job by bypassing the Personnel Department and how to understand the employer's system for screening and selecting candidates. Written in an irreverent and humorous style.

Getting Down to Business: Travel Agency

American Institutes for Research
PO Box 11131
Palo Alto, CA 94302
Phone: (415)493-3550
Fax: (415)858-0958

Rachel L. Rassen. 1981.

Getting Hired: How to Sell Yourself

Carolina Pacific Publishing
7808 SE 28th Ave.
PO Box 02399
Portland, OR 97202

Costanzo, W. Kenneth. 1987. $8.95. 103 pages.

Getting a Job in the Computer Age

Peterson's
PO Box 2123
Princeton, NJ 08543-2123
Phone: (609)243-9111

Compiled by the staff of the National Institute for Work and Learning. $7.95. 101 pages. Describes more than 75 of the most popular occupational categories and the computer requirements for each.

Getting to the Right Job

Workman Publishing
708 Broadway
New York, NY 10003
Phone: (212)254-5900

Cohen, Steve, and de Oliveira, Paulo. 1987. $6.95. 288 pages.

Go Hire Yourself an Employer

Doubleday and Co., Inc.
666 5th Ave.
New York, NY 10103
Phone: (212)984-7561

Irish, Richard K. 1987. $9.95. 312 pages.

Guerilla Tactics in the Job Market

Bantam Books
666 5th Ave.
New York, NY 10103
Phone: (212)765-6500

Jackson, Tom. 1987. $4.50. 384 pages. Provides 79 action-oriented tips for getting the job or changing jobs.

A Guide to Becoming a Flight Attendant

Bob Adams, Inc.
260 Center St.
Holbrook, MA 02343
Phone: (617)268-9570

Douglas K. Kinan. 1987. Job hunting guide for flight attendants. Describes qualifications. Offers advice on getting an interview, writing resumes and cover letters, filling out the application, and interviewing. Contains 45 sample interview questions with sample "preferred" answers.

Guide to Starting and Operating a Successful Travel Agency

Delmar Publishers, Inc.
2 Computer Dr., W.
PO Box 15015
Albany, NY 12212-5015
Phone: (518)459-1150

Stevens, Laurence. 1985. $29.95. Guide to travel agency management. Topics covered include buying and starting a travel agency; hiring and training staff; advertising and promoting; establishing an accounting system; initiating a commercial or group travel unit; escorting tours; and related travel agency management concerns. Includes a glossary and an appendix listing associations, attorneys, automation vendors, franchisors, insurers, and other travel agency suppliers.

Have You Considered.Hotel Management?

Catalyst
250 Park Ave., S.
New York, NY 10003
Phone: (212)777-8900

1987. This pamphlet describes the field of hotel management, the nature of the work, salary, education and training, entering the field, and employment outlook.

Helicoptor Pilots

Chronicle Guidance Publications, Inc.
PO Box 1190
Moravia, NY 13118-1190
Phone: (315)497-0330

1990. This career brief describes the nature of the job, working conditions, hours and earnings, education and training, licensure, certification, unions, personal qualifications, social and psychological factors, location, employment outlook, entry methods, advancement, and related occupations.

Hospitality Industry

AIMS Media, Inc.
9710 DeSoto Ave.
Chatsworth, CA 93111-4409
Phone: (818)773-4300

Videocassette. 1988. 40 mins. A section of the "Career Awareness" series which covers the hotel industry.

Hospitality Industry Compensation Survey

American Hotel & Motel Assn.
1201 New York Ave., NW
Washington, DC 20005-3917
Phone: (202)289-3100

1987. Reports the salaries of 17 managerial positions by region, property size, and revenue.

Hospitality and Recreation

Franklin Watts, Inc.
387 Park Ave., S.
New York, NY 10016
Phone: (212)686-7070

Marjorie R. Schulz. 1990. Part of the Careers for Today series.

Hotel Front Office Management & Operation

William C. Brown Group
2460 Kerper Blvd.
Dubuque, IA 52001
Phone: (319)588-1451
Fax: (319)589-2955

Peter Dukas. Third edition, 1970.

Hotel/Motel Careers: A World of Opportunities

American Hotel and Motel Assn.
Educational Institute
1407 S. Harrison Rd.
PO Box 1240
E. Lansing, MI 48826
Phone: (202)289-3100

1990. Booklet providing an overview of the lodging industry and its job opportunities.

Hotel/Motel Careers: Check It Out!

Educational Institute of the American Hotel and Motel Assn.
PO Box 1240
East Lansing, MI 48826
Phone: (517)353-5500
Toll-free: 800-752-4567

This pamphlet describes career opportunities in the hotel/motel industry, as well as education, training, and scholarships.

Hotel/Motel Clerk

Careers, Inc.
PO Box 135
Largo, FL 34649-0135
Phone: (813)584-7333

1990. Two-page occupational summary card describing duties, working conditions, personal qualifications, training, earnings and hours, employment outlook, places of employment, related careers and where to write for more information.

C ovia, the airline reservation company based in Rosemont, IL, is co-owned by American Airlines and six other carriers. Covia runs Apollo, the second-largest reservation system behind AMR Corp.'s Sabre. The two systems each enjoy about a third of the $1.5 billion market. Technology advances in the field are fast and furious, even allowing travel agents to call up pictures of hotel rooms on their screens. In 1991 Covia made plans for overseas expansion, supplementing joint ventures in Canada and Great Britain with partnerships in Japan and Korea.

Source: *Forbes*

Hotel-Motel Manager

Careers, Inc.
180 5th Ave.
Largo, FL 34649-0135
Phone: (813)584-7333
Toll-free: 800-726-0441

1987. Eight-page brief offering the definition, history, duties, working conditions, personal qualifications, educational requirements, earnings, hours, employment outlook, advancement, and careers related to this position.

Hotel and Motel Managers

Chronicle Guidance Publications, Inc.
Aurora St. Extension
PO Box 1190
Moravia, NY 13118-1190
Phone: (315)497-0330

1987. Career brief describing the nature of the job, working conditions, hours and earnings, education and training, licensure, certification, unions, personal qualifications, social and psychological factors, location, employment outlook, entry methods, advancement, and related occupations.

The Hotel: One Week in the Life of the Plaza

Simon & Schuster, Inc.
Simon & Schuster Bldg.
1230 Ave. of the Americas
New York, NY 10020
Phone: (212)698-7000

Sonny Kleinfield. 1989. Describes the operation of a large hotel; the author spent one week behind the scenes at the New York Plaza Luxury Hotel.

How to Apply for a Job

Acoma Books
PO Box 4
Ramona, CA 92065

Post, L.H. $2.50. 32 pages. Also available in Spanish.

How to Create Your Ideal Job or Next Career

Ten Speed Press
PO Box 7123
Berkeley, CA 94707
Phone: (415)845-8414

Bolles, Richard N. 1990. $4.95. 64 pages. Trade edition of the new job-hunting guide from *What Color Is Your Parachute?*

How to Find and Get the Job You Want

Johnson/Rudolph Educational Resources, Inc.
1004 State St.
Bowling Green, KY 42101

1989. $20.50. 160 pages. Aimed at the college student.

How to Get a Better Job Quicker

Taplinger Publishing Co., Inc.
132 W. 22nd St.
New York, NY 10011
Phone: (212)877-1040

Payne, Richard A. 1987. $16.95. 217 pages.

How to Get a Better Job in This Crazy World

Crown Publishers, Inc.
225 Park Ave., S.
New York, NY 10003
Phone: (212)254-1600

Half, Robert. $17.95.

How to Get and Get Ahead on Your First Job

VGM Career Horizons
4255 W. Touhy Ave.
Lincolnwood, IL 60646-1975
Phone: (708)679-5500

Bloch, Deborah Perlmutter. 1988. $6.95. 160 pages. Details in step-by-step ways how to go about finding that first job, apply for it, write the winning resume, and manage the successful interview.

How to Get Interviews from Job Ads

Elderkin Associates
PO Box 1293
Dedham, MA 02026

Elderkin, Kenton W. 1989. $19.50. 256 pages. Outlines how to select and follow up ads to get the job. Includes unique ways to get interview offers and how to incorporate the use of a computer and a fax machine in arranging interviews. Illustrated.

How to Get a Job with A Cruise Line: Adventure-Travel-Romance - How to Sail Around the World on Cruise Ships & Get Paid for It

Ticket to Adventure, Inc.
PO Box 47622
St. Petersburg, FL 33743
Phone: (813)544-0066

Mary F. Miller. 1990.

How to Land a Better Job

VGM Career Horizons
4255 W. Touhy Ave.
Lincolnwood, IL 60646-1975
Phone: (708)679-5500

Lott, Catherine S., and Lott, Oscar C. 1989. $7.95. 160 pages. Tells the job seeker how to enhance his or her credentials, overcome past weaknesses, uncover job leads, get appointments, organize an appealing resume, and score points in interviews. A special section devoted to getting a better job without changing companies covers the process of transferring departments and gives pointers on moving up to the boss's job.

> areer paths in the future will more closely resemble a series of loosely connected dots than a neat line headed upward. To advance, professionals will have to resist pigeon-holing themselves in one industry, location, company or even career. Instead, they will need to be prepared to move backward and sideways from large companies to small ones, from one city to another, from the corporate womb to their own small enterprises. Those with portable skills may discover opportunity even in struggling industries.
>
> Source: *U.S. News & World Report*

How to Open and Run a Money-Making Travel Agency

John Wiley and Sons, Inc.
605 3rd Ave.
New York, NY 10158
Phone: (212)850-6000
Fax: (212)850-6088

Pamela Fremont. 1983.

How to Seek a New and Better Job

Consultants Bookstore
Templeton Rd.
Fitzwilliam, NH 03447
Phone: (603)585-6544
Fax: (603)585-9221

Gerraughty, William. 1987. $5.95. 64 pages. Presents information on cover letters, resumes, and mailings. Includes a self-analysis, fifty-six questions asked by interviewers, and a variety of forms and lists.

How to Use Job Ads to Land the Job You Really Want

Jeffrey Lant Associates
50 Follen St., No. 507
Cambridge, MA 02138
Phone: (617)547-6372

$4.00. A summary of an interview with Kenton

Elderkin, author of *How to Get Interviews from Job Ads: Where to Look, What To Select, Who to Write, What to Say, When to Follow-up, How to Save Time.*

How to Win the Job You Really Want

Henry Holt and Co.
115 W. 18th St.
New York, NY 10011

Weinberg, Janice. 1988. $10.95. 290 pages.

The bureau of Labor Statistics predicts that 18 million new jobs will be created in the U.S. in the 1990s.

How You Too Can Become a Flight Attendant!: A Step by Step Guide

Ross Publishing Co.
Rte. 3, 188 Forester Rd.
Slippery Rock, PA 16057
Phone: (412)794-2837

Debby Shearer. 1987.

I Got the Job!

Crisp Publications, Inc.
95 1st St.
Los Altos, CA 94022

Chapman, Elwood N. 1988. $7.95. 80 pages. Provides case studies and demonstrates how to plan a targeted job search.

INNovation: Creativity Techniques for Hospitality Managers

John Wiley & Sons, Inc.
605 3rd Ave.
New York, NY 10158
Phone: (212)850-6000

Florence Berger and Dennis H. Ferguson. 1990.

International Employment Hotline

International Employment Hotline
PO Box 3030
Oakton, VA 22124
Phone: (703)620-1972
Fax: (703)620-1973

Monthly. $29.00/year. Covers temporary and career job openings overseas and advice for international job hunters. Entries include: Company name, job title, description of job,

requirements, geographic location of job. Arranged geographically.

Introduction to Management in the Hospitality Industry

John Wiley & Sons, Inc.
605 3rd Ave.
New York, NY 10158
Phone: (212)850-6000
Fax: (212)850-6088

Tom Powers. Third edition, 1988.

Job and Career Building

Ten Speed Press
PO Box 7123
Berkeley, CA 94707
Phone: (415)845-8414

Germann, Richard, and Arnold, Peter. $7.95. 256 pages.

The Job Hunt

Ten Speed Press
PO Box 7123
Berkeley, CA 94707
Phone: (415)845-8414

Nelson, Robert. $2.95. 64 pages. A compact guide with a direct, question-and-answer format with space for notations.

The Job HUNTER

University of Missouri-Columbia
Career Planning and Placement Center
100 Noyes Bldg.
Columbia, MO 65211

Biweekly. $50.00/6 months; $75.00/year. Lists opportunities for college graduates with 0-3 years experience in many fields. Includes information on internships and summer jobs.

The Job Hunter's Final Exam

Surrey Books, Inc.
500 N. Michigan, No. 1940
Chicago, IL 60611
Phone: (312)661-0050

Camden, Thomas. 1990. $8.95. 140 pages. Helps job seeker quiz self about resumes, interviews, and general job-hunting strategies.

The Job Hunter's Workbook

Peterson's
PO Box 2123
Princeton, NJ 08543-2123
Phone: (609)243-9111

Taggart, Judith; Moore, Lynn; and Naylor, Mary. $12.95. 140 pages. Deals with such job-seeking topics as assessing personal strengths, networking, interviewing and answering interview questions, dealing with salaries and benefits, and preparing resumes, cover letters, and portfolios. A combination of self-assessment exercises, work sheets, checklists, and advice.

Job Search: Career Planning Guidebook, Book II

Brooks/Cole Publishing Co.
Marketing Dept.
511 Forest Lodge Rd.
Pacific Grove, CA 93950

Lock. 1988. $9.00. 248 pages. Assists the reader in a production job search.

The Job Search Companion: The Organizer for Job Seekers

The Harvard Common Press
535 Albany St.
Boston, MA 02118
Phone: (617)423-5803

Wallach and Arnold. 1987. $7.95. 160 pages. An organizer with resources and forms to assist in and direct the job search process.

The Job Search Handbook

Bob Adams, Inc.
260 Center St.
Holbrook, MA 02343
Phone: (617)767-8100
Fax: (617)767-0994

Noble, John. $6.95. 144 pages. Identifies and provides advice on the essential elements of the job search, including networking, cover letters, interviewing, and salary negotiation. Aimed at first-time entrants to the job market, those looking for a job in a new field, and middle-level professionals looking to take their next step up.

Job Search: The Total System

Consultants Bookstore
Templeton Rd.
Fitzwilliam, NH 03447
Phone: (603)585-6544
Fax: (603)585-9221

Dawson, Kenneth, and Dawson, Sheryl. 1988. $12.95. 244 pages. A guide that shows how to link networking, resume writing, interviewing, references, and follow-up letters to land the job. Thirty resumes are included.

Personality tests to assess job applicants are too expensive for many companies to administer, but they still want to base hiring decisions on some diagnostic tool. Lately more companies seem to be turning to handwriting analysis in screening job seekers. It's a popular technique in Europe, but not universally accepted or openly used in the United States. In Rhode Island a legislator tried unsuccessfully in 1991 to ban the use of handwriting analysis in job selection. Critics and skeptics abound, but the practice is gaining ground and some companies swear by it.

Source: *Newsweek*

Job Seeking Guide

Delmar Publishers, Inc.
2 Computer Dr., W.
PO Box 15015
Albany, NY 12212-5015
Phone: (518)459-1150
Fax: (518)459-3552

Pautler Jr., Albert J., 80 pages. Covers the job search, from preparation to interviewing to results.

Jobs '92

Prentice Hall Press
15 Columbus Circle
New York, NY 10023

Kathryn and Ross Petras. 1992, annual. Provides career outlook information for 15 career fields, as well as special reports on disabled workers, minorities, and women. Also includes industry forecasts for 29 industry segments and a look at regional conditions in the United States.

JOBS! What They Are, Where They Are, What They Pay

The New Careers Center
1515 23rd St.
Box 297-CT
Boulder, CO 80306

Snelling, Robert, and Snelling, Anne. 1989. $12.95. Covers jobs available in today's job market, their duties and responsiblities, what they pay, and how to pursue them. Focuses on the seven top entry-level job areas.

Airline reservationists are expected to handle 150 to 200 calls per day.

Source: *Harper's*

Journeying Outward: A Guide to Career Development

Delmar Publishers, Inc.
2 Computer Dr., W.
PO Box 15015
Albany, NY 12212-5015
Phone: (518)459-1150
Fax: (518)459-3552

Lynton, Jonathan. 1989. 224 pages. Examines the correct way to present oneself in the job search, covering appearance, interviewing, writing a resume, and completing a job application. Resume writing section illustrates models of various resume formats. Includes sections on planning the job search and working the plan.

Joyce Lain Kennedy's Career Book

VGM Career Horizons
4255 W. Touhy Ave.
Lincolnwood, IL 60646-1975
Phone: (708)679-5500

Kennedy, Joyce Lain. Co-authored by Dr. Darryl Laramore. 1988. $14.95 paperback. $29.95 hardcover. 448 pages. Guides the reader through the entire career-planning and job-hunting process. Addresses how to find the kinds of jobs available and what to do once the job is secured. Provides a number of case histories to give examples.

Kennedy's Career Strategist

Marilyn Moats Kennedy Career Strategies
1153 Wilmette Ave.
Wilmette, IL 60091

Twelve issues/year. $75.00/year. Offers job search guidance.

Liberal Education and Careers Today

The Career Press, Inc.
PO Box 34
Hawthorne, NJ 07507
Phone: 800-227-3371

Figler, Howard. 1989. $10.95 108 pages. Shows job seekers with liberal arts education how to link their majors to the specific needs of employers.

Managing Your Career

Dow Jones and Co.
420 Lexington Ave.
New York, NY 10170

College version of the *National Business Employment Weekly*. Excludes job openings, but provides job-hunting advice.

Martin's Magic Formula for Getting the Right Job

St. Martin's Press
Special Sales Dept.
175 5th Ave.
New York, NY 10010
Phone: (212)674-5151

Martin, Phyllis. 1987. $7.95. 192 pages. A comprehensive approach to the job campaign.

Merchandising Your Job Talents

U.S. Government Printing Office
Superintendent of Documents
Washington, DC 20402

Booklet. 1986. 21 pages. General advice for job seekers. Illustrated.

Network Your Way to Job and Career Success

The Career Press Inc.
62 Beverly Rd.
PO Box 34
Hawthorne, NJ 07507
Phone: 800-227-3371

Krannich, Ron, and Krannich, Caryl. 1989.

$11.95. 180 pages. Based on a comprehensive career planning framework, each chapter outlines the best strategies for identifying, finding, and transforming networks to gather information and obtain advice and referrals that lead to job interviews and offers. Includes exercises, sample interviewing dialogues, and a directory of organizations for initiating and sustaining networking activities.

The New Quick Job-Hunting Map

Ten Speed Press
PO Box 7123
Berkeley, CA 94707
Phone: (415)845-8414

Bolles, Richard N. $2.95. 64 pages. Trade version of *The Quick Job-Hunting Map* in *What Color Is Your Parachute?* Provides a personal blueprint for the job search.

Occupational Outlook Handbook

Bureau of Labor Statistics
441 G St., NW
Washington, DC 20212
Phone: (202)523-1327

Biennial, May of even years. $24.00 hardcover. $22.00 paperback. Contains profiles of various occupations, which include description of occupation, educational requirements, market demand, and expected earnings. Also lists over 100 state employment agencies and State Occupational Information Coordinating Committees that provide state and local job market and career information; various occupational organizations that provide career information. Arranged by occupation; agencies and committees are geographical. Send orders to: Superintendent of Documents, U.S. Government Printing Office, Washington, D.C. 20402 (202-783-3238).

The Official Guide to Airline Careers

Arco Publishing Co.
15 Columbus Circle
New York, NY 10023
Phone: (212)373-8931
Toll-free: 800-223-2348

Alexander Clark Morton. Sixth edition, 1983.

The One Day Plan for Jobhunters

Prakken Publications, Inc.
416 Longshore Dr.
PO Box 8623
Ann Arbor, MI 48107

Segalini and Kurtz. 1988. $9.95. 100 pages.

Online Hotline News Service

Information Intelligence, Inc.
PO Box 31098
Phoenix, AZ 85046
Phone: (602)996-2283

Contains five files, one of which is Joblines, featuring listings of employment and resume services available in voice, print, and online throughout North America.

Large companies can be great schools: Think of them as learn-while-you-earn programs. Hands-on management, for example, is an absolute requirement in today's job market. So people in staff jobs should seek line responsibilities. Seasoned operating managers, on the other hand, should pick up planning or development experience to round out their portfolios.

Source: *Business Week*

The Only Job Hunting Guide You'll Ever Need

Poseidon Press
Simon and Schuster Bldg.
1230 Ave. of the Americas
New York, NY 10020
Phone: (212)698-7290

Petras, Kathryn, and Petras, Ross. 1989. $8.95. 318 pages. Covers the full range of the job search process.

Opportunities in Airline Careers

National Textbook Co.
4255 W. Touhy Ave.
Lincolnwood, IL 60646
Phone: (312)679-5500

Adrian A. Paradis, author. 1987. Surveys trends in the industry and career opportunities with the airlines including management, customer service, flying, and maintenance. Describes pilots job duties, working conditions, and basic educational and training requirements.

Opportunities in Hotel and Motel Management

National Textbook Co.
4255 W. Touhy Ave.
Lincolnwood, IL 60646-1975
Phone: (708)679-5500
Toll-free: 800-323-4900

Shepard Henkin. Revised edition, 1985. Describes jobs in the hospitality industry, employment outlook, personal requirements, educational preparation, apprenticeship and training, salary, and job hunting techniques.

Most people's careers divide into three stages, each with pitfalls and possibilities. The first stage, running from your 20s into your middle to late 30s, is the time to expose yourself to as many varied job situations as possible, assembling a repertory of basic skills. By your late 30s or early 40s, you must be a key player, attuned to your company's strategic goals and fully conversant with customer needs, new-product possibilities, and all the vagaries of your particular marketplace; or else you should switch jobs. Most people reach their career peak in their late 40s or early 50s.

Source: *Fortune*

Opportunities in Non-Profit Organizations

ACCESS/Networking in the Public Interest
96 Mt. Auburn St.
Cambridge, MA 02138

Monthly. Lists opportunities in many fields, including public interest law.

Out of Work but Not Alone

Self-Help Clearinghouse
Publications Dept.
St. Clares-Riverside Medical Center
Pocono Rd.
Denville, NJ 07834
Phone: (201)625-9565

1984. $9.00.

Peterson's Job Opportunities for Business and Liberal Arts Graduates 1991

Peterson's
PO Box 2123
Princeton, NJ 08543-2123
Phone: (609)243-9111

Compiled by the Peterson's staff. 1991. $19.95 paperback. $35.95 hardcover. 300 pages. Lists hundreds of organizations that are hiring new business, humanities, and social science graduates in the areas of business and management. Explores how to match academic backgrounds to specific job openings. Provides information about opportunities for experienced personnel as well. Includes data on starting locations by city and state, summer jobs, co-op jobs, internships, and international assignments.

Professional Job Finder

Planning/Communications
7215 Oak Ave.
River Forest, IL 60305-1935
Phone: (708)366-5200

Daniel Lauber. 1992. Provides information on approximately 2,000 specialized sources of help wanted ads, including periodicals, job hotlines, and computerized databases. Arranged by subject and also by state.

Resort Development and Management

American Hotel & Motel Assn.
1201 New York Ave., NW, Ste. 600
Washington, DC 20005
Phone: (202)289-3100

Chuck Y. Gee; edited by Marjorie Harless. Second edition, 1988. Offers extensive details on the process of planning and development, managing the health club/spa facility, computer systems, security, safety, and risk management.

The Right Place at the Right Time

Ten Speed Press
PO Box 7123
Berkeley, CA 94707
Phone: (415)845-8414

Wegmann, Robert G. $9.95. 192 pages. A comprehensive approach to career planning and job seeking developed to find the right job in the new economy.

Secrets of the Hidden Job Market
Betterway Publications, Inc.
White Hall, VA 22987
Phone: (804)823-5661

Rodgers, Bob; Johnson, Steve; and Alexander, Bill. 1986.

Skills in Action: A Job-Finding Workbook
Univ. of Akron
Adult Resource Center
Akron, OH 44325

Selden, J.H. $12.50. 75 pages. Workbook format; aimed at job seekers looking for initial or transitional employment.

So You Want to Be an Innkeeper
Chronicle Books
275 Fifth St.
San Francisco, CA 94103
Phone: (415)777-7240
Fax: (415)777-8887

Mary E. Davies. 1990.

The Student's Guide to Finding a Superior Job
Slawson Communications
165 Vallecitos de Oro
San Marcos, CA 92069

Cohen, William A. 1987. $9.95. Aimed at the new college graduate.

The Successful Job Hunter's Handbook
Johnson/Rudolph Educational Resources, Inc.
1004 State St.
Bowling Green, KY 42101

1987. $12.95. 150 pages.

Suggestions for Career Exploration and Jobseeking
New York State Dept. of Labor
Div. of Research and Statistics
NY-SOICC
State Office Bldg. Campus, Bldg. 12,
Rm. 488
Albany, NY 12240
Phone: (518)457-6182

Brochure. 1989. Free. Prepared for New York State labor market. Includes roster of state Job Service offices.

Super Job Search: The Complete Manual for Job-Seekers and Career-Changers
Jeffrey Lant Associates
50 Follen St., No. 507
Cambridge, MA 02138
Phone: (617)547-6372

Studner, Peter. $25.95. 325 pages. A step-by-step guidebook for getting a job, with sections on getting started, how to present accomplishments, networking strategies, telemarketing tips, and negotiating tactics.

S ince most savvy air travelers expect problems, what's most important is how such problems are explained and resolved. The best airlines give employees who have contact with customers plenty of leeway to act. Some airlines are allocating trained personnel in airports to enhance communication and focus on solving customers' problems. Douglas C. Birdsall, president of Travelmation Corp., a travel consultant in Stamford, CT, argues that airlines could use computer systems more effectively to track passengers and baggage through their many connections.

Source: *Business Week*

Taking Charge of Your Career Direction: Career Planning Guidebook, Book I
Brooks/Cole Publishing Co.
Marketing Dept.
511 Forest Lodge Rd.
Pacific Grove, CA 93950

Lock. 1988. $13.50. 377 pages. Provides guidance for the job search process.

Ticket Agents
Chronicle Guidance Publications, Inc.
PO Box 1190
Moravia, NY 13118-1190
Phone: (315)497-0330
Toll-free: 800-622-7284

1991. This career brief describes the nature of the work, working conditions, hours and earnings, education and training, licensure, certification, unions, personal qualifications, social and psychological factors, employment outlook, entry methods, advancement, and related occupations.

Training for the Hospitality Industry
American Hotel & Motel Assn.
1201 New York Ave., NW
Washington, DC 20005
Phone: (202)289-3100

Lewis C. Forrest, Jr. Second edition, 1989.

L ester Minsuk and Phyllis Macklin, outplacement specialists in Princeton, NJ, advise clients to dress like the boss of the person you're hoping to work for. They also stress that compromises with your natural inclinations may be necessary, like touching up a greying beard with Grecian Formula, toning down makeup, or buying a serious watch. "You've got to remember that you are a product, and you need to be packaged."

Source: *Fortune*

Travel Agent
Careers, Inc.
PO Box 135
Largo, FL 34649-0135
Phone: (813)584-7333

1990. Two-page occupational summary card describing duties, working conditions, personal qualifications, training, earnings and hours, employment outlook, places of employment, related careers and where to write for more information.

Travel Agent
Vocational Biographies, Inc.
PO Box 31, Dept. VF10
Sauk Centre, MN 56378
Phone: (612)352-6516
Toll-free: 800-255-0752

1989. This pamphlet profiles a person working in the job. Includes information about job duties, working conditions, places of employment, educational preparation, labor market outlook, and salaries.

Travel Agent
Arco/Prentice Hall Press
1 Gulf & Western Plaza
New York, NY 10023
Phone: (212)373-8500

Wilma Boyd. 1989. Introduction to the travel

business. Covers U.S. and foreign travel, time zones, ticketing, world geography, and airline, railroad, and tour bus connections, and accommodations. Outlines entry-level positions in the airline, car rental, and hospitality industries as well as in travel agencies and related travel services. Explains travel agency operations, sales techniques, and the use of computers in travel services. Gives job hunting advice and sales tips.

The Travel Agent: Dealer in Dreams
Prentice Hall Press
1 Gulf & Western Plaza
New York, NY 10023
Phone: (212)373-8500

Aryear Gregory. Third edition, 1989. Comprehensive guide for those interested in the travel industry . Covers the work of the travel agent, agency problems, techniques, and promotion. Describes various jobs within the travel industry including travel consultant, agency manager, and tour operators. Explains the knowledge, skills, training, and educational preparation needed to succeed.

Travel Agents
Chronicle Guidance Publications, Inc.
PO Box 1190
Moravia, NY 13118-1190
Phone: (315)497-0330
Toll-free: 800-622-7284

1988. This career brief describes the nature of the work, working conditions, hours and earnings, education and training, licensure, certification, unions, personal qualifications, social and psychological factors, employment outlook, entry methods, advancement, and related occupations.

Travel Career Development
Houghton Mifflin Co.
1 Beacon St.
Boston, MA 02108
Phone: (617)725-5000

Nona Starr. Fourth edition, 1990.

Travel Free: How to Start and Succeed in Your Own Travel Consultant Business

Prima Publishing and Communications
4970 Topaz Ave.
PO Box 1260
Rocklin, CA 95677
Phone: (916)624-5718

Ben Dominitz. 1984.

Travel Industry Guidelines for Employment

Travel Text Associates
12065 State Fair
Detroit, MI 48205
Phone: (313)527-6971

Chris Hoosen. 1990. Part of Travel Agent Training Series.

U.S. Employment Opportunities: A Career News Service

Washington Research Associates
7500 E. Arapaho Plaza, Ste. 250
Englewood, CO 80112
Phone: (303)694-1259
Fax: (303)770-1945

Annual; quarterly updates. $166.00 per year to libraries; $184.00 per year to others. List of over 1,000 employment contacts in companies and agencies in the banking, arts, telecommunications, education, and 14 other industries and professions, including the federal government. Entries include: Company name, name of representative, address, description of products or services, hiring and recruiting practices, training programs, and year established. Classified by industry. Indexes: Occupation.

What Color Is Your Parachute?

Ten Speed Press
PO Box 7123
Berkeley, CA 94707
Phone: (415)845-8414

Bolles, Richard N. 1992. $12.95 paperback. Subtitled: *A Practical Manual for Job-Hunters and Career-Changers.* One of the best-known works on job hunting, this book provides detailed and strategic advice on all aspects of the job search.

What is a Travel Agent?

American Society of Travel Agents
1101 King St., Ste. 200
Alexandria, VA 22314
Phone: (703)739-2782

This six-panel brochure describes industry outlook, education, training, job duties, and working conditions.

Where Can I Find Help With. . .

Ready Reference Press
PO Box 5249
Santa Monica, CA 90405
Phone: (213)474-5175

$95.00. Two-volume set. Subtitled: *The Sourcebook of Career Services and Programs.* Lists extensive resources aimed at the young job seeker, including job banks, resume preparation services, testing programs, job referral sources, career training programs, and others. Entries provide organization name, type of service, description, audience served, costs (if any), hours, address, and telephone number. Subject and geographic indexes.

Where Do I Go from Here with My Life?

Ten Speed Press
PO Box 7123
Berkeley, CA 94707
Phone: (415)845-8414

Crystal, John C., and Bolles, Richard N. $9.95. 272 pages. A planning manual for students of all ages, instructors, counselors, career seekers, and career changers.

Where the Jobs Are: A Comprehensive Directory of 1200 Journals Listing Career Opportunities

Garrett Park Press
PO Box 190
Garrett Park, MD 20896
Phone: (301)946-2553

1989. $15.00; $14.00, prepaid. Contains list of approximately 1,200 journals that publish advertisements announcing job opportunities. Arranged alphabetically. Indexes: Occupational field.

Where to Start Career Planning

Peterson's
PO Box 2123
Princeton, NJ 08543-2123
Phone: (609)243-9111

Lindquist, Carolyn Lloyd, and Feodoroff, Pamela L. 1989. $15.95. 315 pages. Lists and describes the career-planning publications used by Cornell University's Career Center, one of the largest career libraries in the country. Covers more than 2,000 books, periodicals, and audiovisual resources on topics such as financial aid, minority and foreign students, overseas employment and travel, resources for the disabled, second careers, study-and-work options, summer and short-term jobs, women's issues, and careers for those without a bachelor's degree. Includes a bibliographic title index.

At least 75% of employers surveyed by the American Productivity & Quality Center, a consulting, training, and research firm in Houston, TX, now use contingent-pay plans. The employers include banks, steelmakers, and hospitals. "We do 1500 executive searches a year in North America, and I can't remember the last the jobs didn't include some kind of variable bonus component," asserts Robert Rollo, a managing director at the Korn/Ferry recruiting firm in Los Angeles, CA.

Source: *U.S. News & World Report*

Which Niche?

Bob Adams, Inc.
260 Center St.
Holbrook, MA 02343
Phone: (617)767-8100
Fax: (617)767-0994

Shingleton, Jack. $4.95. 164 pages. Subtitled: *Answers to the Most Common Questions about Careers and Job Hunting.* Designed to convey essential job-hunting information without adding unnecessary jargon. Each section is accompanied by a humorous cartoon illustrating the lighter side of job prospecting.

Who's Hiring Who

Ten Speed Press
PO Box 7123
Berkeley, CA 94707
Phone: (415)845-8414

Lathrop, Richard. $9.95. 268 pages. Provides advice on finding a better job faster and at a higher rate of pay.

Work in the New Economy: Careers and Job Seeking into the 21st Century

The New Careers Center
1515 23rd St.
Box 297-CT
Boulder, CO 80306

1989. $15.95.

Your Career in Hotel Management

Arco Publishing Co.
15 Columbus Circle
New York, NY 10023
Phone: (212)373-8931

Susan Gordan. 1983. Part of Arco's Career Guidance series. Includes an index.

Professional and Trade Periodicals

1830 Arrived

Russ Moore & Assoc.
4151 Knob . Dr., Ste. 200
Eagan, MN 55122
Toll-free: 800-728-3213

Diane Steen, editor. Quarterly. Trade magazine covering the hospitality industry.

Air Line Pilot

Air Line Pilots Assn.
535 Herndon Pkwy.
PO Box 1169
Herndon, VA 22070
Phone: (703)689-4176
Fax: (703)689-4370

Esperison Martinez, Jr., Editor. Monthly. Magazine covering industry trends and developments, flight technology, and air safety.

Air Transport (ATA)
Air Transport Assn. of America
1709 New York Ave., NW
Washington, DC 20006
Phone: (202)626-4000

Annual.

Airline, Ship & Catering
International Publishing Co. of America
PO Box 188
Hialeah, FL 33011
Phone: (305)887-1701
Fax: (305)885-1923

Jim O'Neal, Editor. 8x/yr. Travel magazine.

Airport Journal
PO Box 273
Clarendon Hills, IL 60514
Phone: (708)318-6872
Fax: (708)986-5010

John Andrews, Editor and Publisher. Monthly. Magazine serving the air transport industry in the Chicago area.

Airport Services
Lakewood Publications
50 S. 9th St.
Minneapolis, MN 55402
Phone: (612)333-0471
Fax: (612)333-6526

Patrick Barry, Publisher. 2x/mo.

Amusement Business
BPI Communications
1515 Broadway
New York, NY 10036
Toll-free: 800-648-1436

Weekly. $75/annual subscription. Includes information on jobs available at amusement parks.

AOCS News
Airline Operational Control Society
131 Pilgrim Dr.
Sewicklem, PA 15143
Phone: (412)741-5349

Steve Mineck, editor. Quarterly. Publishes news of the association, which is "dedicated to the preservation and advancement of civil aviation through the concept of ground-based operational control." Offers information on activities of government agencies in civil aviation, new procedures, and equipment for the aircraft dispatcher.

ARTAFACTS
Assn. of Retail Travel Agents
1745 Jefferson Davis Pkwy., Ste. 300
Arlington, VA 22202-3402
Phone: (703)553-7777
Toll-free: 800-969-6069
Fax: (703)486-0228

Monthly. Reviews developments in the travel industry for retail travel agents. Covers topics such as ethics, tour operations, transportation services, educational opportunities, commissions, and political action in pertinent issues. Includes chapter and association news.

While most of a hotel concierge's work is routine—travel reservations, theater tickets, restaurants—some problems require creative solutions. Like returning an embarrassed and elusive naked guest to his locked room, finding a belly dancer for a party, procuring a mobile dry cleaning team for a guest's automotive upholstery, outfitting a private jet for a guest's personal zoo, sending 4,000 roses to Cairo, or arranging a guest's cosmetic surgery.

Source: *Smithsonian*

ASTA Agency Management
Yankee Publications
666 5th Ave.
New York, NY 10103
Phone: (212)765-5454

Patrick Arton, Editor. Monthly. Magazine reporting and analyzing the business of the travel industry with special reference to travel agency profitability.

ASTA Stat (ASTA)
American Soc. of Travel Agents
1101 King St.
Alexandria, VA 22314
Phone: (703)739-2782

Monthly. Newsletter containing current travel industry statistics.

ASTA Travel Agency Management Magazine (ASTA)
American Soc. of Travel Agents
1101 King St.
Alexandria, VA 22314
Phone: (703)739-2782

Monthly.

AstaNotes (ASTA)
American Soc. of Travel Agents
1101 King St.
Alexandria, VA 22314
Phone: (703)739-2782

Weekly. Newsletter.

ATCA Bulletin
Air Traffic Control Assn.
2020 N. 14th St., Ste. 410
Arlington, VA 22201
Phone: (703)522-5717

Monthly. Features news of the association, which is interested in the establishment and maintenance of a safe and efficient air traffic control system.

> ■ n pay-for-knowledge systems, factory workers and ladder climbers whose careers have plateaued can boost pay by mastering new skills that help them make lateral moves. Such strategies pay off for companies as well, by allowing them to divide responsibilities among fewer people.
>
> Source: *U.S. News & World Report*

Atterbury Letter
Kirby and Renee Atterbury
PO Box 1197
Bethel Island, CA 94511
Phone: (510)684-3142

Editor(s): Kirby and Renee Atterbury. 6/yr. Carries personal opinions from readers and writers on their experience in various locales integrating wine, dining, and travel. Reports on travel fares, accommodations, conditions, tours, restaurants, and vineyards. Recurring features include specific recommendations, off-beat travel ideas, and discussions of seasonal differences in prices and services.

Aviation News
Aviation News, Inc.
6885 NW 25th St.
Miami, FL 33122
Phone: (305)871-8113
Fax: (305)871-6487

Steve Davis, editor. Monthly. An independent newspaper covering the general and commercial aviation industries.

Bulletin Voyages
Editions Acra Ltee.
Succursale E.
C.P. 85
Montreal, PQ, Canada H2T 3A5
Phone: (514)287-9773
Fax: (514)842-6180

Etienne Ozan-Groulx, Editor. Weekly. Travel trade magazine (French).

The Cornell Hotel and Restaurant Administration Quarterly
Cornell School of Hotel Administration
Statler Hall
Ithaca, NY 14853
Phone: (607)255-5093
Fax: (607)257-7608

Glenn Withiam, editor. Quarterly. Magazine of applied research and ideas for hotel and restaurant managers.

CTCs Newsletter (ICTA)
Institute of Certified Travel Agents
148 Linden St.
PO Box 82-56
Wellesley, MA 02181
Phone: (617)237-0280

Monthly.

CTO News for Travel Agents
Caribbean Tourism Organization
20 E. 46th St.
New York, NY 10017
Phone: (212)682-0435
Fax: (212)697-4258

6/yr. Instructs travel agents on how to effectively sell the Caribbean for greater profit. Reviews developments in Caribbean tourism, providing information on air flights, hotels, restaurants, and other attractions. Recurring features include editorials, news of members, and a calendar of events.

European Edition OAG Travel Planner Hotel & Motel RedBook
Official Airline Guides
2000 Clearwater Dr.
Oak Brook, IL 60521
Phone: (708)574-6000
Fax: (708)574-6667

Richard A. Nelson, Publisher. Quarterly. Directory containing information on travel to and through Europe, including country basics, city destination data, hotel/motel listings, airport diagrams, city and country maps, and reservation directories.

Flightlog
Assn. of Flight Attendants, AFL-CIO
1625 Massachusetts Ave., NW
Washington, DC 20036
Phone: (202)328-5400
Fax: (202)328-5424

Editor(s): Mary Ann Forbes. Bimonthly. Covers aviation industry news, aviation safety, legislative and government issues affecting flight attendants, union activities, and related topics.

Foodservice East
The Newbury St. Group, Inc.
545 Boylston St., No. 605
Boston, MA 02116-3606
Phone: (617)267-9080

Susan Holaday, editor. Seven issues/year. Tabloid covering restaurant, hotel, school, college, and hospital food service in the Northeast.

General Aviation News
PO Box 98786
Tacoma, WA 98498-0786
Phone: (214)248-0928

Daryl E. Murphy, editor. Biweekly. General aviation newspaper for aircraft pilots and owners.

The Hideaway Report
Harper Associates, Inc.
PO Box 50
Sun Valley, ID 83353-0050
Phone: (208)622-3183

Editor(s): Andrew Harper. Monthly. Provides informative critiques on small, secluded resorts and executive retreats around the world. Composed of 12-15 hotel descriptions per issue. Recurring features include Hideaway of the Year Awards in December issue and columns titled Reader Requests and Hotel & Travel Watch.

Hotel Industry Focus
Laventhol & Horath
1845 Walnut St.
Philadelphia, PA 19103
Phone: (215)299-1600
Fax: (215)299-8645
Editor(s): Carol Greenberg. Quarterly. Provides

econometrically based forecasts on the lodging industry.

Hotel & Motel Management
Edgell Communications, Inc.
7500 Old Oak Blvd.
Cleveland, OH 44130
Phone: (216)243-8100
Fax: (216)891-2726

Robert Nozar, editor. Eighteen issues/year. Magazine covering the lodging industry.

Hotel & Travel Index
500 Plaza Dr.
Secaucus, NJ 07096
Phone: (201)902-1600
Fax: (201)319-1628

Melinda Bush, Publisher. Quarterly. Magazine serving as a worldwide hotel directory.

Hotels
Cahners Publishing Co.
1350 E. Touhy Ave.
PO Box 5080
Des Plaines, IL 60017-5080
Phone: (708)635-8800

Donald T. Lock, Publisher. Monthly. Magazine covering management and operations as well as foodservice and design in the hospitality industry.

ICTA News
Institute of Certified Travel Agents
148 Linden St.
PO Box 56
Wellesley, MA 02181-0503
Phone: (617)237-0280
Toll-free: 800-542-4282
Fax: (617)237-3860

Editor(s): Dawn Ringel. 10/yr. Covers the educational activities of the Institute, which grants the Certified Travel Counselor (CTC) designation to travel industry personnel. Offers special news stories on topics relevant to the travel industry. Recurring features include news of members, management tips, and names of newly certified agents.

Innkeeping World

Charles Nolte
PO Box 84108
Seattle, WA 98124
Phone: (206)284-4247

Ten issues/year. Dedicated to providing information "to enhance the hotel executive's skillful management of all aspects of hotel operation through concisely written articles incorporating ideas and case-histories which communicate useful knowledge for lasting benefit." Features regular columns covering market and industry developments, marketing advice, personnel concerns, and other topics of interest to management level staff.

 o-called "gold-collar" workers are those valued for their brainpower and problem-solving abilities.

Inside Preferred Hotels

Preferred Hotels Worldwide
1901 S. Meyers Rd., Ste. 220
Oakbrook Terrace, IL 60148
Phone: (312)953-0404

Editor(s): Mary Foley. Monthly. Provides information for executives and general managers of the independently-owned Preferred Hotels. Reports personnel changes, statistics, and meeting and convention dates and locations.

Journal of the American Helicopter Society

American Helicopter Society
217 N. Washington St.
Alexandria, VA 22314
Phone: (703)684-6777
Fax: (703)739-9279

David A. Peters, editor. Quarterly. Technical journal on helicopters.

Lodging

American Hotel & Motel Association
1201 New York Ave., NW, Ste. 600
Washington, DC 20005
Phone: (202)289-3100

Monthly.

Lodging Briefing

Walter Mathews Associates, Inc.
28 W. 38th St.
New York, NY 10018
Phone: (212)921-4314
Fax: (212)719-9382

Editor(s): Walter Mathews. 10/yr. Remarks on industry developments, consumer trends, and economic performance in the area of travel. Carries information to help travel agents increase their sales, develop their promotional techniques, and to better manage both their employees and finances. Recurring features include travel price indexes.

Lodging Hospitality

Penton Publishing
1100 Superior Ave.
Cleveland, OH 44114
Phone: (216)696-7000
Fax: (216)696-7658

Ed Watkins, editor. Monthly. Magazine serving managers of independent, franchise, chain-owned, and referral groups in the hospitality industry.

Lodging Industry: National Trend of Business

Laventhol & Horwath
1845 Walnut St.
Philadelphia, PA 19103
Phone: (215)299-1600
Fax: (215)299-8645

Monthly. Compiles statistics and data on the hotel industry. Covers occupancy, room rates, and food and beverage sales, both nationally and by local regions throughout the country.

Meetings & Incentive Travel

Maclean Hunter Ltd.
777 Bay St.
Toronto, ON, Canada M5W 1A7
Phone: (416)596-2697
Fax: (416)596-5810

Tommi Lloyd, Editor. 7x/yr. Magazine for corporate meeting planners, incentive travel executives, and travel agents.

Motel/Hotel Insider

Magna Publishing
2718 Dryden
Madison, WI 53704
Phone: (608)249-2455

Editor(s): Robert Reis. Weekly. Covers motel/hotel management, travel and vacation trends, business travel, new products and services for the hospitality market, motel/hotel chains, and trends and changes in the lodging industry.

North American Edition OAG Business Travel Planner

Official Airline Guides
2000 Clearwater Dr.
Oak Brook, IL 60521
Phone: (708)574-6000
Fax: (708)574-6667

Richard A. Nelson, Publisher. Quarterly. Official lodging directory of the American Hotel and Motel Association includes city destination information, hotel listings, airport diagrams, city, metro, resort area and country maps, travel basics, and reservation directories.

Official Tour Directory

Thomas Publishing Co.
5 Penn Plaza
New York, NY 10001
Phone: (212)629-2175
Fax: (212)629-1544

Ester Reiter, editor. Lists 2,000 tour operators that offer tours and vacation packages to over 700 destinations worldwide.

PATA Travel News (Americas Edition)

Baxter Publications, Inc.
310 Dupont St.
Toronto, ON, Canada M5R 1V9
Phone: (416)968-7252

Timothy Baxter, Editor. Monthly. Magazine for the travel trade, emphasizing travel to the Pacific-Asia region. Includes news from the Pacific Asia Travel Association and its 35 chapters in the Americas.

Prairie Hotelier

Naylor Communications Ltd.
100 Sutherland Ave.
Winnipeg, MB, Canada R2W 3C7
Phone: (204)947-0222
Fax: (204)947-2047

Lisa Kopochinski, Editor. 6x/yr. Hotel industry magazine.

U pstart Alaska Airlines has created something of a cult following by providing upscale meals and gracious cabin attendants. But while the market demands service, it is driven by price. Nearly all the new carriers built on *haute cuisine* and high prices have failed quickly.

Source: *Fortune*

Private Pilot Magazine

Fancy Publications, Inc.
PO Box 6050
Mission Viejo, CA 92690
Phone: (714)855-8822
Fax: (714)855-3045

Dennis Shattuck, editorial director. Monthly. Magazine covering general aviation interests.

Professional Pilot

Queensmith Communications Corp.
3014 Colvin St.
Alexandria, VA 22314
Phone: (703)370-0606
Fax: (703)370-7082

Murray Q. Smith, publisher. Monthly. Magazine serving pilots of corporate, charter, commuter, and major airlines.

Recommend

Worth International Communications Corp.
5979 NW, 151 St., Ste. 120
Miami Lakes, FL 33014
Phone: (305)828-0123
Fax: (305)826-6950

Hal Herman, Pres./Editor-in-Chief. Monthly. Travel industry magazine.

Southeast Travel Professional

1200 NW 78th Ave., Ste. 201
Miami, FL 33126
Phone: (305)592-6133
Fax: (305)592-9741

Larry Cafiero, Editor. Monthly. Travel magazine (tabloid).

Tour & Travel News
CMP Publications, Inc.
600 Community Dr.
Manhasset, NY 11030
Phone: (516)365-4600
Fax: (516)562-5472

Linda Ball, Editor. Weekly Magazine for the travel industry, covering issues of interest to travel agents. Jerry Landress, Publisher; Irwin Barnett, Advertising Mgr.

A ccording to the Bureau of Labor Statistics, the working population will steadily age between 1992 and 2005, which will boost productivity as the experience level of the workforce increases. Manufacturing's share of total national output is projected in the BLS study to remain around 19%, with considerable growth in the nondefense sector to make up for defense cuts. But while output will remain steady, productivity gains will allow the share of employment taken by manufacturing to continue to decline, from 24% in 1975 to 17.5% in 1990, and to 14% in 2005.

Source: *Forbes*

TOURISME
Publications Transcontinental, Inc.
465, rue St-Jean, 9e etage
Montreal, PQ, Canada H2Y 3S4
Phone: (514)842-6491
Fax: (514)842-8557

Michel Villeneuve, Editor. Weekly. Magazine (tabloid) serving travel industry professionals (French).

Travel Agent Magazine
Universal Media
801 2nd Ave.
New York, NY 10017
Phone: (212)370-5050
Fax: (212)370-4491

Irwin M Barnett, Publisher. 2x/wk. Travel industry magazine.

Travel Courier East
Baxter Publishing Co.
310 Dupont St.
Toronto, ON, Canada M5R 1V9
Phone: (416)968-7252
Fax: (416)968-2377

Rob Wilson, Editor. Weekly. Magazine (tabloid) serving the travel industry.

Travel Digest
1654 SW 28th Ave.
Fort Lauderdale, FL 33312-3949
Phone: (305)792-2234

Jurgen Hartmann, Publisher. Monthly. Magazine for travel agents.

Travel Industry Honors (ASTA)
American Society of Travel Agents
1101 King St.
Alexandria, VA 22314
Phone: (703)739-2782

Periodic.

Travel News
Travel Agents International, Inc.
111 2nd Ave., NE, 15th Fl.
Box 31005
St. Petersburg, FL 33731-8905
Phone: (813)895-8241

Roger E. Block, Publisher. Monthly Travel publication.

Travel People Magazine
CMP Publications, Inc.
600 Community Dr.
Manhasset, NY 11030
Phone: (516)562-5000
Fax: (516)562-5472

Jerry Landress, Group Publisher. Monthly. Lifestyle magazine targeted for travel agents.

Travel Trade
15 W. 44th St.
New York, NY 10036
Phone: (212)730-6600
Fax: (212)730-7137

Joel M. Abels, Editor and Publisher. Weekly. Travel industry magazine.

Travel Trainers Network (ICTA)
Institute of Certified Travel Agents
148 Linden St.
PO Box 82-56
Wellesley, MA 02181
Phone: (617)237-0280

Semiannual. Newsletter providing information of interest to those teaching travel courses.

Travel Weekly

Reed Travel Group
500 Plaza Dr.
Secaucus, NJ 07096
Phone: (201)902-2000
Fax: (201)319-1947

Alan Fredericks, Editor. 2x/wk. (Mon. and Thurs.). Travel industry magazine.

Winston's Travel Discoveries

Winston's Travel Discoveries
PO Box C
Sausalito, CA 94966
Phone: (415)332-9612

Editor(s): Isabella Winston. Bimonthly. Features "refreshingly critical" reviews of the better resorts, hotels, and restaurants in the U.S. and abroad, with all establishments being reviewed anonymously and in-person by the editor. Recurring features include "travel planners," for particular areas, which carry data on typical weather conditions, major airlines, and tourist information sources.

Basic Reference Guides

Africa's Top Wildlife Countries

Global Travel Publishers, Inc.
First Union Bank Bldg.
1620 S. Federal Hwy., Ste. 900
Pompano Beach, FL 33062
Phone: (305)781-3933
Toll-free: 800-882-9453
Fax: (305)781-0984

Mark W. Nolting, President, editor. Biennial, April of even years. List of parks, accommodations, banks, tourist camps and offices, and automobile associations and clubs in 14 African countries; African embassies; airlines that fly to Africa. Entries include: Name, address, phone, services. Arrangement: Classified by service. Indexes: Product/service, geographical.

Airline Companies Directory

American Business Information, Inc.
American Business Directories, Inc.
5711 S. 86th Circle
Omaha, NE 68127
Phone: (402)593-4600
Fax: (402)331-1505

Annual. $125.00. Number of listings: 3,045.

Entries include: Name, address, phone (including area code), year first in "Yellow Pages." Arrangement: Geographical.

American Bus Association's Motorcoach Marketer: Complete Directory of the Intercity Bus & Travel/Tourism Industry

American Bus Assn.
1015 15th St. NW, No. 250
Washington, DC 20005
Phone: (202)842-1645
Toll-free: 800-283-2877
Fax: (202)842-0850

Tom Jackson, Publisher, editor. Annual, September. Over 2,000 hotels and sightseeing services, convention information centers, visitors' centers, and similar businesses and organizations of interest to motorcoach tour organizers; includes about 1,000 companies which operate intercity scheduled and charter buses; coverage includes Canada. Entries include: Company name, address, phone, name and title of contact. Arrangement: Classified by line of business.

American Express Pocket Guides

American Express Publishing Corp.
1120 Ave. of the Americas
New York, NY 10036
Phone: (212)382-5600

Series of guides that list hotels, restaurants, and shopping and entertainment centers throughout the world, including guides to England, Mexico, Paris, Spain, and Venice. Entries include: Business name, address, phone, days and hours of operation; travel access to hotels, restaurants, shops; highlighted descriptions of all major cities and points of interest. Indexes: Product/service, subject, trade name.

ASTA Officials Directory

American Soc. of Travel Agents
1101 King St.
Alexandria, VA 22314
Phone: (703)739-2782

Annual. Lists information on committee, council, and task force activities and members. Includes antitrust compliance guidelines, code of ethics, and bylaws.

Aviator's Guide to Flight Planning

TAB Books
PO Box 40
Blue Ridge Summit, PA 17294-0850
Phone: (717)794-2191
Toll-free: 800-822-8138

Donald J. Clausing. 1989. Includes illustrations.

Business of Travel: Agency Operations & Administration

Macmillan Publishing Co., Inc.
866 3rd Ave.
New York, NY 10022
Phone: (212)702-2000

Dennis L. Foster. 1990.

Job-search scams are springing up all over the country, charging advance fees ranging from $2,000 to $30,000, with 25 to 30 percent paid up front; complaints against such scams rose 75% between 1990 and 1991. Ask your state attorney general's office whether any complaints have been filed against a placement agency before you contact it; be wary if a fee is required before services are rendered or if a job is guaranteed within 6 to 12 weeks.

Source: *Working Woman*

CMAA Yearbook

Club Managers Association of America
1733 King St.
Alexandria, VA 22314
Phone: (703)739-9500
Fax: (703)739-0124

Free to members. Membership directory.

Consolidators Handbook: Guide to Low Cost International Travel

Hammond Publishing
PO Box 12924
Gainesville, FL 32604
Phone: (904)378-8780

Kriss Hammond, President, editor. Annual, January. Companies worldwide that offer discount airfare, hotel packages, and tour packages for international travel. Entries include: Company, location, phone. Arrangement: Geographical.

Corporate Travel—Directory Issue

Gralla Publications
1515 Broadway, Ste. 3201
New York, NY 10036
Phone: (212)869-1300
Fax: (212)302-6273

Laurie Berger, editor. Annual, January. Approximately 2,000 airlines, hotels, and other businesses offering travel packages to corporations. Entries include: Company name, address, phone. Arrangement: Geographical.

Directory of Hotel and Motel Systems

American Hotel & Motel Assn.
1201 New York Ave., NW, Ste. 600
Washington, DC 20005
Phone: (202)289-3100

Annual.

Flight International World Airline Directory Issue

Reed Business Publishing Group
3700 Campus Dr., Ste. 203
Newport Beach, CA 92660
Phone: (714)756-1057
Fax: (714)756-2514

Annual, March/April. $4.35. Publication includes: Over 500 scheduled airlines and charter companies operating commercial fixed and rotary wing aircraft for passenger and freight service, worldwide. Entries include: Airline name, address, phone, telex, date established, names of subsidiaries, major routes flown, number of employees, number and type of aircraft in service and on order. Arrangement: Alphabetical. Indexes: Geographical.

Hotel and Motel RedBook

American Hotel Assn. Directory Corp.
1201 New York Ave., NW, 6th Fl.
Washington, DC 20005-3917
Phone: (202)289-3100

Quarterly. $81.00, plus $4.00 shipping. The official directory of the American Hotel and Motel Association. Entries include property name, address, and phone number.

IAAF Membership Directory
International Agricultural Aviation Foundation
405 Main St.
Mt. Vernon, WA 98275
Phone: (206)336-9737
Fax: (206)336-2506

Annual.

IAHA Roster
International Association of Hospitality
Accountants (IAHA)
Box 27649
Austin, TX 78755
Phone: (512)346-5680

Periodic. Membership directory.

The Lodging and Food Service Industry
American Hotel & Motel Assn.
1201 New York Ave., NW, Ste. 600
Washington, DC 10106
Phone: (202)289-3100

Gerald W. Lattin. Second edition, 1989. Describes the lodging industry; covers growth and development, organization, and structure, as well as such areas as operations, maintenance, marketing, and personnel. Describes career opportunities.

Lodging Hospitality - 400 Top Performers Issue
Penton Publishing Co.
1100 Superior Ave.
Cleveland, OH 44114
Phone: (216)696-7000

Annual, August. $5.00. Includes top 400 hotels, motels, inns, and lodges based on total sales per room, and top 25 chains and franchises based on number of rooms. Lists hotel names, locations, number of guestrooms and suites, and number of employees.

Macmillan Directory of Leading Private Companies
National Register Publishing Co.
Macmillan, Inc.
3004 Glenview Rd.
Wilmette, IL 60091
Phone: (708)441-2202

Annual, March. $427.00, plus $6.45 shipping. Covers: Over 6,400 privately owned companies. Entries include: Company name, address, phone, telex, year founded, financial assets and liabilities, net worth, approximate sales, names and titles of key personnel, number of employees, number of U.S. and foreign offices, and other information. Arrangement: Alphabetical. Indexes: Geographical, parent company, Standard Industrial Classification number.

Managing Front Office Operations
American Hotel & Motel Assn.
1201 New York Ave., NW, Ste. 600
Washington, DC 20005
Phone: (202)289-3100

Charles E. Steadman and Michael L. Kasavana; edited by Matthew O. Rowe. Second edition, 1988. Explains guest registration, accounting, and how to evaluate and manage the operations and staff of the front office.

NAI Membership Directory
Negro Airmen International
PO Box 1340
Tuskegee, AL 36008

Annual.

National Air Transportation Association Official Membership Directory
National Air Transportation Assn.
4226 King St.
Alexandria, VA 22302
Phone: (703)845-9000

Annual, April. $25.00. Covers: More than 1,000 regular, associate, and affiliate members; regular members include airport service organizations, air taxi operators, and commuter airlines. Entries include: Company name, address, phone, name and title of contact. Arrangement: Regular members are classified by service; associate and affiliate members are alphabetical in separate sections. Indexes: Geographical.

Ninety-Nines, International Women Pilots Membership Directory
Ninety-Nines, International Women Pilots
Will Rogers Airport
PO Box 59965
Oklahoma City, OK 73159
Phone: (405)685-7969

Annual. Free.

Official Hotel and Resort Guide

News Group Publications, Inc.
Murdoch Magazines Div.
500 Plaza Dr.
Secaucus, NJ 07096
Phone: (201)902-2078

Four times/year. $250.00 for set of three volumes. Roster of 30,000 hotels, resorts, and motor hotels, worldwide. Lists hotel/motel/resort names, addresses, phone numbers, name of managers, and number of rooms or units.

What airline passengers value: good service, plenty of flights, impeccable safety standards, a new generation of ultramodern planes.

Source: *Fortune*

Private Pilot Directory of Aviation Clubs Issue

Fancy Publications, Inc.
Box 6050
Mission Viejo, CA 92690
Phone: (714)855-8822
Fax: (714)855-3045

Biennial. $2.95. Publication includes: List of aviation clubs and pilot organizations. Entries include: Organization name, address, contact person, phone, number of members, annual fees, publications, purpose, date of annual meeting. Arrangement: Alphabetical.

Resorts Directory

American Business Information, Inc.
American Business Directories, Inc.
5711 S. 86th Circle
Omaha, NE 68127
Phone: (402)593-4600
Fax: (402)331-1505

Annual. $375.00. Number of listings: 11,305. Entries include: Name, address, phone (including area code), year first in "Yellow Pages." Arrangement: Geographical.

Standard and Poor's Register of Corporations, Directors and Executives

Standard and Poor's Corp.
25 Broadway
New York, NY 10004
Phone: (212)208-8283

Annual, January; supplements in April, July, and October. $498.00, lease basis. Covers: Over 50,000 corporations in the United States, including names and titles of over 400,000 officials (Volume I); 70,000 biographies of directors and executives (Volume 2). Entries include: For companies - Name, address, phone, names of principal executives and accountants; number of employees, estimated annual sales, outside directors. For directors and executives - Name, home and principal business addresses, date and place of birth, fraternal organization memberships, business affiliations. Arranged alphabetically. Indexes: Volume 3 indexes companies geographically, by Standard Industrial Classification number, and by corporate family groups.

The Student Pilot's Flight Manual

Iowa State Univ. Press
2121 S. State Ave.
Ames, IA 50010
Phone: (515)292-0140
Fax: (515)292-3348

William K. Kershner. Sixth edition, 1990. Includes illustrations.

Travel Agency Communications Reports—North American Edition

Cabell Travel Publications
2235 E. Flamingo Rd., No. 100-F
Las Vegas, NV 89119
Phone: (702)796-0040

Quarterly. Travel agents, wholesale tour operators, motor coach-sightseeing companies, airlines, steamships, railroads, car rental companies, foreign auto sales, state and government tourist offices, foreign consulates, hotel/motel chains and systems, hotel and travel representatives, and special service companies throughout North America. Entries include: Company name, address, phone, fax, telex, cable address, association memberships, number of employees, head office, location, names of executives. Arrangement: By type of business, then geographical. Indexes: Alphabetical index of travel agencies; classified index of wholesale tour operators by destination areas.

Travel Agent—Domestic Tour Manual Issue

American Traveler, Inc.
Fairchild Publications
Capital Cities Media, Inc.
7 W. 34th St., 6th Fl.
New York, NY 10003
Phone: (212)630-3880

Annual. Lists of leading motorcoach tour companies offering over 500 escort vacation tours with 9,000 departures throughout the U.S. and Canada. Entries include: For tour companies—Name, address, phone. For tours—Dates offered, name of tour, costs, number of days. Arrangement: Alphabetical. Indexes: Chronological, destination.

Travel Industry Association of America—International Travel News Directory

Travel Industry Assn. of America
2 Lafayette Center
1133 21st St., NW
Washington, DC 20036
Phone: (202)293-1433
Fax: (202)293-3155

Shawn Flaherty, editor. Biennial. Travel editors of major newspapers, magazines, and broadcast outlets; consumer and travel industry magazines and publications, including guide books, in-flight publications, in-room publications; news and photo services; international coverage for travel trade and consumer travel editors. Entries include: Generally, publication title, address, phone, fax, telex, names of editorial and advertising contacts, target audience, editorial and advertising deadlines. Arrangement: Classified by media, then in separate section for United States and international. Indexes: Media title, geographical.

Travel Industry Personnel Directory

Fairchild Books
7 E. 12th St.
New York, NY 10003
Toll-free: 800-247-6622

Annually, in the spring. Includes contact information for more than 20,000 hotel sales and marketing personnel in the United States and Canada. Also covers people working for airlines, railroads, bus lines, cruise lines, and car rental companies.

Travel and Tourism Research and Marketing Directory

Travel and Tourism Research Assn.
Box 58066
Salt Lake City, UT 84158-0066
Phone: (801)581-3351
Fax: (801)581-3354

Mari Lou Wood, editor. Irregular; 1990. More than 200 organizations engaged in research and consulting on travel and tourism, including government agencies, university departments and private firms. Entries include: Company name, address, phone, fax, date founded, chief officer, name of member, type of organization, number of employees, services available, publications. Arrangement: Alphabetical. Indexes: Alphabetical, geographical, company category.

Travel & Vacation Discount Guide

Pilot Books
103 Cooper St.
Babylon, NY 11702
Phone: (516)422-2225

Paige Palmer, author. 1990. Nearly 335 sponsors of discount travel programs, including discount travel clubs, hotels, airlines, and other travel industry firms; also lists tourist information agencies in the United States and abroad. Entries include: Sponsor name, address, phone, description of program. Arrangement: Alphabetical.

Ward's Business Directory of U.S. Private and Public Companies

Gale Research Inc.
835 Penobscot Bldg.
Detroit, MI 48226
Phone: (313)961-2242
Toll-free: 800-877-GALE
Fax: (313)961-6083

1992, annual. Five-volume directory that provides information on more than 133,000 businesses in the United States, over 90 percent of which are privately held. Includes all major companies, as well as companies with an annual sales volume of less than $50,000. Entries include: company name, address, telephone, and fax; financial information and employee figures; four-digit SIC codes; fiscal year end; year founded; import/export information; immediate parent; and up to five company officers. Arrangement: Volumes 1, 2, and 3 list the companies in alphabetical order. Volume 4 lists companies in ZIP Code order by state and includes a number of other indexes. Volume 5 ranks companies by sales volume withing four-digit SIC classifications.

Who's Who in the Lodging Industry

American Hotel and Motel Assn.
1201 New York Ave., NW
Washington, DC 20005
Phone: (202)289-3100
Fax: (202)289-3199

Annual, May. $39.95. Covers hotels, motels, suppliers, corporations, and individuals affiliated with the lodging industry. For individuals, entries include name, address, phone, and name of affiliated company. For properties and corporations, entries include name, address, phone, and names and titles of key personnel.

World Aviation Directory

McGraw-Hill, Inc.
Aerospace and Defense Group
1156 15th St., NW
Washington, DC 20005
Phone: (202)822-4600
Fax: (202)293-7482

Semiannual, March and September. $140.00. Covers: Airlines; air freight companies; support services (repair stations, fuel companies, etc.); aviation, aerospace, and missile manufacturers, including manufacturers of aircraft, spacecraft, piston and jet engines, and component manufacturers and major subcontractors; government agencies and associations; airline caterers; international scope. Entries include: Company or organization name, address, phone, names of key executives, annual sales, number of employees. Arrangement: Classified by major activity (manufacturers, airlines, etc.). Indexes: Company and organization, personnel, product.

Worldwide Travel Information Contact Book

Gale Research Inc.
835 Penobscot Bldg.
Detroit, MI 48226-4094
Phone: (313)961-2242
Toll-free: 800-877-GALE
Fax: (313)961-6083

Burkhard Herbote, author. Biennial, September of even years; first edition 1990. Approximately 25,000 contacts and sources for travel information including: travel agents, associations, tourist authorities, tour operators, lodging associations, and publications. Entries include: Name, address, phone, fax, telex. Arrangement: Geographical, then by subject heading. Indexes: Travel destination.

MASTER INDEX

Master Index

The Master Index provides comprehensive access to all four sections of the Directory by citing all subjects, organizations, publications, and services listed throughout in a single alphabetic sequence. The index also includes inversions on significant words appearing in cited organization, publication, and service names. For example, "Ward's Business Directory of U.S. Private and Public Companies" could also be listed in the index under "Companies; Ward's Business Directory of U.S. Private and Public."